THE PHILOSOPHY OF MIND

T0204211

THE
PHILOSOPHY OF MIND
An Introduction

PETER SMITH and O. R. JONES

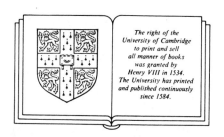

The right of the
University of Cambridge
to print and sell
all manner of books
was granted by
Henry VIII in 1534.
The University has printed
and published continuously
since 1584.

CAMBRIDGE UNIVERSITY PRESS
CAMBRIDGE
NEW YORK   NEW ROCHELLE
MELBOURNE   SYDNEY

Published by the Press Syndicate of the University of Cambridge
The Pitt Building, Trumpington Street, Cambridge CB2 1RP
32 East 57th Street, New York, NY 10022, USA
10 Stamford Road, Oakleigh, Melbourne 3166, Australia

First published 1986
Reprinted 1987, 1988

Printed in the United States of America

British Library cataloguing in publication data
Smith, Peter, 1944–
The Philosophy of Mind: an introduction
1. Mind and body   2. Intellect
I. Title   II. Jones, O. R.
128'.2   BF161

Library of Congress cataloging in publication data
Smith, Peter, 1944–
The philosophy of mind.
Bibliography
Includes index.
1. Dualism.   2. Perception (Philosophy)
3. Belief and doubt.
4. Thought and thinking.   I. Jones, O. R.
II. Title.
B812.S65   1986   128'.2   86–9571
ISBN 0 521 32078 X hard covers
ISBN 0 521 31250 7 paperback

CONTENTS

Contents

PREFACE

This book is aimed principally at undergraduates who are taking a first course in the philosophy of mind, though it should be readable by anyone with a serious interest in the issues we discuss. It has developed from a course of lectures for complete beginners in philosophy which we have given together for some years.

We have tried to keep our intended audience firmly in mind without succumbing to the temptation of addressing our professional colleagues instead. We certainly haven't aimed to get all the way to the 'frontiers'; our main concern is to present clearly some introductory arguments in the philosophy of mind, in such a way as to make them available to someone new to the area. Those who think that these familiar arguments are to be vigorously criticised in one way or another will still, we hope, welcome a book which presents them frankly and perspicuously.

We can't pretend that the book is consistently an easy read, and the discussions inevitably get significantly more difficult as the book proceeds, particularly in Part III. Real philosophy in our preferred analytical style requires following the twists and turns of complex chains of argument, and to the uninitiated this process can seem a little intimidating. But we have tried to keep the pace fairly gentle, especially in Part I.

Instead of breaking up the text with cryptic section-headings, we have provided a descriptive Analytical Table of Contents; this rather old-fashioned device should prove much more helpful in using the book. We have also appended a Chronological Table for those hazy about the dates of the 'great dead philosophers' and a brief Guide to Further Reading. Cross-references within the book are by chapter and section: the system of references to other works is explained in the preamble to the Bibliography.

We are extremely grateful to the friends and colleagues who have generously commented at length on drafts of this book. We should mention in particular David Cockburn, Jonathan Dancy, Lucy Littlehailes, Gregory McCulloch, Susan Mendus, Fred Stoutland and Ian Tipton. John FitzGerald gave advice about translations and George Botterill helped us to see what we meant in Chapter VIII. We have had helpful comments from three (officially anonymous) readers for C.U.P. And many first-year Aberystwyth students have – less voluntarily – provided written comments on individual chapters which have been very useful. Real thanks to everyone.

We are also grateful to Professor T.A. Roberts whose support resulted in our being very well provided with word-processing facilities, without which this project would undoubtedly have taken very much longer and been considerably less enjoyable.

Last, but certainly not least, special thanks are due to our wives, Patsie and Jean, who had to put up with us being even more preoccupied with philosophy than usual.

Aberystwyth   P.J.S.
April 1986   O.R.J.

ANALYTICAL TABLE OF CONTENTS

PART I : DUALISM, FOR AND AGAINST

Chapter I: Introduction

1 Questions about the nature of the mind arise very naturally. 2 They are philosophical questions insofar as they force us to re-examine critically what we ordinarily take for granted. 3 We begin with the question: are we composed of two distinct components, a physical body plus an immaterial self? 4 On the two-component view, mental characteristics belong to our immaterial component, and physical characteristics to the body. 5 This theory was defended by Plato and Descartes. 6 To dispute their theory is not to say that people don't have minds in the ordinary sense. 7 The question whether dualism (as it will be called) is true cannot be settled by searching to find our alleged immaterial components. We cannot directly observe other people's Cartesian Minds; nor, as Hume remarked, can we find our own by introspection. We must resort to argument.

Chapter II: Arguments for Dualism

1 We examine eight arguments for dualism. (A) Mental properties and physical properties are so different that they must be had by different things. (B) Merely material things cannot think or feel at all, so we are not merely material. (C) Material things cannot have higher mental characteristics like the capacity to appreciate art, so we are not merely material. 2 Argument (A) is hopeless. 3 Arguments (B) and (C) also fail. 4 Underlying (B) and (C) is the thought (D) that things made of physical stuff alone

could not exhibit the degree of behavioural complexity characteristic of thinking beings. But (D) is unsupported.   5 Argument (E) appeals to the alleged fact that people sometimes have out-of-body experiences. But are such experiences any more than an interesting variety of hallucination?   6 Can we establish dualism by (F) noting that the expressions 'Jack' and 'Jack's body' are not used equivalently? No – the linguistic facts in question can also be explained by the anti-dualist.   7 We cannot (G) prove dualism by claiming that we have disembodied life after death, for the anti-dualist will dispute the claim. Can we infer dualism from (H) reflections on the imaginability of life after death? This raises similar issues to those discussed in the next chapter.

Chapter III: Descartes's Argument

1 Descartes asks how we know that we are not permanently deceived by an evil demon.   2 He is interested in discovering which of our beliefs are absolutely sceptic proof.   3 Each of us has a cast-iron proof of his own existence – 'I think, therefore I am'. But we haven't such a sceptic-resistant proof that our bodies exist: for couldn't they be an illusion created by the evil demon?   4 This suggests Descartes's Argument: I can feign that my body does not exist; I cannot feign that I myself do not exist; hence I myself am entirely distinct from my body.   5 This is logically valid if argument (H) of II.7 is.   6 But these arguments are both invalid: cf. the Prime Minister's Argument, which is of the same form but patently bogus.   7 Descartes's Argument belongs to a wider family of invalid arguments.

Chapter IV: Difficulties for the Dualist

1 To attack pro-dualist arguments doesn't disprove dualism: but there are the following objections.   2 The 'Many Minds' problem: how can a dualist defend his view against bizarre rival hypotheses (e.g. a person consists of one body and seventeen minds all thinking in unison)?   3 The evolution problem: the dualist is committed to imposing a black/white distinction on the graduated evolutionary facts.   4 Further, the dualist has a double difficulty in accommo-

a decisive objection. 9 Despite the inevitable loose ends of this discussion, the prospects for the revised belief-acquisition theory of perception are good.

Chapter IX: Action and Volition

1 Focus on the topic of intentional action. 2 A genuine action differs from a mere bodily movement by having the right kind of mental causes. 3 What are the initiating causes of an intentional action? 'Acts of will' or 'volitions' is the answer given by Locke, Berkeley, Hume and many others. 4 But if there is a puzzle about the nature of ordinary outer actions then there is an exactly parallel puzzle about the nature of inner 'acts' of will. 5 It isn't any better to identify the mental causes of actions as 'choices', 'tryings' or '(considered) intentions'. 6 We should say instead that an intentional action flows from the agent's reasons for action, where having reasons consists in having appropriate beliefs and desires. 7 But if so, can our actions really be 'up to us'? The objection defused. 8 So the mental causes of actions are appropriate beliefs and desires.

Chapter X: Two Theories of Belief

1 Belief and desire are the most basic 'propositional attitudes'. 2 Hume held that (A) having a belief involves having ideas ('faint images' of impressions) in mind, and (B) these ideas are more 'vivid' or 'lively' in cases of belief than of imagination. (B) is a hopeless theory of the belief/imagination distinction. 3 Hume's much better second thought (B*) that beliefs are the 'governing principles of all our actions' needs to be disentangled from (A). 4 Beliefs dispose us to act in various ways: we might therefore say that beliefs are dispositions. Ryle held that for someone to have a disposition is just for a package of 'iffy' propositions to be true of his behaviour. 5 An aside on soft vs. hard behaviourism. 6 Three difficulties with Ryle's behaviourism: first, it misrepresents the explanatory role of beliefs. 7 Second, it makes a mystery of our 'inside knowledge' of our own beliefs. 8 Third, we cannot analyse talk about beliefs in terms of 'iffy' talk which is purely about

behaviour; we are always forced to go round in circles and mention more beliefs. 9 So neither Hume's account nor Ryle's will do.

Chapter XI: The Function of Beliefs

1 A belief is a disposition in Armstrong's sense of being a state which is causally responsible for a lot of 'iffy' facts about one's behaviour. 2 Properly understood, this revised theory avoids the circularity objection which sinks Ryle's dispositional theory. 3 It sidesteps the difficulty concerning The Asymmetry between first-person and third-person routes to knowledge about beliefs. 4 It also avoids the objection to the Rylean theory based on considerations about explanation. 5 Given our earlier criticisms of dualist ideas, we can reasonably assume that a belief-state is some physical state (presumably of the brain). 6 Different cases of believing that it is about to rain can be constituted by different types of physical state. To describe a state as a belief is to describe its function in producing behaviour, and the same functional role can be played by physically different states at different times or in different people. 7 The 'matter' of a belief-state is physical, its 'form' is its function.

Chapter XII: Functionalism and Folk Psychology

1 How do we know what functional role a given belief has? How do we know which 'iffy' facts about behaviour correspond to which belief? We appeal to some implicit general principles. 2 Such principles of everyday folk psychology play a very important role in our everyday understanding of each other. 3 But the question of their precise form and status is difficult. 4 In summary: beliefs are brain-states identified not by their intrinsic physical constitution but by the role they play in interaction with other states in producing behaviour. Parallel remarks apply to desires. 5 The distinction between hard and soft functionalism: the latter defended. 6 This sort of theory discourages scepticism about our knowledge of other minds.

Chapter XVII: Reasons and Causes

1 Some philosophers have argued that the beliefs and desires that explain our actions do not cause them.   2 Two bad arguments for this view discussed and dismissed.   3 A third bad argument rests on a flawed contrast between causal explanation and 'explanation by redescription'.   4 The most interesting argument for the thesis that reasons are not causes is based on Hume's Principle combined with the Logical Connection Thesis. Hume's Principle asserts that any causal statement about particular events must be backed up by a contingent general law.   5 The Logical Connection Thesis maintains that the principles relating beliefs and desires to action involve logical connections between concepts and are quite un-Humean.   6 It is far from clear that either Hume's Principle or the Logical Connection Thesis is true as it stands.   7 And in any case, they do not entail the desired conclusion that reasons are not causes. So we can maintain the common-sense view that beliefs and desires are the causes of action.

Chapter XVIII: Causality and Freedom

1 On a physicalist theory of the mind, humans are made only of physical stuff, and are thus as susceptible to the laws of physics as anything else. But is the implication that our doings are entirely caused compatible with the idea that we sometimes act freely?   2 Aristotle gives accounts of voluntary action...   3 ...and of the subclass of deliberated actions which define these types of act precisely in terms of the way they are caused. For Aristotle, appropriate causality, far from ruling out freedom, actually constitutes freedom.   4 His causal theory of freedom does not presuppose psychological determinism, which may indeed be inimical to freedom.   5 'But if our acts are caused we couldn't have done otherwise than we did, and so are not free.' The attractions of this argument rest on a slide between different senses of 'could have done otherwise'.   6 An aside on the complications caused by quantum indeterminacies, and why we can ignore them.   7 It is often said that if all our doings are physically caused, then we are automata, or the world is a prison. But this is mere rhetoric, unless it is based on the rejected dualist conception of the person.   8 The

issue of free will is large and difficult: but perhaps enough has been said to show that it is not obvious that a physicalist cannot accommodate freedom in a broadly Aristotelian way.

Part I

DUALISM, FOR AND AGAINST

I

INTRODUCTION

1   There can be few people who are not occasionally prompted to puzzled reflection about human beings and their actions. Perhaps a long-standing friend does something that strikes us as wildly out of character, even quite incomprehensible. It is brought home to us how resistant to our understanding other people can be; we are forcefully reminded that another person's mental life is largely hidden from us. And we may well begin to wonder whether we can ever really know what someone else thinks and feels. After all, when we ascribe thoughts and feelings to another person, it seems that all we have by way of supporting evidence is what we observe, namely his external behaviour. But how can we know in the case of someone else which outward behaviour patterns are signs of which inner states? Perhaps the similarity of his behaviour to our own may lead us to conjecture that he thinks and feels as we do; but are we ever really entitled to be sure what is going on in his mind?

Such sceptical thoughts come to us very readily; so too do speculations about the nature of whatever it is that has those elusive inner states. And here we seem to be torn in two directions. On the one hand, thinking and feeling surely require the possession of a self or soul or mind, which we tend to think of as something distinct from a gross material body. If body and soul *are* two distinct things, then the one could in principle exist without the other: indeed, many people believe that our souls do continue to exist, do continue to have conscious thoughts and experiences, even after the death and destruction of our bodies. It is evidently very tempting to think in this way of persons as really comprised of two distinct components, the physical body that we can see or touch, and a non-physical soul or mind that may perhaps survive independently. And this picture of the mind as something quite distinct from the observable body may further encourage doubts concerning the possibility of knowing anything about other people's mental states.

On the other hand, this tempting 'two-component' picture of the person goes clean against the contemporary scientific view of man as part of the natural world. No doubt humans are peculiarly complex organisms; but from the sober view-point of the biological sciences it appears gratuitous to suppose that humans are marked off from the rest of nature by possessing an extra non-physical component, which somehow underlies and explains their actions. The working presumption of the sciences is that human behaviour can in principle be explained without any reference to non-bodily entities. And this presumption seems very well supported by the continuing development of progressively more detailed accounts of the biological bases of behaviour.

Should we therefore just take the second, tough-minded stance, and reject all talk of the mind as a non-physical entity? Perhaps: but this naturalistic stance has its own problems. For a start, if human beings are simply part of the natural world, subject to the same physical, chemical and biochemical laws as anything else, then isn't the idea of free will an illusion? If what Jack did is explicable in physical terms by means of scientific laws, it seems to follow that Jack was causally determined to behave as he did and wasn't really free to do otherwise. So how can we reasonably hold him responsible for what he did? The hard-headed, purely scientific, view of persons seems to undermine something very central to our ordinary conception of a person – namely, the idea of being a responsible free agent: and this idea is obviously not one we can readily abandon.

We have touched here on three problems which must have occurred to most people in reflective moments. First, can we ever really know what someone else is thinking or feeling? Second, are we ourselves something quite distinct from our bodies, so that we may possibly survive bodily death? And third, are we really free to act as we choose, or are our actions determined by causal factors outside our control, such as our environment or physical make-up? These three problems are distinctively philosophical ones, and they are just some of the central questions about the nature of the mind which we will be tackling in this book.

2   Why do these problems about the mind count as *philosophical* ones? Well, all three arise from clashes between basic

assumptions which seem to be embedded in our everyday thinking. Thus there is a special problem about our knowledge of other minds because – as we will show in Chapter XIV – some apparently common-sense assumptions about such hidden, inner things as pains turn out to clash with the equally reasonable presumption that we can sometimes know whether someone else is in pain (just try doubting, in a real-life case, whether the child who comes crying with a badly grazed knee is really in pain). Again, the problem of the relation between mind and body arises because some familiar ways of thinking of ourselves as contrasted with our bodies seem to conflict with what we are inclined to say in our more scientific moments. And thirdly, as we have already suggested, these more scientific reflections seem in turn to undermine our conception of people as free agents, giving us the problem about whether we really have free will. In each of our examples, apparent conflicts underlying our everyday ways of thought and talk force us to re-examine critically what we ordinarily take for granted. Such re-examinations have always been the characteristic business of philosophy.

Of course, in everyday life we get by pretty well in an unreflective way and cheerfully suppress our fleeting philosophical qualms. But the price of trying to muddle through is the perpetual risk of error and confusion: and going wrong about, say, immortality or freedom would plainly not be a trivial matter. So it hardly needs to be argued that it is worth embarking on a philosophical scrutiny of what normally goes unexamined in our everyday ways of thought about ourselves and each other.

Yet even if it is agreed that philosophical issues arise in a natural way from tensions in our ordinary modes of thought, it might still be protested that there is something rather peculiar about our problems. After all, haven't philosophers been arguing about them for hundreds, if not thousands, of years? For example, the question whether we ourselves are distinct from our bodies was discussed by Plato, and has remained on the agenda of philosophy ever since. Surely there is something extremely odd about a problem that resists intensive investigation for so long! And indeed, it *would* be highly suspicious if there were no real progress in philosophy, if down the ages even the greatest philosophers had merely run in circles around the same grooves first cut by the Greeks. But in the course of this book it should become clear that we are not engaged in a fruitless enquiry into perennially unanswerable questions. On the contrary, by displaying some of the fruits of both ancient and contemporary philosophical enquiry into the nature of the mind, we aim to show that progress is discernible and that our questions are answerable.

3   We will set aside until very much later in this book the questions about our knowledge of other people's minds and about free will. Instead, we begin by concentrating on what seems at first sight to be the most basic of the issues we have already mentioned, namely the question whether or not we are really comprised of two distinct components, a body plus a non-physical self or mind. Let's spell out in rather more detail how this crucial issue arises.

Even the dullest of us has a remarkably rich and varied mental life. We have beliefs and desires, hopes and intentions, moods and emotions. We make conjectures, think out plans, come to decisions. We perceive the world around us by means of a continuous flux of visual, auditory and tactile experiences. And we are aware of our own bodies when we feel pains and itches, tinglings and churnings. All this is entirely familiar, and yet it immediately suggests a question. How is it possible for creatures like us to be subject to such a range of mental states, processes and events? What is it about human beings as contrasted with (say) geraniums, grasshoppers and goats, which gives us a mental life of such absorbing diversity?

One possible response is this: the reason that our mental lives are so rich is that we are extraordinarily complex organisms. In particular, our behavioural control system – the human brain – is comparatively massive and quite staggeringly intricate. The most superficial acquaintance with the results of twentieth-century research in human neuro-physiology reveals an organ with a bewildering complexity of structure and function. Our cerebral cortex consists of a network of some ten billion neurones, each one 'wired up' to as many as ten thousand others, giving us many thousand billion interconnections. With all this (quite literally) in our heads, is it after all any wonder that our mental life is correspondingly complex? By comparison with us, the humble geranium is a very simple organism; and again, to put it very crudely, you can't pack much grey matter into a grasshopper. Even a goat's brain is discernibly smaller and simpler in structure than our own; so it should be no surprise that its wits are dull and its intellectual horizons distinctly limited. Humans are built to a noticeably more intricate pattern, and that is what accounts for our distinctive mental prowess.

Now, this could be no more than the very beginning of an answer to our question about what makes it possible for us to think and feel as we do. We still need to be told a lot more about *how* our mental life is supposed to be based in the complex activity of our brains. Is it the case, for example, that mental states just *are* brain states, differently described, rather as water is H_2O differently described? Or is it perhaps that talk about mental happenings stands to talk about the brain rather as talk of a computer's program stands to talk about its physical hardware? We certainly need some way of understanding how a convoluted sequence of neural happenings can show up as a pang of jealousy or a whimsical speculation, a thought about the weather or a desire for a pint of beer. More generally, we need to understand how purely material creatures can possibly be capable of a mental life. And on further reflection it may very well be doubted whether we can achieve such an understanding. It is tempting to protest: how could some mere bodily complexity bring into existence something so remarkable as a conscious inner life? How could a physical heap of brain cells, however intricately structured, be solely responsible for the ebb and flow of our mental experiences? How could a thinking being really be made of nothing but unconscious brute matter? On second thoughts it can easily begin to look utterly implausible to suppose that the drama on our mental stage can in any way be reduced to a stream of chemical and electrical events in the brain. We seem to have a sense of ourselves as something apart from the physical world, with a spark of consciousness which marks us off from the merely material. And this maybe suggests that our first line of thought pointed in exactly the wrong direction. What crucially underpins our mental life and makes it all possible is perhaps not a bodily phenomenon at all, but something entirely different.

This vague notion that our mental experiences have a non-physical basis leads very naturally to the following somewhat more precise thought. We can think and feel as we do because we are not mere chunks of matter, however intricately structured: rather, we are physical beings plus an essential additional component – a soul, a self, a mind (call it what you will). In other words, the 'something entirely different' which is needed for our distinctive kind of mental life is some sort of non-physical entity, which is superadded to the gross material body to give us that composite being, a human person. As we remarked before, this idea that a person consists of two components, one mental and one physical, has evident attractions. After all, in ordinary discourse we often appear to distinguish ourselves from our bodies – thus Jill might say 'Jack isn't interested in me but only my body!' Consider too the familiar fantasy of finding oneself waking up in someone else's body. It is very tempting to suppose that this idea of body-hopping makes sense; indeed, by science fiction standards, it is a very modest fantasy. But it is plainly only coherent if we ourselves are indeed in some crucial sense separable from our bodies.

In summary: we have outlined, albeit still in the most sketchy and impressionistic way, two kinds of initial reaction to our question concerning what it is about us humans that enables us to think and feel as we do. The first type of reaction, which might be dubbed the *naturalistic* response, looks for an answer that postulates no entities beyond those of kinds recognised in the natural sciences, and talks in hard-headed terms about brain-complexity and the like. The second kind of reaction, the *two-component* response, regards its rival as leaving out of the story exactly what is most important – namely the non-physical self or soul which exists in tandem with our physical body, and may perhaps survive independently.

Since both these responses have roots deep in our everyday ways of thinking about ourselves it would be tendentious to dismiss either as being obviously mistaken. However, the two-component response initially strikes very many people, when they first come to think philosophically about these things, as the more immediately compelling. We will therefore leave the further development of a naturalistic theory of the mind until Part II, and instead begin our investigations with an extended critical discussion of the seemingly attractive two-component view. We first develop this view a little and explore some of the considerations that seem to lend it weight. We then examine some of the difficulties that the two-component picture has to face. We will be able to arrive at some pretty firm conclusions.

4   The leading idea of what we have called the 'two-component' picture is that we are a composite of two entities, one corporeal and one non-physical: and the presence of the second non-physical component is essential if we are to function as thinking, feeling beings. The obvious way of developing this story is to suppose that there is a *division of labour* between the two components. The body (including, of course the brain) is the locus of purely physical phenomena and processes, while it is the self or mind (or whatever we call the second component) which does the thinking and feeling. Thus, strictly speaking, it is Jack's body which weighs a hundred and eighty pounds, but it is Jack's inner self that thinks that that is too much, and wishes he weighed less; likewise, it is Jack's body that absorbs the digested meat, after Jack's mind has chosen steak rather than fish. Again, suppose Jill imagines being in Venice, and is also at the same time in a certain complex neurophysiological state. Then, on the view we are describing, it is one component of Jill, her physical part, which is in the neurophysiological state in question, and it is the other incorporeal component which is doing the imagining. The idea implicit in the rival naturalistic view, namely that the state of Jill's brain could somehow itself constitute the thinking is thus entirely ruled out as a gross confusion – the physical state and the mental state belong to quite different elements of the composite being who is Jill.

The position we are describing can perhaps be put in the following terms. A human person such as Jill (at least in her normal embodied state) consists of two distinct entities somehow yoked together: one of these, the body, possesses physical properties but not mental properties; the other, incorporeal, component lacks physical characteristics but has mental ones.

This summary is attractively tidy, but it requires us to draw a very sharp distinction between mental and physical properties. And this distinction is not at all easy to draw cleanly, at least if we try to do it in a way that accords with our everyday intuitions about what counts as mental and what counts as physical. (The difficulty in producing a neat criterion or test for what counts as a 'mental property' explains why we earlier resorted to giving lists of examples in order to illustrate the sort of thing which we want to discuss.) We can see straight away that many quite ordinary properties straddle the mental/physical boundary. Consider, for example, the property of being a competent tennis player: this doesn't fall neatly on one side or the other of the supposed great divide between the mental and the physical. The defender of the two-component theory must reply that the property of being a competent player is a 'mixed' property which can be resolved into physical elements belonging to the body (e.g. the capacity to run speedily about the court) and mental elements belonging to our incorporeal part (e.g. good anticipation in rallies). This manoeuvre looks worryingly contrived; but we need not press this point. For even if there isn't a clean distinction between the mental and the physical recognised in everyday thought, we certainly cannot debar the theorist from introducing some sharp distinctions where previously things were more hazy. So, for the time being, let's grant the two assumptions that we can neatly demarcate purely mental properties from purely physical ones, and that we can resolve 'mixed' properties into their mental and physical elements; and let's proceed to examine the theory that the two basic sorts of properties are had by two quite different sorts of things.

5   The two-component theory has had many vigorous proponents throughout the history of philosophy. For instance, in one of Plato's dialogues, Socrates is portrayed on the day of his death arguing about immortality and the nature of the soul. And he starts off by defining death in a way that plainly seems to presuppose a two-component conception of the person:

> being dead is this: the body's having come to be apart, separated from the soul, alone by itself, and the soul's being apart, alone by itself, separated from the body.   (*Phaedo*: 64c)

And later Socrates sums up his view like this:

> Consider, then, ... if these are our conclusions from all that's been said: soul is most similar to what is divine, immortal, intelligible, uniform, indissoluble, unvarying, and constant in relation to itself; whereas body, in its turn, is most similar to what is human, mortal, multiform, non-intelligible, dissoluble, and never constant in relation to itself. Have we anything to say against those statements ... to show that they're false?   (80a-b)

The suggestion, then, is that a man has two parts, the body which is of earthly stuff, and the soul which has a touch of the divine. Elsewhere in the *Phaedo* our mental functions (or at least the higher ones) are attributed to this non-material soul. So we find here a clear presumption in favour of the sort of two-component picture of the person which we outlined in the previous sections.

This picture is repeatedly endorsed by later philosophers, most notably by the founding father of modern philosophy, René Descartes. Thus the very title page of Descartes's *Meditations* announces that one of the two central aims of that work is to demonstrate 'the distinction between the human soul and the body'; and a key passage halfway through the Sixth Meditation concludes

> It is true that I may have (or, to anticipate, that I certainly have) a body that is very closely joined to me. But nevertheless, on the one hand I have a clear and distinct idea of myself, in so far as I am simply a thinking, non-extended thing; and on the other hand I have a distinct idea of body, in so far as this is simply an extended, non-thinking thing. And accordingly, it is certain that I am really distinct from my body, and can exist without it. (*Writings* II: 54)

So here again we find a very clear presentation of the now familiar story – a sharp contrast is drawn between two entities, one of which has physical characteristics such as being extended (i.e. taking up a certain amount of space) but is not conscious, the other of which has mental characteristics such as consciousness but lacks physical properties, the two separable entities being normally 'closely bound up' together to give us that composite being, the embodied human person.

We could considerably extend the list of defenders of this idea beyond Plato and Descartes. But for our purposes it is enough to note that these two, who rank among the very greatest of philosophers, were – for their very different reasons – devotees of the two-component picture. This fact, combined with the intuitive appeal of the picture, certainly makes it worth our dwelling at some length on their shared conception of what it is to be a person.

6   It will be useful at this point to introduce some brisker jargon. We will use the standard term *dualism* to refer to any version of the two-component theory which postulates a division of labour between the two components, and assigns at least such key mental phenomena as beliefs, desires, intentions, feelings of pain, and visual and tactile experiences to the incorporeal component. And we will officially refer to the non-physical component which is

supposedly the seat of mental functions as the *Cartesian Mind* ('Cartesian' in honour of Descartes, and capital 'M' to emphasise that we are using the word 'Mind' to introduce an entity postulated by a perhaps disputable theory).

So, is some kind of dualism correct? Do people have Cartesian Minds?

We must immediately make it absolutely clear that we are not now asking whether, in the *ordinary* sense, people have minds. In other words, we are not currently concerned with any outlandish scepticism: we can for the moment assume that people do think and feel, perceive the world around them, display intelligence and have all sorts of other mental capacities and aptitudes – in short, we can assume that people have minds. When we ask whether dualism is correct we are not questioning whether people think and feel, but raising the quite different issue of what exactly is involved in being a thinking, feeling person. Both the dualist and his opponent can agree that people do have feelings and thoughts; but both parties go beyond this truism to make a further, more controversial, claim. According to the dualist, to have feelings or thoughts requires having not just a body (however complex) but also an extra non-bodily component, an immaterial Cartesian Mind. And the anti-dualist maintains, not that we don't have mental states as we ordinarily understand them, but that having mental states doesn't require the possession of a non-physical extra something. Our question is who is right?

7   How can we decide this issue? We want to know whether there are such things as Cartesian Minds. But how in general do we settle such questions?

Let's start by comparing the question whether Cartesian Minds exist with another, more banal, question about what exists: are there such things as unicorns? We know well enough how to go about settling this second question; just look for some unicorns. We know at least roughly what would count as finding a unicorn, and so to search for unicorns is not an aimless project. However, the search proves fruitless, and we are prepared on this basis to say that unicorns are merely fabulous beasts and do not really exist. Now, can we settle the question about Cartesian Minds in a parallel way, by again engaging on a search? There would seem to be two reasons why not, one rather obvious, the second more subtle.

The first and obvious difficulty in searching for Minds (as we will unofficially call them for short) is that we don't really know yet what would count as finding one. We have been told what Minds are not: they are not our bodies, or even some part of our body like our brain – rather they are non-material entities. And perhaps we can go on to say other negative things, such as that they don't possess a size or shape. But we are as yet very far from any clear idea of what Minds actually are.

Let's waive this first point, however, because there is a much more interesting difficulty with the idea that we can set out to search for Minds. Note, for a start, that we can't hope to discover by direct observation any Minds other than our own. For all we can directly see of other people are their physical bodies: we certainly can't perceive any immaterial Minds attached to their bodies! What about our own case? Well, even the project of looking for one's own Cartesian Mind seems to be fruitless: this point is nicely caught in a justly famous passage by the Scots philosopher David Hume. He begins by describing the view that we can, as it were, observe our own Minds – or in his terminology 'selves' – in action:

> There are some philosophers, who imagine we are every moment intimately conscious of what we call our SELF; that we feel its existence and its continuance in existence; and are certain, beyond the evidence of a demonstration, both of its perfect identity and simplicity. The strongest sensation, the most violent passion, say they, instead of distracting us from this view, only fix it the more intensely, and make us consider their influence on *self* either by their pain or pleasure. To attempt a farther proof of this were to weaken its evidence; since no proof can be deriv'd from any fact, of which we are so intimately conscious; nor is there any thing, of which we can be certain, if we doubt of this. (*Treatise*: I.iv.6)

But Hume immediately goes on to suggest that it is in fact very far from obvious that we can in this way identify an inner self or Mind by some act of introspection:

> For my part, when I enter most intimately into what I call *myself*, I always stumble on some particular perception or other, of heat or cold, light or shade, love or hatred, pain or pleasure. I never can catch *myself* at any time without a perception, and never can observe any thing but the perception. When my perceptions are remov'd for any time, as by sound-sleep; so long am I insensible of myself ... And were all my

> perceptions remov'd by death, and cou'd I neither think, nor feel, nor
> see, nor love, nor hate after the dissolution of my body, I shou'd be
> entirely annihilated, nor do I conceive what is farther requisite to make
> me a perfect non-entity. If any one upon serious and unprejudic'd
> reflection, thinks he has a different notion of *himself*, I must confess I
> can reason no longer with him. All I can allow him is, that he may be in
> the right as well as I, and that we are essentially different in this
> particular. He may perhaps, perceive something simple and countinu'd,
> which he calls *himself*; tho' I am certain there is no such principle in
> me.   (*Treatise*: I.iv.6)

Hume's concluding remarks here are surely heavily ironic: he
believes that in everyone's case introspection may reveal thoughts
or feelings, but not the immaterial Cartesian Mind or self which
allegedly does the thinking and feeling. Hume isn't offering an
argument here so much as an observation put before us for our
agreement. His opponents assert that introspection reveals a Mind
or self behind our thoughts and feelings; and Hume is casting doubt
on this, and querying whether we are ever directly aware of our
'selves' as opposed to the thinking and feeling we engage in. But
though there is no real argument here, the Humean doubt is very
persuasive.

Of course, we do ordinarily talk of a person knowing herself well
– but Hume would say (surely rightly) that this is a matter of her
knowing the sort of things she feels in various circumstances,
understanding her own motives etc.; it does *not* involve her being
acquainted with a mysterious something in addition to her thoughts
and feelings.

Still, this Humean point is not enough to scotch Cartesian
dualism. For the dualist can easily countenance the fact that Hume
cannot find his self introspectively. Consider an analogy: there is
one thing which we cannot directly see, namely our eye itself. Our
eye is what we see with; we have evidence of its existence from
mirror images, and from the sense of touch, and so on – but we
cannot directly see it. Likewise, the dualist might urge that our
Cartesian Mind is what enables us to be aware of other things, and
can no more be directly aware of itself than the eye can directly see
itself. But he might still claim that we have compelling indirect
grounds for believing in the existence of Minds.

In short, then, it seems that direct observation – either of other
people or of ourselves – cannot by itself establish the truth or falsity
of dualism. But that point obviously doesn't settle anything: it only

shows that we need to resort to inference and argumentation. So we must turn next to the task of examining some pro-dualist arguments that might be thought to lend weight to the two-component picture.

II

ARGUMENTS FOR DUALISM

1   The dualist, as we have seen, propounds a version of the two-component theory according to which our non-bodily component, our Cartesian Mind, is the true seat of such key mental phenomena as beliefs and desires, pains and visual experiences. But as soon as we start seriously thinking about it, this initial characterisation of the dualist position begins to look extremely vague and thoroughly problematic. What precisely is meant by talk of a 'non-bodily component'? Where are such things to be found? What are they made of? How are they supposed to interact with our bodies? Are we unique among the animals in having them? When and how did they emerge onto the evolutionary scene? The questions crowd in and, as we shall see in Chapter IV, no easy answers present themselves. Yet dualism retains a very powerful appeal; and many are initially tempted to think that, despite the sort of difficulties which we have just raised, some version of dualism must be correct because there are compelling arguments in its favour. So in the present chapter we will begin to unravel some of the considerations that seem to give dualism its undoubted appeal.

Let's start by examining a few lines of thought which hardly qualify as fully-fledged arguments, but which try to articulate the dualist's sense that the mental is quite distinct from anything physical. Such thoughts are perhaps suggested by the loaded rhetorical questions (such as 'how can a conscious being be made of unconscious stuff?') which we raised in I.3 when motivating the dualist position. So consider:

(A)   Mental properties (like being conscious, for example) are so different from physical properties (like weighing two hundred pounds, for example) that they clearly cannot be had by the same thing: so the physical properties are had by the body and the mental ones by something else.

and

(B) Merely material things cannot think or feel. Obviously, we can think and feel. Hence we are not merely material objects, but something else besides.

The first premise of (B) involves the sweeping claim that mere chunks of physical stuff cannot think or feel at all. There is a variation on the argument which appeals instead to the rather more modest premise that there are some particularly deep or impressive thoughts and feelings which merely material things cannot have. Consider for example:

(C) A merely material being could not appreciate *The Marriage of Figaro*, fall in love, believe in God, ... We evidently can appreciate *Figaro*, fall in love, believe in God, ... So again it follows that we are not mere chunks of physical stuff but something else besides.

Perhaps no major philosopher has officially appealed to exactly these crude considerations to support a dualist position. However, such thoughts quite certainly underlie the kind of thing that many apprentice philosophers are inclined to say in defence of their initial pro-dualist inclinations. So it is very well worth expending some effort bringing these thoughts frankly out into the open and exposing their extreme weakness. We will discuss them in turn.

2   A moment's reflection shows that (A) as it stands will not do. Suppose we grant for the sake of argument that there is some good sense in which mental properties are radically different from physical properties. Why on earth should we accept that it follows that the two sorts of properties cannot be had by the same thing? After all, we normally allow that one and the same thing can have a wide variety of properties. A cathedral, for example, may be built of limestone, be seven hundred years old, be of great beauty, and be visited by thousands of people a year. These various characteristics certainly seem at first sight to be very different in type one from another: yet for all that, one and the same thing – the cathedral – has the temporal characteristics, the aesthetic ones and so forth. So why shouldn't we be able to agree that mental properties and physical properties are likewise very different in type, but again go on to insist that they are had by one and the same unitary thing –

this time the human organism which is Jack or Jill? Why shouldn't things have properties of the two diverse kinds?

To add to our questions here, suppose we do get squeamish about saying that mental and physical properties can be had by the same thing; why should we then stop at dualism? For mental properties are themselves a pretty mixed bunch. Compare, for instance, the properties of being in pain and of understanding quantum field theory. We cannot readily be mistaken about whether we are in pain, but it is all too easy to be mistaken about whether one understands a scientific theory. Again, understanding quantum field theory would seem to be a state only open to a rational language-using creature, while even a mouse can feel pain. These contrasts suggest that mental properties can in turn be divided into notably distinct classes. So if we are in the mood to multiply entities and infer a two-component picture from the alleged split between physical and mental characteristics, why not go one better and infer a three-component picture from the equally impressive contrasts between physical, intellectual and sensory properties? Thus we might suppose that a person consists of a body plus an intellect plus a centre of sensation. Why stop at a neat marriage between body and Cartesian Mind, when more exciting relations between three or more partners beckon?

Of course, these remarks do not show that there is anything actually wrong with dualism; but they do show that argument (A) is not enough by itself to establish the dualist case. The advocate of (A) owes us a reasoned defence of his assumption that the supposed divide between our mental and physical properties requires us to be beings comprised of exactly two components, no more and no less. Mere assertion is not good enough.

3   Turning next to arguments (B) and (C), what are we to make of their talk of 'merely material things'? One possibility is that the word 'merely' is intended to function simply as a kind of verbal sneer. If that is how the word is being used in (B), then the first premise is just another, rather dismissive, way of saying that material things (i.e. things made of physical stuff alone) cannot think or feel. But the dualist can hardly help himself to *that* as a starting-point for an argument against a naturalistically inclined opponent. For this opponent is immediately going to retort: no,

some material things can think and feel – namely those entirely physical organisms which are human beings! So, if (B) is to get off the ground as an argument, we had better read its first premise in some alternative way that does not dismissively beg the question against the anti-dualist.

Suppose therefore that we understand talk of 'merely material things' to refer to fairly unorganised lumps of stuff like sticks and stones which lie about the world in a quite insensate and boringly inert way. Then of course we can all accept that 'merely material things', on this second understanding of the term, cannot think or feel, while we humans can think and feel. So it certainly follows that we are not in the present sense merely material beings. However, argument (B) tries to reach the much stronger conclusion that we are not merely material things *but something else besides*; and if this strengthened conclusion is to be read in a dualist way, it has no warrant at all. For what justifies the move from the thought that we are not inert and unorganised lumps of stuff to the desired conclusion that we are chunks of physical stuff *plus* some other non-material thing? Why shouldn't we agree that we are not *simple* lumps of stuff, but go on to assert (with the anti-dualist) that we are extremely *complex* material beings? The premises of argument (B), on our second understanding of the phrase 'merely material things', in fact give no more support to the dualist position than to its naturalistic rival.

So on either of our interpretations of its initial premise, argument (B) collapses. On the first understanding of that premise, it entails the desired dualist conclusion but is unacceptable because question-begging: on the alternative reading, the premise can be freely granted but it doesn't imply dualism. It is only by muddling the two interpretations that one could possibly come to see argument (B) as persuasive.

Does (C) fare any better? Well, the anti-dualist will presumably reply to its assumption that material things cannot appreciate *Figaro* (for example) with the bald counter-claim that some material things *can* appreciate Mozart's opera – namely human beings. So the initial premise of (C) again begs the question against the anti-dualist. However, the defender of argument (C) might protest that his opponent's counter-claim is in this case wildly implausible. We can imagine him arguing like this:

> How can you possibly think that some purely physical system could appreciate such sublime music? I can just about see how

you might come to hold that merely material things could have some types of mental state, such as mundanely factual beliefs – though speaking as a dualist I must disagree with this supposition. I can for instance understand that, if you are over-impressed with the capacities of computers, then you might perhaps start attributing to them some thoughts. However, soul-less physical systems certainly cannot respond to Mozart (or fall in love, etc.). Only something that itself rises above and is distinct from brute matter can appreciate the sublime.

Now, this rhetoric has an enticing ring; but it really should not shake the anti-dualist. Let's frankly agree that it is not immediately plain exactly how physical systems might be capable of aesthetic responses. But this in no way supports a dualist two-component picture of the person. For it is equally unclear how *non*-physical systems might be capable of aesthetic responses. Indeed, while there is something of a mystery about the nature of those aesthetic experiences which can be so profoundly important to us, this mystery is not instantly dissolved but merely compounded by ascribing the experiences to a puzzling non-physical entity. It is a major task for philosophy (one that has not been sufficiently pursued) to investigate what is involved in such experience: and it is certainly not obvious at the outset, in advance of any detailed investigation, that the capacity for aesthetic experience can only be explained by locating it in an immaterial Cartesian Mind. Hence the simple appeal to our ability to respond to *Figaro* cannot by itself establish the dualist case.

In short, what we might call 'the *Figaro* argument' fails. The other versions of (C) fail for analogous reasons – so overall (C) indeed fares no better than argument (B).

4   The dualist proponent of (B) or (C) might perhaps protest that we are perversely missing his essential point. He might vigorously argue that his claim that we are more than merely material objects is not question-begging prejudice, but is based ultimately on the thought that

(D)   It is obviously true that things made of physical stuff alone could not exhibit all the complexities of behaviour distinctive of human beings. Hence the thinking and feeling that underlies our behaviour must be due to some non-physical component.

But once again this really will not do at all. For we quite certainly do not understand the workings of the body so well that we can say 'human behaviour *must* be due to non-physical causes'. As Spinoza remarked long since:

> Experience has not yet taught anyone what the body can do from the laws of nature alone, in so far as Nature is only considered as corporeal.
> (*Ethics*: 3 Prop.ii Note)

And this remains true: experience has not yet taught us that a purely corporeal being couldn't exhibit the behavioural complexity of a human being. On the contrary, as research in the biological sciences and in the field of artificial intelligence progresses, we increasingly get to understand how purely physical systems can be capable of more and more complex behaviour. In short, the anti-dualist can rightly protest that (D)'s premise is not obviously true as it stands.

The moral of these preliminary skirmishes is very simple but extremely important: we must not give the game to the dualist too readily by allowing him to assume straight off that the rival naturalistic position is wrong. We may grant that there is some plausibility in saying that mental and physical properties are very different from each other. But the dualist mustn't assume, as in (A), that one and the same thing cannot have both kinds of property. Again, we are of course not merely material things, in the sense of being brute unthinking lumps of stuff; but that doesn't mean that we are a combination of some brute physical thing with a special kind of additional entity which does the thinking, namely a Cartesian Mind. The anti-dualist will obviously agree that we are not unthinking physical objects; his view is that we are *thinking* physical beings and nothing in (B) shows that this view is untenable. Again, we can agree that there is something of a mystery about the nature of our aesthetic experiences (and likewise for many other aspects of our mental lives): but we cannot simply assume with (C) that this establishes the dualist case. For we need to investigate what is involved in our aesthetic responses (or whatever), and we have no business to be prejudging the results of such an investigation by supposing that it must turn out that only immaterial Minds could have such responses. Finally, the dualist cannot just assume what needs to be argued, namely (D) that the complexity of human behaviour is to be explained by ascribing it to non-physical causes.

5   We turn now to discuss a rather more interesting argument which again seems to have a very considerable attraction for many when they begin to think about these matters, but which also proves to be entirely resistible. It goes roughly like this:

(E)   Dualism must be true because people sometimes have experiences in which they perceive themselves from a point outside their bodies. But in that case we can hardly be the same thing as our bodies − for a thing cannot leave itself!

There is a very obvious difficulty with this line of reasoning. Suppose we agree that it occasionally seems to people as if they are perceiving their body from a point located outside it. In such cases, it will no doubt *seem* to the person in question that she herself is somewhere other than where her body is. However, it plainly does not follow from this that she really *is* out of her body. This might merely be a kind of illusion to which people are rather prone.

This point is worth expanding. Suppose that Jill says 'Yesterday, I had the strange experience of seeing my recumbent body as if from a spot six feet above the bed; I watched myself for some time and then ...' We need not impugn Jill's sincerity; we may grant that she is describing exactly how things seemed to her. Yet why shouldn't we say that she is simply reporting an interesting hallucination? And if she did hallucinate, then it obviously does not follow that she in fact 'left her body'. Even if Jill's story about how the world appeared to her during her 'out-of-body experiences' contains details which turn out to be correct, this still does not show that she left her body. For presumably the course of an hallucination can be governed by environmental cues, just as our dreams can often contain elements cued by happenings which occur while we are asleep. If Jill's story is to have any chance at all of providing the basis of a pro-dualist argument, her experiences need to resist being classified as hallucinatory: in a word, her experiences need to be genuine cases of reliable perception. But we have very little reason to suppose that anyone ever has out-of-body experiences of *that* kind.

This is enough to rebut argument (E). However, there is perhaps some residual interest in going on to make a further critical point.

Suppose for the sake of argument that we grant the defender of out-of-body experiences what is really far too much, and pretend that people do sometimes genuinely perceive the world in a reliable way *as if* from a point external to the body. This still would not force us to agree that people (or rather their Minds) sometimes leave their bodies and hence are distinct from their bodies. For note that the occurrence of out-of-body perceptions only establishes that a person can leave her body given the assumption (L), that a person herself is always to be located at the point from which she 'sees' the world. And while this assumption is of course true in ordinary circumstances, we are presently engaged in considering *extra*ordinary circumstances. In such cases, it is doubtful whether we can retain the assumption, as will perhaps become clear if we indulge in a little science fiction fantasy. Suppose that our eyes worked by sending radio signals the short distance to the brain rather than by sending impulses up the optic nerve. Our eyes would then continue to function when removed from their sockets and placed in artificial holders some distance away from the body, and we would in such circumstances be able to see the world (including the rest of our body) from a point outside our main body. There would plainly be very little temptation in this case to preserve assumption (L) and say without qualification that we are still simply located just where our *eyes* are. And once our faith in the necessary truth of (L) is loosened, we certainly cannot presume that it holds good in the case of alleged out-of-body experiences. Thus, even if Jill mysteriously developed the perceptual capacity for reporting on happenings in remote places while remaining physically situated here with us, this would not conclusively prove that Jill herself was travelling around the world in a disembodied state. After all, here she still seems to be, reporting to us her strange experiences. So why not say that Jill is here, but she can (as it were) see further than us?

To sum up. Seeming to perceive the world from a place outside the body proves nothing at all. And we have no good reason to suppose that anyone ever does better than seem to have out-of-body perceptions. Furthermore, even if we did apparently encounter a case of thoroughly reliable perception of events from a point of view remote from the body, this still would not conclusively demonstrate that a person had left her body. So argument (E) collapses.

6   We now turn, at last, to a much more substantial argument, whose treatment requires more care. We are normally prepared in ordinary discourse to say both things like 'Jack is thinking about Vienna' and also things like 'Jack weighs two hundred pounds'. In other words, we normally appear to ascribe both mental and physical characteristics to the same thing. The naturalistically inclined might be tempted to seize on this point and claim that our ordinary ways of thought and talk are quite inimical to the two-component picture of the person. But this would be far too quick. For the dualist can easily retort that such everyday habits of speech are merely a trifle slapdash. On his view, 'Jack weighs two hundred pounds' is simply a familiar shorthand for 'Jack's body weighs two hundred pounds', just as 'Jack had a puncture' is short for 'Jack's car had a puncture'. On the other hand, when we assert that Jack is thinking about Vienna, we are referring to Jack himself, the Cartesian Mind or soul that constitutes the inner man, rather than his body. By taking this line, the dualist need not be the least abashed by our everyday habit of apparently assigning mental and physical states to the same subject – he can explain away this routine speech habit as an entirely understandable shorthand device.

Can the dualist now turn the tables and appeal to other elements of our everyday linguistic practices which in fact favour his two-component picture? Well, consider the following argument:

(F)   According to the naturalistic view, there is nothing more to the person Jack than that complex physical organism which is Jack's body. So on this view the name 'Jack' and the phrase 'Jack's body' pick out one and the same thing. But if these two expressions do stand for the same thing, then surely we should be able to use one expression or the other as the fancy takes us, without radically changing the content of what we say. However, these two expressions are clearly not merely alternative means for picking out the same thing. There is all the difference in the world between saying, for example,

I admire Jack

and

I admire Jack's body.

Indeed, the first could be true while the second is false. And there are many other contexts where substituting the expression 'Jack's body' for 'Jack' significantly changes what is said, even turning a truth into a falsehood. So the name 'Jack' and the phrase 'Jack's body' do not pick out the same thing. Hence the naturalistic alternative to dualism must be false. This is certainly a much more serious pro-dualist argument than its predecessors; as we shall see, it exploits an incontrovertible linguistic fact combined with a plausible principle. But are we forced to accept its conclusion?

First, we must agree that the expressions 'Jack' and 'Jack's body' are not mere stylistic variants which can be freely interchanged without affecting the significance and truth of what is said. Thus contrast 'I met Jack' with 'I met Jack's body', or 'Jack solved a quadratic equation' with 'Jack's body solved a quadratic equation'. Or consider once more the sentence 'I admire Jack's body': if we try substituting the phrase 'Jack's body' for the occurrence of the name 'Jack' in that sentence we arrive at the absurd 'I admire Jack's body's body'. Such examples can be multiplied indefinitely; so we must grant the defender of (F) his starting-point, namely the observation that the expressions 'Jack' and 'Jack's body' are not freely interchangeable.

Second, we must also grant that if two expressions do simply pick out the same thing then they can normally be substituted one for the other without affecting the truth of what is said (they can, in short, be intersubstituted *salva veritate*). For example, if 'Jack' and 'Jill's father' pick out one and the same person, then the claims 'Jack solved an equation' and 'Jill's father solved an equation' stand or fall together – one is true if and only if the other is. While the claims may differ in respect of such things as the politeness of their phraseology, they cannot differ in respect of their truth or falsity. Similarly with the pair of claims 'I met Jack' and 'I met Jill's father' and a vast number of further examples.

The principle involved here is an extremely important one, so let us try to make it absolutely clear. It will be useful to introduce two bits of jargon. First, a *designator* is (roughly speaking) an expression whose standard function is simply to refer to or pick out a particular individual person or thing. So sample designators might be 'Jack', 'that table', 'Jill's father', 'the third book from the left', 'the man in the corner drinking a martini' and so on. Second, we will say that two designators '*a*' and '*b*' are *co-referential* if the claim '*a* is *b*' is true (so that the designators actually refer to the same thing). Accordingly, the pair of designators 'Jack' and 'Jill's father' are co-referential if Jack *is* Jill's father. Now, suppose we have a pair of claims of the form '*a* is *P*' and '*b* is *P*', where '*a*' and '*b*' are designators, and '*P*' specifies some property; then the first claim ascribes the property of being *P* to the thing picked out by '*a*', and the second claim ascribes the same property to the thing denoted by '*b*'. If the two designators '*a*' and '*b*' are co-referential and happen to pick out the *same* thing, then our two claims will be ascribing the same property to the same thing – and so in this case either both claims are true (because the designated item actually has the property in question), or both are false (because the designated item actually lacks the property in question). For example, if the designators 'Jack' and 'Jill's father' are co-referential, then the two claims 'Jack is bald' and 'Jill's father is bald' must stand or fall together, for both claims ascribe baldness to one and the same person. Likewise the pair of claims 'Jack smokes' and 'Jill's father smokes' must also stand or fall together; and so on.

An immediate corollary is this: if some claim of the form 'Jack is *P*' is true and the corresponding claim of the form 'Jill's father is *P*' is false, then it follows that the two designators in question are not co-referential after all but pick out distinct individuals (i.e. it follows that Jack is *not* Jill's father). If two things can be distinguished in respect of *P*-ness, if one is *P* and the other isn't, then we must indeed be dealing with *two* distinct things.

So, to sum up and generalise the point, co-referential designators can be interchanged without affecting the truth of what is said. This principle is one version of what is standardly called *Leibniz's Law*, in honour of the great German philosopher who propounded it. As we shall see in the next chapter, there is actually an important class of exceptions to the principle as we have stated it. However, this fact is largely irrelevant to the point currently at issue; for present purposes we can allow Leibniz's Law to stand in its unrestricted form. But if we accept the principle that two designators which pick out the same thing can be interchanged *salva veritate*, and also grant (as we have done) that the two expressions 'Jack' and 'Jack's body' cannot always be interchanged *salva veritate*, then we obviously have to agree that the two expressions do not simply pick out the same thing. So how can we possibly avoid the dualist's conclusion that the expressions pick out *different* things?

This is not a straightforward matter. But the anti-dualist can perhaps adequately reply to (F) along roughly the following lines. He can maintain that the terms 'Jack' and 'Jack's body' do pick out the same thing, but the latter expression is conventionally reserved for use when one is focusing on the more obviously bodily aspects of Jack. In other words, the phrase 'Jack's body' functions rather like the longer phrase 'Jack, so far as his more obviously corporeal aspects are concerned'. Thus when Jill asserts 'I admire Jack's body', she is thereby conveying the carnal nature of her appreciation of Jack. She is not saying she admires something distinct from Jack himself, but she is revealing what aspects of Jack her admiration is based on (as we might put it, she admires Jack bodywise). We can agree, then, that the expression 'Jack's body' does not *merely* denote Jack. It isn't a designator pure and simple, but instead has a *double* function: it both picks out the living organism which is Jack and also focuses our attention on Jack's more evidently corporeal aspects. This explains why the claims 'I admire Jack' and 'I admire Jack's body' can easily peel apart: since you can admire someone for other than carnal reasons, the first claim may well be acceptable even when the second is not (Jill can admire Jack without admiring him bodywise). Further, given that the phrase 'Jack's body' *does* work rather like 'Jack, so far as his more obviously corporeal aspects are concerned', this perhaps explains why the assertions 'I met Jack's body' and 'Jack's body solved an equation' are distinctly odd, and why the phrase 'Jack's body's body' looks ill-formed.

The important point, the anti-dualist will insist, is that the expression 'Jack's body' does *not* have to be regarded as serving the same sort of function as the expression 'Jack's house'. The latter phrase is indeed a pure designator which simply denotes an object quite distinct from Jack himself: and perhaps the grammatical similarity between the two expressions tempts us into thinking that the phrase 'Jack's body' also picks out something quite distinct from Jack himself. But according to the anti-dualist we should not succumb to this temptation: as we have just seen, there is an alternative, 'double-function', explanation of the use of the phrase 'Jack's body' which does not involve us in supposing that it picks out anything other than Jack after all. That phrase does not designate something distinct from Jack, but rather it serves *both* to designate Jack *and* to focus on Jack's more obviously corporeal characteristics. By adopting some version of this 'double-function' explanation of the linguistic behaviour of the phrase, we can successfully defuse argument (F).

It is worth stressing one further, but absolutely crucial, point. Argument (F) purports to prove the dualist case by reference to features of our everyday ways of talking about people. We have suggested that the argument fails to show that we are linguistically committed to dualism: but even if we were so committed, even if our everyday ways of talking did presuppose a dualist theory, that of course would not show that dualism is true. Our common-sense ways of thought and talk about the matter could just be wrong.

7   In the very first section of Chapter I, we noted that one source of the attractiveness of the two-component picture of the person lies in reflections about the possibility of surviving death. So let's return to consider arguments for dualism that start from premises about life after death.

Obviously we can't argue for dualism like this:

(G)   I myself will survive the (final and total) destruction of my body: but my body will of course not survive its own destruction. So I and my body are two different things.

The move from the premises of this argument to its conclusion looks safe enough: if someone survives the destruction of his body, then clearly he is not the same thing as his body. The trouble with the argument is its first premise. No one who holds a naturalistic view of the person according to which people are complex organisms (and nothing else besides) is likely to agree that a person can survive final and total organic destruction! So the initial premise of the pro-dualist argument (G) just begs the question against the opposition.

It might be protested that we have gone too quickly, and that there are independent reasons for accepting the disputed premise, namely the authority of religious revelation. But this would betray a (rather popular) confusion. The Christian scriptural promise is of eternal life, and this promise can be redeemed even if we could not survive the total and final destruction of our bodies. For note first that there is an important religious tradition which insists that talk of 'eternal life' does not refer to a future life which lasts for ever but rather speaks of the possibility of an ordinary earth-bound life of a certain spiritual quality. This tradition is straightforwardly consistent with a naturalistic view of the person, and lends no support at all to dualism: we will not discuss this tradition any further here. Let's concentrate instead on a very literalistic understanding of the phrase 'eternal life' and interpret the scriptural promise as holding out the prospect of a life continuing after what ordinarily passes for death. Then note secondly that we can *still* have eternal life in this sense, we can enjoy life after death, even if we do not (and could not) survive the total and final destruction of our bodies: for it may be that our ordinary death does not (as we might reasonably assume) entail the final destruction of our bodies. Perhaps we undergo bodily resurrection. And of course, one central Christian tradition involves a faith in just such a resurrection of the body. Jack, this very man, this very corporeal being, will be raised in glory on the Last Day. By adhering to this tradition, the religious believer can deny dualism, can agree that he could not survive the total and final destruction of his body, yet still look forward to everlasting life. His faith is that ordinary death is not the final dissolution of the body.

Christian scriptural authority and the authority of the Church fathers promise us eternal life – but this promise can be redeemed even if dualism is false. We do not have to think of life after death in terms of the Platonic picture we met in the previous chapter which envisages a soul continuing to exist independently of any body. So we certainly have no conclusive scriptural grounds for accepting dualism.

Argument (G) started from the presumption that we can survive total bodily destruction: and this presumption rendered the argument unacceptably question-begging. Can we construct a better argument that starts from a less contentious premise about life after death? Well, even if we lack (G)'s confident faith in the hereafter, we might be tempted to concede that disembodied life after death is some sort of possibility, even if only a remote one. And perhaps this much weaker concession is enough to secure the dualist case. For if we can imagine being disembodied then we can conceive of continuing to exist even after the destruction of our present body. So consider the following argument:

(H) I can imagine myself surviving the destruction of my present body. But of course I cannot imagine my body continuing to exist even when it has been destroyed – that supposition is simply nonsensical. So there is a difference between myself and my body. The first has the property of being imaginable-by-me-as-existing-after-the-destruction-of-my-body, and the second lacks this property. This means that we have found a feature, albeit a complex one, which distinguishes myself from my body. Hence, as the dualist maintains, they must be distinct things.

This argument – which seems to involve another application of Leibniz's Law – looks ingenious and subtle. But on reflection doesn't it rest on rather shaky foundations? Is it really possible to coherently imagine continuing to exist without any body at all? If you try to perform the required imaginative feat then you will find that you rather quickly run into puzzles and difficulties. There threatens to follow an extremely unprofitable dispute about the limits of what we can imagine.

We can, however, support the first premise in (H) without appealing to the troublesome notion of disembodied existence. For while it is difficult to imagine just what it would be like to exist without any body at all, it seems much easier to imagine existing in a different body from the one you have at present. In other words, it seems possible to imagine completely 'swapping bodies' with someone else: and if you can imagine swapping bodies, then you can again imagine continuing to exist (in some other body) even though your present body no longer exists. And this again gives us the first premise of (H).

The basic thought underlying (H) is that we can clearly separate ourselves from our bodies in thought, and then infer from the possibility of separating them in thought that these things must be genuinely distinct items in reality. The very special interest of this idea is that it is one that Descartes himself is standardly interpreted as having used to support his dualism. So, before we pursue (H) any further, it will be well worth seeing how Descartes develops the same underlying idea: indeed, his argument deserves a chapter to itself.

III

DESCARTES'S ARGUMENT

1   The opening pages of Descartes's *Meditations* are among the most impressive in all philosophy. They set before us, in a marvellously compelling way, questions such as these: How do you know that you are not dreaming now? How do you know that the whole course of your experience is not just one long hallucination? Descartes conjures up a

> malicious demon of the utmost power and cunning [who] has employed all his energies in order to deceive me,

and he goes on to imagine

> that the sky, the air, the earth, colours, shapes, sounds and all external things are merely the delusions of dreams which [the demon] has devised to ensnare my judgement.   (*Writings* II: 15)

And how do you know that *you* are not in thrall to such a demon, who even at this moment is orchestrating illusions which fool you into thinking that you are sitting on a chair, reading a book?

These questions – looked at coldly – might seem to involve just the sort of idle speculation that gets philosophy a bad name. So, in discussing the *Meditations*, we first need to show why these apparently absurd Cartesian questions are worthy of serious consideration. Then second, we must explain the relation between the issues raised by these questions and 'the distinction between the human soul and the body' (which, together with the existence of God, is Descartes's announced topic).

2   You currently have a vast and varied range of beliefs about the world around you. Some of these are probably held in a rather tentative way and would be readily abandoned in the light of

countervailing evidence; but others will doubtless seem to be about as certain as anything possibly could be. Take for example your belief that there is a book currently in front of you. You are no doubt as sure of that as you are of anything: but what gives you the right to be sure? The obvious reply is that you can see the book, touch it, hear the rustle of its pages (and, if you are so inclined, pick it up and smell it, and even taste it). In short, you have the overwhelming evidence of your five senses for the existence of the book. And this answer is fine as far as it goes: but – having got ourselves into a questioning frame of mind – it does immediately suggest another more vexing question, namely what gives you the right to be sure that your senses really are trustworthy? It is a familiar enough fact that our senses do let us down from time to time; mightn't they let us down a lot more often and a lot more systematically than we usually suppose them to do?

Consider for example the following science fiction story, a modern-dress version of Descartes's 'evil demon' fantasy. Some time ago, you were abducted in your sleep by a mad scientist, who took you unconscious to his laboratory. While you were still unconscious, he removed your brain from its housing in your body, and placed it in a vat of nutrients; the nerves which respectively supply input signals to the brain and carry output signals from the brain were then connected to apparatus controlled by his mega-computer. This computer is so programmed as to stimulate your input nerves just as if you were perceiving some scene in a perfectly normal way: and in particular everything is cunningly arranged in such a way that when your output nerves send a signal as if to raise an arm (for example) your sensory input nerves are stimulated so that it looks and feels to you exactly as if your arm has actually gone up. In other words, our mad scientist has rigged things up so that, as far as your brain can tell, you are still perceiving and reacting to what you perceive in the ordinary way; there will be no way of telling 'from the inside' that you are actually in the power of the mad scientist and reduced to being a manipulated brain in a vat. But if this is correct, if there really would be no way of telling that you were in this awful situation, then *how do you know that you aren't a brain in a vat right now?* Of course, everything seems normal enough; it certainly seems to you as if you are sitting on a chair reading a book. But how do you know that this isn't because you are currently being fooled by the fiendish devices of some madman?

We should hasten to reassure you straight away that we are not suggesting that there is a real sporting chance that you actually are a brain in a vat, being fed the illusion of reading a book. Of course that isn't how things are! The point of our science fiction story – or equally of Descartes's fantasy of the evil demon – is not to produce in you a real anxiety about whether you are currently reading a book, but rather to get you puzzled about the grounds for the entirely proper confidence you feel in the existence of the book in front of you. As we noted before, the challenge to defend your right to be confident about such things is naturally met by citing the evidence of your senses. But we have now seen that this sort of evidence is not only compatible with the existence of a book in front of you but is also consonant with a very different story in which you are the victim of a systematic hallucination engineered by the mad scientist. This shows that invoking the evidence of your senses to support your everyday beliefs about the world around you wouldn't be enough on its own to defeat the challenge of the determined sceptic: he will simply retort 'Ah, but you could still be completely mistaken about how the world really is, you could be systematically deluded!' Further, it isn't at all clear what we could add which *would* satisfy the sceptic here. For how can we show that our experiences are not all part of some delusion? It is no good blankly appealing to the way the world appears to be. The sceptic will of course agree that our experience *seems* to be of a real external world of books, chairs and so on; but he will just repeat his challenge to demonstrate that this appearance isn't delusory.

At this point, therefore, we are going to have to resort to some more sophisticated argument if we are to defeat the sceptic; and the task of finding a decent argument turns out to be a gripping and absorbingly difficult one which has been at the very centre of philosophical dispute ever since Descartes. It would unfortunately take us too far away from our central concern with the nature of the mind to describe the twists and turns of the debate here (though we will briefly mention below some features of Descartes's own approach). However, all we need for our present purposes is the following crucial point. While you are of course quite sure that you are sitting on a chair, reading a book and so forth, and while you are no doubt right to be sure, it seems that at the moment – in advance of any sophisticated philosophical enquiry – you are *not* going to be in conscious possession of a cast-iron, sceptic-proof defence of your right to be sure about such things.

3   Descartes's reaction to this crucial point is fascinating and (once you understand it) deeply attractive. He suggests the following strategy for dealing with the sceptic. We should first set to one side all those beliefs for which we *don't* actually possess at the outset an absolutely cast-iron guarantee of their truth, so that we are initially left with a core of entirely safe beliefs which can resist even the extravagant challenges of the most fanciful sceptic. Then, from this secure redoubt beyond the reach of any attack, and armed with a set of sound principles with which we can defend our beliefs, we must try to break out again onto the ground we temporarily ceded to the sceptic and refortify most of our old positions in a way which will render them now less vulnerable to sceptical attack. Or, to switch metaphors, having dismantled the ramshackle structure of our beliefs until we are left with some rock-solid foundations, we must then try to build up again a new structure which will no doubt be much the same in broad outline, but which cannot now be shaken by the attempts of the sceptic to undermine it. The Cartesian strategy therefore has two stages, a temporary suspension of belief in those things for which we don't initially have a cast-iron proof, and then a constructive phase in which we seek to re-establish at least the bulk of our old beliefs.

Not surprisingly, it is the second, positive, phase which causes the most trouble for Descartes: it is one thing to set certain beliefs aside for the sake of argument, it is quite another thing to try to re-establish them on a firmer footing. Descartes's own attempt at the positive part of his programme went roughly like this. He first argued for the existence of God, holding (rather implausibly) that this could be established on the basis of some absolutely certain, sceptic-proof principles: and he then suggested that a good God would plainly not have so ordered His creation that our senses would radically deceive us about the nature of the world He has given us. Few have found this terribly convincing! However, it is the first, negative part of the Cartesian project that will concern us here. So let's consider what sort of beliefs you will be left with if you *do* try to follow Descartes in temporarily setting aside all those beliefs for which you haven't readily to hand a cast-iron, absolutely sceptic-proof defence.

As we argued above, it seems that – while engaged in the Cartesian project – you will have to set aside the great bulk of your everyday beliefs about the world around you; for it seems that you just don't have at the outset any immediate knock-down retort to the determined sceptic who continues to insist that your experiences could be completely misleading about how things really are in the world. You will even have to put aside your belief in the existence of your own body: for our tale about the mad scientist seemed to show that you could in principle be deceived about that too – in the story you continued to have experiences as of seeing and feeling your arm, for example, although all that was left of you physically speaking was a brain in a vat. Admittedly, in this first fanciful tale, you do still at least have a brain; but we can easily imagine alternative stories which the sceptic might use to cast doubt on your warrant for believing in the existence of brains. After all, how do you know that you have one? To revert to Descartes's own fantasy, couldn't it be that you are a disembodied spirit who is being completely fooled about *everything* physical – including the existence of brains – by a malicious demon? Doubtless this hypothesis is bizarre: but have you readily to hand a knock-down argument against the sceptic who suggests that you could be deluded about whether you have a brain? So it seems that, at least at the outset, even the existence of your own brain is not beyond sceptical challenge.

So, various fanciful tales can be used by the sceptic to challenge your right to be sure that you have a body (or any bodily part such as a brain – a qualification we will omit henceforth). Hence, if you are following Descartes in setting aside any belief that is initially open to sceptical challenge, then it seems that one belief that will temporarily have to go is your belief in your own body. But if even *that* belief has to be set aside, what can possibly remain standing? Obviously not very much. However, there is one quite crucial belief each of us shares that does seem to be resistant to even the most inventive sceptical challenge, namely our belief in our own individual existence. We may be able to spin a tale according to which we are possibly deceived about the existence of our own body, along with the rest of the physical world. But none of us can coherently suppose ourselves to be in error in holding that we ourselves exist. The very fact that you can so much as raise the question whether you exist proves conclusively that you *do* exist, because you have to exist in order to think at all!

At the beginning of his Second Meditation, Descartes develops exactly this line of thought:

> I have just said that I have no senses and no body. This is the sticking point: what follows from this? Am I not so bound up with a body and

with senses that I cannot exist without them? But I have convinced myself that there is absolutely nothing in the world, no sky, no earth, ... no bodies. Does it not now follow that I too do not exist? No: if I convinced myself of something then I certainly existed. But there is a deceiver of supreme power and cunning who is deliberately and constantly deceiving me. In that case I too undoubtedly exist, if he is deceiving me; and let him deceive me as much as he can, he will never bring it about that I am nothing so long as I think that I am something. So after considering everything very thoroughly, I must finally conclude that this proposition, *I am, I exist*, is necessarily true whenever it is put forward by me or conceived in my mind.   (*Writings* II: 16-17)

Descartes sums up the same point in Part Four of his *Discourse on the Method*:

I noticed that while I was trying thus to think everything false, it was necessary that I, who was thinking this, was something. And observing that this truth '*I am thinking, therefore I exist*' was so firm and sure that all the most extravagant suppositions of the sceptics were incapable of shaking it, I decided that I could accept it without scruple as the first principle of the philosophy I was seeking.   (*Writings* I: 127)

In short, while Descartes's belief in the existence of his own body is vulnerable to the evil demon fantasy, his belief in his own existence is absolutely secure. And what goes for Descartes here goes for each one of us.

4   If you follow Descartes in attempting to set aside any belief for which you do not currently have an absolutely rock-solid proof, then (we have suggested) you are going to have to suspend judgement about the existence of your own body; on the other hand, you can retain your belief in your own existence. *But doesn't this imply that you yourself must then be something distinct from your body?* – for we seem to have shown that the two things are distinguishable, at least in respect of how far their existence can be thrown into question. Here at last we seem to have the makings of a sophisticated argument for dualism, and one which looks as if it can indeed be attributed to Descartes.

For example, in the *Discourse* (immediately after the passage just quoted) Descartes writes

I saw that while I could feign that I had no body and that there was no world and no place for me to be in, I could not for all that feign that I did not exist. I saw on the contrary that from the mere fact that I thought of doubting the truth of other things, it followed quite evidently and certainly that I existed; whereas if I had merely ceased thinking, even if everything else that I had ever imagined had been true, I should have had no reason to believe that I existed. From this I knew I was a being whose whole essence or nature is simply to think, and which does not require any place, or depend on any material thing, in order to exist. Accordingly this 'I' – that is, the soul by which I am what I am – is entirely distinct from the body, and indeed is easier to know than the body, and would not fail to be whatever it is, even if the body did not exist. (*Writings* I: 127)

Here we indeed seem to have a straight inference from the absolute certainty of one's own existence as contrasted with the existence of one's body to the dualist conclusion that one's self or soul or Cartesian Mind is something quite distinct from the body and the existence of one does not require the existence of the other. The same argument for the Mind/body distinction can be found in an even brisker form in Descartes's unfinished dialogue *The Search after Truth*. There, the character Polyander, speaking for Descartes, says that he is quite certain that he exists and that he is not a body:

Otherwise, if I had doubts about my body, I would also have doubts about myself, and I cannot have doubts about that. (*Writings* II: 412)

It is this neat, and really rather pleasing, line of argument that we shall refer to below as *Descartes's Argument*.

We should perhaps note straight away that Descartes did offer other arguments for his dualist position which we will not be discussing here. So when we talk of Descartes's Argument we mustn't be taken to be implying that he had only one. More annoyingly, it also has to be admitted that some expert commentators deny that Descartes actually meant to use what we will be calling Descartes's Argument (though others insist that he did). Again we will not enter into the details of the scholarly debate. Our excuses for pressing on regardless are that, first, the Argument is intrinsically fascinating and well worth discussing whether or not it was one of Descartes's own defences of dualism. And second, Descartes certainly *seems* to use the Argument; so even if it is a mistake to attribute it to him in its initial simple version, it would still be absolutely essential to get clear about the Argument as a step towards seeing how Descartes might possibly be read as providing a more complex and perhaps better argument along similar lines.

Descartes's Argument, then, may be summarily stated as follows:
   (a) I can feign that my body does not exist,
   (b) I cannot feign that I myself do not exist,
hence (c) I myself am entirely distinct from my body.
It should not need repeating that Descartes does not mean by (a) that
there is a real element of practical doubt about the existence of his
body; he means of course that *while engaged in the project of setting
aside all beliefs which initially appear vulnerable to sceptical attack* he
can suspend belief in his own body's existence. Interpreted in this way,
the first premise of Descartes's Argument looks very plausible. The
second premise looks even more secure for the reasons that Descartes
himself gives. So, for the sake of the present discussion, we will accept
the two premises (a) and (b) without further argument. Our assessment of Descartes's Argument will therefore turn on whether or not
we think the argument is a valid one, i.e. on whether we think that
accepting the premises logically forces us to accept the dualist
conclusion.

5   We should pause very briefly at this point to compare
Descartes's Argument with what we called argument (H) in the last
chapter. That argument could be briskly summarised in an analogous way as follows:
      (a′) I can imagine myself surviving the destruction of my
           body,
      (b′) I cannot imagine my body surviving the destruc-
           tion of my body,
   hence (c) I myself am entirely distinct from my body.
This argument is not of exactly the same form as Descartes's, but it
is plainly a close relation; in each case we are invited to infer the
distinction between body and self from the observation that there is
something we can imagine or feign with respect to the one which
we cannot imagine or feign with respect to the other. As far as
validity is concerned, the two arguments would therefore seem to
be very much on a par (ignoring some nice quibbles). In other
words, it is reasonable to suggest that the move from the premises
to the conclusion in (H) is legitimate if and only if the parallel move
in Descartes's Argument is acceptable.
   The obvious difference between the arguments is not in respect
of their joint validity or lack of it, but in respect of the plausibility

of their premises. In particular, (a') invites dispute. Is it *really* the case that we can coherently imagine existing without a body at all or continuing to exist in some other body? By contrast, Descartes's premise (a), properly understood, isn't about what is imaginatively possible but about what is required in a certain intellectual project. The claim is that, if we are temporarily retreating from ground which we cannot at the outset defend against the sceptic, then we will have to suspend belief in the existence of our bodies. In short, (a') makes a bold positive claim about what we can imagine; (a) encapsulates a much more modest negative claim about the difficulty of defending our belief in the physical world against sceptical challenge. Put that way, Descartes's (a) looks quite a lot more attractive than (a'). The other premises of the arguments seem roughly equally secure: so, since the premises of Descartes's Argument are safer overall than the premises of (H), while the arguments seem to be on a par as far as validity is concerned, we will continue to concentrate on the Cartesian variation on the common theme.

6   Is Descartes's Argument logically valid? If we accept the premises are we compelled to accept its conclusion?

Leibniz, with his typical logical acumen, saw that the Argument won't do. He wrote

> It is not valid to reason: 'I can assume or imagine that no corporeal body exists, but I cannot imagine that I do not exist or do not think. Therefore I am not corporeal, nor is thought a modification of the body.' I am amazed that so able a man [as Descartes] could have based so much on so flimsy a sophism. ... Someone who thinks that the soul is corporeal ... will admit that you can doubt (as long as you are ignorant of the nature of the soul) whether anything corporeal exists or does not exist. And as you nevertheless see clearly that your soul exists, he will admit that this one thing follows: that you can still doubt whether the soul is corporeal. But no amount of torture can extort anything more from this argument.   (*Papers*: 385)

In short, Descartes's premises about what we can feign to be the case show – at most – that we can *feign* that we are distinct from our bodies: and this isn't sufficient to show that we really *are* separate from our bodies.

This straightforward riposte to the Argument, which was first offered by Descartes's correspondent Antoine Arnauld, is sound enough. But it can usefully be supplemented by some further considerations.

One standard and familiar technique for assessing the validity of a problematic argument is as follows: we seek a second argument which has the same overall form or shape, which should work if the problematic argument works, but which is patently bogus. If we do find such an argument, that will show that the original argument was itself fallacious (the underlying idea here is that an argument's validity is a matter of its form, so finding a second argument of the same form which quite obviously doesn't work will show that the original argument is also a failure). Let's put this technique to work in the present instance. Can we find an argument of the same form as Descartes's Argument which is patently invalid?

Well, suppose Margaret Thatcher wakes up one morning during her premiership stricken by partial amnesia, having forgotten who she actually is, but remembering her Descartes. It then occurs to her that she *might* be the Prime Minister, and she wonders whether this rather improbable proposition is true. Now, could she resolve this question by arguing in the following way?

Let me follow Descartes in temporarily setting aside anything that is vulnerable to sceptical attack. Then it is only too easy to spin sceptical tales according to which *no one* is presently Prime Minister (say, because there has been a revolution overnight)! Indeed, all my beliefs about the constitutional arrangements of Britain may perhaps have been brought about by the machinations of an evil demon. On the other hand, like Descartes, I can be absolutely certain that I exist. That gives me the following two premises,

(a″) I can feign that the Prime Minister does not exist,

(b″) I cannot feign that I myself do not exist.

From these I can infer in the manner of Descartes's Argument that

(c″) I myself am entirely distinct from the Prime Minister.

So that at least settles that I am not the Prime Minister!

Quite obviously, the Prime Minister's Argument – as we will call it – is hopeless. In the imagined situation where the Argument is propounded by Margaret Thatcher herself during her premiership, the premises are true (or at least they are true if the similar premises of Descartes's Argument are true, as we are currently supposing for the sake of our discussion); the conclusion, however, is simply false, for Margaret Thatcher is indeed none other than the Prime Minister. But an argument cannot be valid if it has true premises and a false conclusion. So the Prime Minister's Argument is invalid. And since the Prime Minister's Argument is invalid, and Descartes's Argument has exactly the same form, it follows immediately that the latter is equally invalid.

There would seem to be only one way in which Descartes could side-step this attack, and that is by denying that his Argument *is* genuinely parallel to the specious Prime Minister's Argument. But how could this be done? The single difference between the two arguments is that in the second one the phrase 'the Prime Minister' replaces the phrase 'my body'; so the two arguments are apparently as alike in form as could possibly be. The only escape route would be to say that the parallel breaks down because the interchanged phrases have a quite different sort of function in the two arguments. So let's consider two attempts to pursue this escape route.

First, harking back to the discussion of II.6, it might be suggested that the arguments are not strictly parallel because 'the Prime Minister' is a straightforward designator while the phrase 'my body' functions in a more complex fashion, in keeping with our 'double-function' story. Now, this is in a way right: but of course, this riposte is not available to the dualist, for the 'double-function' account is precisely part of his *opponent's* armoury, and belongs to a line of attack *against* the dualist's theory that 'Jack's body' is a designator which refers to something different from 'Jack himself'.

Alternatively, it might be suggested that while the phrase 'my body' is intended to pick out an entity in Descartes's Argument, the phrase 'the Prime Minister' is used in the second argument merely to locate a social role, and this difference is enough to break the alleged parallel between the two arguments. But again this suggestion does not help the dualist. Suppose we agree that, when Margaret Thatcher asserts (a″), she is saying, in effect, that she can feign that there is nothing which currently occupies the role of being Prime Minister. Well, Descartes's assertion (a) can be equally properly understood in an exactly parallel way; *he* is saying precisely that he can feign that there is nothing which currently occupies the role of being his body. So the suppositions are analogous after all.

There thus seems to be no avoiding Leibniz's conclusion that Descartes's Argument – like the Prime Minister's Argument – is simply invalid; we can accept its rather enticing premises without being at all committed to accepting its dualist conclusion.

7   Fatal damage has already been done to Descartes's Argument; and if that argument is invalid then so too is the analogous argument (H). But as a coda to our discussions – which can be omitted on a first reading – it is perhaps of some interest to say a little more about exactly *why* these arguments are invalid. And the first point to note is that they both belong to a much wider family of invalid arguments that involve exceptions to the principle introduced in the last chapter which we labelled 'Leibniz's Law' (II.6). Let us explain.

Consider the following arguments:

(d) Jill believes that George Orwell wrote *1984*,

(e) Jill does not believe that Eric Blair wrote *1984*,

hence (f) George Orwell is not Eric Blair.

(d′) Jack expects the milkman to call today,

(e′) Jack does not expect his wife's lover to call today,

hence (f′) The milkman is not Jack's wife's lover.

(d″) Oedipus wants to marry Jocasta,

(e″) Oedipus does not want to marry his mother,

hence (f″) Jocasta is not Oedipus's mother.

Each of these arguments is evidently invalid; in each case the premises could be true yet the conclusion false. From the fact that Jill is averagely ignorant about literary history it certainly doesn't follow that George Orwell and Eric Blair are different people. Likewise, from the fact that Jack does not think of the milkman as his wife's lover it certainly does not follow that the milkman is not in fact his wife's lover! Similarly with the third argument.

Now, how do these elementary observations square with our remarks in the last chapter about Leibniz's Law? You will recall that we noted then that two co-referential designators can normally be interchanged *salva veritate* – i.e. they can be swapped one for the other without making a difference to the truth or falsity of what is said. Or, what comes to exactly the same thing, if swapping two designators *does* affect the truth of what is said, then (as a general rule) this shows that they denote distinct items. Consider, for example, the simpler argument

(g) George Orwell wrote *1984*,

(h)   Eric Blair did not write *1984*,
       hence (i) George Orwell is not Eric Blair.

This little argument is plainly valid: if both the premises had happened to be true, then the conclusion would have had to be true too. If plugging the designator 'George Orwell' into the empty slot in '... wrote *1984*' produces a truth while plugging in the designator 'Eric Blair' produces a falsehood, then the designators must indeed pick out distinct things. Now, the three arguments we have just spelt out evidently attempt to exploit the same general rule; for in each case the premises record that something holds true when stated with one designator and is false when stated using another designator – and in accord with the rule it is inferred that the things picked out by the designators are distinct. The invalidity of these arguments illustrates that there are exceptions to the rule.

To take just the first example again, consider the premise (d); we obviously cannot substitute the designator 'Eric Blair' for the occurrence of 'George Orwell' in *this* context and rely on preserving the truth, despite the fact that the two designators are actually co-referential (i.e. despite the fact that Eric Blair *is* George Orwell). On the contrary it may be true that Jill believes that George Orwell wrote *1984* and yet false that she believes that Eric Blair wrote *1984*. Similarly with the other examples. So it seems that we need to amend the rule about the interchangeability of designators which denote the same thing; we now must say something like this – two co-referential designators can be swapped one for the other without affecting the truth of what is said *except when they occur after a psychological verb like 'expects', 'believes', 'wants', etc.* In other words, the fact that two particular designators '*a*' and '*b*' cannot be interchanged *salva veritate* after a psychological verb is quite compatible with the truth of '*a* actually is *b*'.

But why should the rule need amending in this way? This question raises some surprisingly sticky issues which we won't be able to go into properly here. Putting it *very* crudely, we can say that when a designator occurs after a psychological verb, it (often) no longer functions in the normal way to pick out some item in the real world. Rather it functions instead as part of the specification of what someone expects, believes, desires or whatever, and locates – so to speak – an element of that person's mental world. To go back to another of our examples above: suppose that the designators 'the milkman' and 'Jack's wife's lover' in normal contexts do indeed pick out one and the same person – i.e. suppose the milkman *is*

Jack's wife's lover. When the designators occur after the psychological verb in the premises of the argument, however, they no longer straightforwardly refer to a particular man but function differently, to give the conceptual content of Jack's expectation (i.e. to specify how he is thinking about things). And obviously it may be the case that in Jack's mental world his concept of *the milkman* may be different from his idea of *my wife's lover*. Thus, the two designators may well locate different conceptual contents when used after psychological verbs; and then – in those special psychological contexts – they cannot be freely interchanged.

Returning now to Descartes's Argument we can see straight away that it involves an attempt to invoke Leibniz's Law in one of those contexts which create exceptions to the general rule. Descartes's idea is that since he can feign that his body does not exist but cannot feign that he himself does not exist it follows that he is something distinct from his body. In other words, Descartes thinks that since the expressions 'I myself' and 'my body' cannot be freely interchanged in the context 'I can feign that ... does not exist' it follows that they pick out different things. But 'I can feign ...' is, of course, a psychological context; and designators which occur in this setting function as part of the specification of a mental state. And, as we have just seen, we cannot infer from the fact that two designators cannot be interchanged in this sort of setting that they do not pick out one and the same thing in their standard use. In brief, Descartes's Argument is invalid for exactly the same sort of reason that the obviously bogus arguments about Jack, Jill and Oedipus are invalid.

IV

DIFFICULTIES FOR THE DUALIST

1   In the last two chapters we have seen that a number of
initially attractive pro-dualist arguments fail to establish the existence of Cartesian Minds as entities distinct from our bodies. But it
can't be emphasised too strongly that this is not yet to show that
dualism is actually false. It is a simple but fundamental point of
logic that bad arguments can have conclusions which happen to be
true; knocking down even eight or nine arguments for a theory
doesn't prove that the theory is wrong – for that still leaves open
the possibility that a tenth argument will turn up trumps and
conclusively demonstrate the soundness of the theory in question.

We now turn, however, to the anti-dualist case, and we will
consider in this chapter a number of arguments that are designed to
show that dualism is indeed a mistaken theory of the mind. But
before doing so, it is perhaps worth stressing once more that the
issue here is an issue about a particular *theory* concerning what it is
to have a mind in the ordinary sense. To argue that this theory is a
bad one isn't to suggest that we are really mindless zombies. On the
contrary, in debating whether Cartesian Minds really exist, we will
still be taking it for granted that we do have the capacities for
thought and feeling: our question is about what makes it possible
for us to have them.

The obvious place to begin our discussions is with the dualist's
conception of the soul or self or mind as an *immaterial entity*
distinct from (and in principle separable from) the body. It might be
tempting to be rather brusque with this idea and assert that the
claim that there exist non-physical things is simply nonsensical.
However, this would be far too hasty. For the dualist's idea is, at
bottom, that there exist entities of a kind that are not recognised by
physics (the science of matter): and it would surely be outrageous to
dismiss as nonsense the thought that there could perhaps be more
things in heaven and earth than are dreamt of in the physicist's

philosophy. In other words, we can't immediately damn dualism as meaningless just because it is a theory which speaks of entities which are not recognised by physics: we must proceed more cautiously. So let's set aside for the moment worries about the immateriality of Minds – we will return to take up the issue in § 4 – and concentrate first on the even more basic dualist assumption that Minds are genuine *entities* in their own right.

2   What is it to be a genuine entity? At first sight, this question might seem far too general, far too abstract, to admit of any contentful answer. But we can lay down some minimal requirements that any genuine entity should fulfil. In particular, if Xs are to count as genuine objects in their own right, then the question 'how many Xs have we got here?' must have a certain legitimate application. Let us explain.

There are many things (in a very loose and generous sense of the word) which no one would care to treat as genuine objects in their own right. Take, for example, *sakes* and *builds*. We certainly talk of such things, as when we say that Jack went to the party for Jill's sake, or that his build prevents him from being a really good fast bowler. But we are not in the least tempted to suppose that sakes or builds are genuine entities. We certainly don't think that Jill is one item, her sake another, and that there is a mysterious relation between the two which prevents Jill passing on her sake to someone else. Questions like 'can Jill exist without a sake?' or 'how many sakes has Jill got?' are more or less senseless. However, such questions can quite sensibly be raised about genuine objects like Jill's heart or her coat. Likewise, no one thinks for a moment that Jack's build is a distinct entity from Jack, or gets puzzled about why the two always go around together (if he can leave his coat at home, why can't he leave his build there too?) A question like 'how many has Jack got?' cannot be asked about builds in the entirely serious way that it can be asked about genuine objects like coats.

It is very plausible to suggest, therefore, that in the case of genuine entities (unlike builds or sakes) the question 'how many?' can be sensibly applied. And it is perhaps worth adding that, at least when we are dealing with entities which persist through time, the question 'is it the same one again, or merely an exact replica?' should also have a parallel application. For example, the question 'is this the golf ball I lost yesterday, or merely an exactly similar one?' makes perfect sense: but the question 'is Jill's sake today the same sake that she had yesterday or merely an exactly similar one?' is just nonsense. Turning then to the dualist's claim that Cartesian Minds are genuine entities in their own right, entirely distinct from bodies, it seems that he must allow that our two test questions will have application to Minds. In other words, he must grant that on his view it makes sense to ask 'how many Cartesian Minds are associated with this particular human body?' and also 'is the Mind which is now associated with this body the same one as was associated with it a few moments ago, or is it only a (more or less) exactly similar replacement?'

To keep things simple, we will only discuss the first of our two questions: a discussion of the other question would run closely parallel. So, how will the dualist respond to the question 'how many minds?' Well, obviously, what he wants to say is that there is one and only one Mind associated with each normal living human body. *But what entitles the dualist to this view?* To quote Strawson, who is developing a variation on a theme in Kant:

> Suppose I were in debate with a Cartesian philosopher, say Professor X. If I were to suggest that when *the man*, Professor X, speaks, there are a thousand souls simultaneously thinking the thoughts his words express, having qualitatively indistinguishable experiences such as he, the man, would currently claim, how would he persuade me that there was only one such soul? (How would each indignant soul, once the doubt has entered, persuade itself of its uniqueness?)   (1966: 174)

If Minds are genuine entities in their own right, what is to stop us advancing the supposition that there are *many* Minds associated with a given body, all thinking away more or less in parallel? This supposition must make as good sense as the original Cartesian hypothesis of one Mind per body. In that case, as Strawson says, it is very difficult to see how the dualist could claim to know that his 'One Mind' theory is true. As he looks inside his own Mind, how can he tell whether it is unique or whether it is one of a community of similar Minds attached to the same body? But if there is no way of experientially deciding between the official Cartesian story and its fanciful 'Many Minds' rival, has Descartes any right to insist that his tale is the correct one?

It is very important to see that the dualist cannot simply protest that a normal human being has one Mind 'by definition'. We might reasonably say, by contrast, that a person only has one build at a time by definition: and we might perhaps say that someone has just one sake by definition. But this is because builds or sakes make no pretence of being genuine entities in their own right. Cartesian Minds, on the other hand, are supposed to be entities distinct from bodies – as distinct as a car from the garage which houses it. So it must be an open question, which cannot airily be settled 'by definition', how many are associated with each body – just as it is an open question, which can't be settled by definition, how many cars are in a particular garage. Part of the price of insisting that Minds are genuine entities in their own right (like cars or coats, not builds or sakes) is that Minds have to be counted independently of bodies.

How, then, is the dualist to defend his answer to the question 'how many Minds per body?' It seems that about the best that he can do is to claim that his 'One Mind' theory is to be preferred to the extravagant 'Many Minds' alternative because it is simpler and more economical. However, although simplicity is a virtue in theories, it is certainly no guarantee of truth. So our Cartesian must grant that he is going well beyond the bounds of certainty. His claim that a person such as himself consists of one body plus one Mind now has the status of a rather chancy hypothesis which is at most a reasonable bet. To admit this is – to say the least – to retreat a very long way from Descartes's confident certainty in the existence of his own unique Mind.

We can press the attack further. For it is really quite unclear whether the Cartesian can even make sense of the difference between his story being true and Strawson's 'Many Minds' story being true. What makes the difference between there being one Mind and there being many exactly similar Minds? It would seem that there must be a difference if Minds are entities in their own right. In the case of physical objects, such as billiard balls, it is spatial location which distinguishes one ball from another qualitatively identical one: even if the two red balls on the table are as similar as can be, there are still two of them, which are distinguished by being in two different places. But Minds, at least according to Descartes's official story (cf. *Writings* I: 339), are non-spatial entities – so what can distinguish qualitatively identical Minds one from another?

It might be suggested that different souls are made of different lumps of soul-stuff. But what on earth is *that*? To allow that talk of non-physical entities perhaps makes sense certainly doesn't commit us to countenancing the idea of non-physical stuffs. (Perhaps numbers and other mathematical abstractions are non-physical things: but it would be nonsense to suppose that *they* are made of non-physical stuff!) And in any case, there would remain the problem of how we are to distinguish two qualitatively similar parcels of soul-stuff.

Difficulties for the dualist are now beginning to mount up. And note that they are difficulties *only* for the dualist – his naturalistic opponent need have no problems here at all. Since the anti-dualist denies that the mind is an entity distinct from the body, *he* can construe talk of someone's mind as being – so to speak – rather like talk of his build. The anti-dualist can maintain that a normal human has one mind 'by definition', so that for him embarrassing questions about how to count minds just don't arise (we will see in Chapter VI how to develop this point). But the Cartesian can't avoid the problems, which seem fundamentally challenging and yet also pretty intractable.

There is doubtless more to be said: however, we can't pursue this damaging but increasingly abstract line of attack any further here. Instead, in order to keep the argument going, let's give the benefit of any residual doubts to the dualist and simply *pretend* from now on that the Cartesian can at least see off the field the alternative 'Many Minds' hypothesis. Plenty of other telling difficulties remain.

3   On the dualist view, there is an absolutely sharp distinction to be drawn between (i) being a merely physical entity, and (ii) having both a physical body and an immaterial Mind. Sticks and stones fall into the first category, we humans supposedly fall into the second: but where do animals fit into this scheme of things? We normally suppose that non-human animals can perceive the world around them and have desires for food and sex; indeed we credit many animals with quite a rich mental life. So should we say that they too have Cartesian Minds?

Descartes himself bluntly supposes that animals belong in the first category of Mind-less, purely physical things. In Part Five of the *Discourse* he argues that animals are indistinguishable from automata;

they have no intelligence at all, and ... it is nature which acts in them according to the disposition of their organs.   (*Writings* I: 141)

Now, from a post-Darwinian perspective, Descartes's attempt to draw an absolutely clear line between us and the brutes by reference to the presence or absence of Minds looks utterly misguided – there just doesn't seem to be that sort of all-or-nothing difference between us and other animals. But it is interesting to note that Leibniz and Locke, writing the better part of two centuries before Darwin, also found Descartes's position quite unsatisfactory. Thus Leibniz protests that

the opinion of those who transform or degrade beasts into pure machines ... goes beyond appearances, and is even contrary to the order of things.   (*Papers*: 454)

And Locke, alluding to the old doctrine of a Great Chain of Being, writes

in all the visible corporeal world we see no chasms or gaps. All quite down from us the descent is by easy steps and a continued series of things, that in each remove differ very little one from the other. ... There are some brutes that seem to have as much knowledge and reason as some that are called men; and the animal and vegetable kingdoms are so nearly joined that, if you will take the lowest of one and the highest of the other, there will scarce be perceived any great difference between them; and so on, till we come to the lowest and most inorganical parts of matter, we shall find everywhere that the several *species* are linked together and differ but in almost insensible degrees.   (*Essay*: III.vi.12)

If there is, in particular, no chasm between men and such animals as the higher apes, then it really can't be plausible to describe the differences which do exist in terms of the stark Cartesian picture (i.e. in terms of the quite radical difference between having a Mind and lacking one). And although Locke rather fudges the issue here as he wants to tread carefully around the Christian doctrine of the soul, his sense of discomfort with the Cartesian view is clear.

Locke's idea that there are no presently existing gaps in nature has, of course, been superseded by the idea that there are – so to speak – no gaps in the history of species; there is an evolutionary story to be told which starts with the primordial slime and runs through to the emergence of human beings. Of course, there is much controversy about the details of this story, and in particular there is considerable argument about the exact *mechanism* of evolution. Fortunately, we don't need to get embroiled in the debates here: all we need for present purposes is the thought that there is a non-gappy series of organisms of increasing behavioural complexity linking the two ends of the spectrum through time. This gives a corresponding temporal twist to the problem for Descartes: when, in the evolutionary story, do Minds first come onto the scene? And why should they emerge? The proto-organisms in the slime presumably don't have Minds, while rational creatures such as ourselves do: it would seem to be quite arbitrary to point to any one place on the gradually rising evolutionary curve and say 'Minds suddenly emerge here', and it will be equally puzzling *why* they should emerge at exactly that point. It's not just that Descartes's own placing of a sharp divide between humans and all other animals is unsatisfactory; *any* sharp demarcation along the evolutionary curve will be equally implausible. In particular, the distinctive mental capacities for perception, desire, thought and feeling emerge gradually, not in one revolutionary leap.

Now, it would be one thing for the Cartesian to ignore complaints based on the pre-scientific idea of a Great Chain of Being; it would be something else entirely to take an equally cavalier attitude to the problems set by evolutionary theory. Unless the dualist rejects post-Darwinian science out of hand, he is going to have to admit that on the material front there is a gradual development of organic complexity, while insisting that on the mental front there is at some point a radical jump between creatures without Minds and creatures with them. This position is not contradictory, but it is difficult to find anything to be said for it: what can possibly explain the existence and location of that alleged jump? The Cartesian operates with a sharp, black/white distinction between bodies which lack associated Minds and those which have them; but the facts of evolutionary development seem to need depicting in graduated shades of grey. Faced with the developmental facts, the latter-day dualist must be embarrassed.

It might be suggested that there is a way out. The dualist could reply that *all* physical things have incorporeal entities associated with them, so there is after all no divide anywhere between things with and without Cartesian components. Thus proto-organisms, the large organic molecules which precede them on the evolutionary tree, and even their component inorganic molecules, atoms and atomic particles, all have proto-Minds, albeit much simpler ones than ours; and there is a process of parallel evolution in both the material and the immaterial realms. But this last-ditch suggestion is wildly fanciful, postulating as it does a whole shadow universe in parallel to the physical world: the idea has the ring of sheer desperation!

4   Let's again pretend as we did in the case of the earlier 'Many Minds' challenge, that the dualist can somehow wriggle off the hook here. It is worth going on to show that there are further difficulties still confronting the dualist, arising from the putative immateriality of Minds.

On the face of it, mental events can cause physical events. For example, you decide to raise your arm and as a result your arm goes up. Or you suddenly remember an embarrassing incident and as a result you blush. Or you feel a stab of pain and that causes you to wince. The deciding, remembering and feeling are mental happenings, and they surely cause the various physical upshots. It seems equally obvious that physical events can cause mental ones. For example, light stimulates the retina and you have a visual experience. The dentist's probe hits a nerve and you feel pain. The sugar level in your blood drops and you start to want food. Here, the retinal stimulation, the prodding of the nerve and the decline in sugar level are all physical happenings, and they cause various mental upshots. We can sum up these apparent truisms by saying that mind and body causally interact. This causes no difficulty at all for that kind of anti-dualist who thinks of mental occurrences as (in some sense) nothing other than events in the brain: for him, mind/body interaction is just a particular kind of physical transaction. But for the dualist, it is a matter of a physical body interacting with an immaterial Cartesian Mind. And that raises two problems. First, *the Philosophical Problem*: without going into physiological details, how much sense can we make of the idea that two things as different as a physical brain and an immaterial Mind can causally interact? And second, *the Scientific Problem*: even if the idea of such interaction makes sense, can we square the claim that it occurs with our knowledge of neuro-physiology? The Philosophical Problem will be our topic in the next section: but the issue is tricky to handle, and the somewhat inconclusive discussion may be omitted on a first reading. We discuss the Scientific Problem in §6.

5   If we say of two events that the first caused the second, then the question '*how* did the one cause the other?' is usually in order. Suppose we assert that a mosquito bite caused the onset of malarial fever; if this causal statement is to be true, then there must exist some causal mechanism which leads from the bite to the fever. Of course, the observed correlation between mosquito bites and fever may make us very confident that there is some underlying causal mechanism at work, even when we have not yet discovered what it is. Still, in claiming that there is a real causal relation here, we do commit ourselves to there being some linking mechanism or other; and it should in principle be discoverable what it is – in other words, there should in principle be some answer to the question '*how* did the mosquito bite bring about a malarial attack?' Until we get an answer, the causal claim will remain merely a promissory note.

Turn now to the dualist who claims that events in our immaterial Mind (which is what he thinks deciding, remembering or feeling are) can cause bodily happenings. On his view, an immaterial cause and a physical upshot are even less like each other than a mosquito bite and a fever attack, so in this case the question 'how does the causal mechanism work?' seems even more urgent. But what can the dualist possibly say to relieve our puzzlement?

Consider an example: Jack wants to vote for Jill, and it is that desire which causes his hand to go up at the appropriate moment. The dualist conceives this as involving a state of an immaterial Mind bringing about a physical upshot, so we ask him '*how* did the immaterial desire bring about the physical arm movement?' Well, he can tell us more about what happens on the mental side of things – perhaps Jack's desire to vote combines with his belief that raising an arm now would count as voting, and so produces a desire to raise his arm; and perhaps this desire in turn combines other beliefs and desires to produce a decision to raise the arm. There is another story to be told on the physical side: neural occurrences lead to the transmission of impulses down nerves, causing muscle contractions, causing the arm to rise. But however much the dualist fills out his tale about what happens between the initiating desire and the final bodily movement, there must on his view be a last immaterial event in the causal sequence (perhaps a decision) and a first physical event (perhaps a neurone firing): and we can now ask of *those* disparate events 'but how does the first cause the second?' We are left with a problem of exactly the same kind as the one we started with.

The general difficulty is this: if we ask the dualist to explain how some particular immaterial event causes a physical upshot then, whatever tale the dualist spins for us, he can only mention further happenings that fall squarely on one side or the other of the great divide between physical events and events in immaterial Minds. If we start off by being puzzled about how the realm of the Mind can influence the physical realm, nothing the dualist can say will make matters any clearer.

There is, of course, an exactly similar difficulty in understanding how physical happenings can have immaterial consequences. The dentist jabs in his probe, and causes you to wish you were elsewhere. On the dualist's view, this is a matter of a physical event having a causal upshot in an immaterial Mind. Suppose we ask once more how the one causes the other. The dualist can tell us more about what happens on the physiological side, tracing the causal sequence of events in your peripheral nervous system on up to the brain. And there is, on his view, a story about the Mind to be told as well — for instance, the occurrence of an excruciating pain prompts the wish. But however fully the links in the causal mechanism leading from the jab to the wish are described, there will be a last physical link in the chain which supposedly causes the first immaterial event in the Mind. And we are left with nothing to say about how *those* two events can be causally linked. In short, then: given that causation requires the existence of causal mechanisms, and that there can be no such mechanisms linking across the body/Mind divide, it follows that there can after all be no causal interaction between physical bodies and immaterial Minds.

Now, as we shall see very shortly, the dualist has a plausible reply to this argument as it presently stands. But it is worth noting that Descartes's theory was thought from the outset to be vulnerable to criticism along these general lines. Of course, Descartes recognised that he had to say something about the interaction of Minds with bodies, and he suggested that the Mind brings its influence to bear on the body in the pineal gland. However, to specify the location of the putative Mind/body interface is not to specify how the causal interaction is supposed to work. We might still want to know, as did Descartes's correspondent Princess Elizabeth of Bohemia, '*How* can the soul of man, being only a thinking substance, determine his bodily spirits to perform voluntary actions?' (Descartes *Letters*: 136). Descartes's replies to Elizabeth survive, but are distinctly unhelpful. It is tempting to agree with Leibniz, who also 'found no way to explain how the body causes anything to take place in the soul, or vice versa', when he judges that 'Descartes gave up the struggle over this problem, so far as we can know from his writings' (*Papers*: 457).

Yet the dualist *can* rebut this line of criticism, at least in the form we have presented it. He needs to undermine the general claim that, where there is causality, there must always be an underlying causal mechanism – and this can be done quite plausibly. For consider again the mosquito bite which causes a malarial attack. Let's grant that it is at least in principle possible to specify the causal mechanism at work, and describe the linking events involving the transmission of a virus, its multiplication, its interaction with the body's immune system, and so on. Further, if we want to take a closer look at some part of the causal chain just described, then we can no doubt go on to explain how one event in the chain causes the next by moving to a more detailed examination of the underlying mechanisms. For example, we could hope in principle to explain the process of viral multiplication in biochemical terms. And then looking at these biochemical processes, we might hope to explain *them* in term of quantum chemistry. However, we might reasonably suppose that this process of explaining coarse-grained causal processes in terms of increasingly more fine-grained constituent processes has got to come to a stop sometime. Eventually – for example when we are dealing with the most fundamental elementary particles – we will reach the rock-bottom level of causal analysis. At this level, we may still want to say of two events that one is the cause of the other, but there will be no further, yet more fine-grained, sub-structure in terms of which this causal relation can be explained. In other words, we must in the end get down to the level of the most basic causal processes, for which questions about underlying mechanisms do not arise.

But once this point is conceded for the case of physics, the dualist can leap to the defence of his position. He can argue along the following lines: 'If we recognise that there *can* be cases of basic, rock-bottom, causal relations which can't be further explained, why shouldn't I maintain that causation across the Mind/body interface is exactly such a case? Why shouldn't I say that here too we have basic causal relations without there being any linking causal mechanisms which could be further described? So the fact that I can't explain what happens at the interface is by itself no objection to my position.' Well, let's grant without further ado that this *is* an adequate reply to the argument which appealed to the sweeping principle that causality requires underlying causal mechanisms. The Cartesian, however, is still not out of trouble.

Consider again the sorts of interaction which, according to our dualist, are instances of basic causal relations between Minds and bodies. Suppose, for the sake of argument, that an example of Mind-to-body causality is provided by a conscious decision and its neural upshot. Thus, you decide to gently wiggle your right index finger, and as a result there is an appropriate neural event (which eventually leads in normal cases to your index finger moving): this, says our dualist, is a case of a basic causal relation, not further to be explained. You now decide to wiggle your second finger, and as a result there is a different neural upshot: this too is supposed to be a case of basic causality. You next decide, not on a gentle wiggle, but on a more vigorous movement of your fingers (or of your whole hand, or your arm, or your toes, or ...): and each of these different decisions in turn results in a different neural upshot – yet another case of basic causality. Carrying on in this way we will obviously end up with a very large number of different basic causal relations, linking particular events in the Mind with their respective bodily consequences. We will have a multiplicity of connections between decisions and neural results which cry out to be systematised and causally explained; but our dualist has insisted on treating these as basic relations which *cannot* be further explained. Now, nothing here seems to depend on our assumption that it is decisions which lie at the Mind/body interface; whatever the Cartesian locates there, similar considerations would suggest that he is going to have to admit that the interface is causally very complex indeed. Yet at the same time – in order to avoid our earlier argument – the Cartesian must hold that there are no underlying causal linkages which could explain this complexity.

While this isn't an incoherent position, it seems a deeply unattractive one. It is one thing to allow a very limited number of types of not-to-be-further-explained interactions between fundamental physical particles, governed by a small number of laws: it is surely something else to postulate a burgeoning family of basic Mind/body causal relations. This would seem to count, not as problem-solving, but as puzzle-creating: we are apparently faced with just the sort of complexity which cries out for further causal explanation, but we are simultaneously told that no such explanation is possible. Now, maybe this complaint can be met, and the alleged parallel between fundamental physical interactions and fundamental Mind/body relations can be restored: so our arguments here are perhaps not conclusive. But until we do get a clearly developed response from the dualist which makes some physiological sense, it is tempting to agree with Ryle's blunt assessment:

> the connection between [events in the Mind and bodily events] is ... a mystery. It is a mystery not of the unsolved but soluble type, like the problem of the cause of cancer, but of quite another type. The episodes supposed [by the Cartesian] to constitute the careers of minds are assumed to have one sort of existence, while those constituting the careers of bodies have another sort; and no bridge-status is allowed. Transactions between minds and bodies [in order to be explicable] involve links where no links can be. (1949: 66)

In short, the dualist theory of the Mind seems to have a serious and intractable puzzle at its very heart.

6   Let's for the third time let the Cartesian off the hook, and give him the benefit of the doubt. We will pretend that he can side-step the 'Many Minds' challenge, sensibly accommodate the evolutionary facts, and outface the Philosophical Problem of how there can be Mind/body interaction. There is worse yet to come, in the form of the Scientific Problem for dualism.

If the Cartesian holds that mental events, which he conceives to be happenings in an immaterial Mind, can cause physical events such as the movements of human bodies, then this commits him to holding that there are some physical events which have immaterial causes. These physical events will presumably include events in the brain, involving changes in brain cells. For we know that bodily movements are caused in the first place by neural events; so if these neural events were not themselves caused by events in the Mind, then the Mind would after all have no part to play in the generation of action. Hence the dualist must hold that there are some changes in brain cells which are brought about, at least in part, by prior non-physical changes in immaterial Minds. More precisely, he must hold that there are changes in the biochemical and electrical properties of cells which are not uncaused, but which are also not purely the causal result of prior changes in the biochemical and electrical properties of cells. *And this goes clean against a fundamental principle of the physical sciences, namely that the causes of physical changes are other entirely physical events.* Biochemical and electrical changes are to be explained in biochemical and electrical terms; the governing laws allow no room for extraneous immaterial causal influences.

Putting it schematically: it is a fundamental principle, deeply entrenched in the practice of science, that the physical world is 'causally closed' − i.e. there are no causal influences on physical events besides other physical events. The Cartesian who believes in Mind/body interaction has to deny this.

We need to be clear about the status of the scientists' closure principle. It plainly isn't the sort of thing that can be demonstrated outright by experimental test; however many cases we find of physical events whose causes are also entirely physical, it won't follow that *all* physical events must be like that. And the closure principle can't be experimentally refuted either. Suppose we locate a neural event for which we cannot at the moment find any explanation in terms of current physical theory: it doesn't follow that there really isn't any physical explanation − perhaps our current theory just needs revision. However, this sort of resistance to easy verification or falsification is typical of high-level scientific principles, so the closure principle is none the worse for that.

Putting it crudely, the principle says 'whatever the current difficulties in the case of the particular physical phenomenon type *P*, don't give up the search for purely physical causes for *P*, because there are such causes to be found!' And the rationality of sticking to this principle − even when doing neurological research − has been demonstrated by the continuing successes of scientists in their search for purely physical explanations of neural occurrences. Principles of cell biology, and more general principles of biochemistry, that have proved their worth in the study of non-human cell structures have been further developed and applied to the study of human cells in general and brain cells in particular. Not surprisingly, given the enormous complexity of the brain, there is a great deal about its functioning that we do not yet understand; but at no point in our neuro-physiological investigations have we encountered the slightest reason to deviate from the closure principle that has so successfully guided research into the non-human world. In brain science, as elsewhere, the presumption that physical changes have purely physical causes has remained triumphantly successful in guiding research. Yet for all that, the interactionist dualist must say that the principle is false.

'So much the worse', the dualist might think, 'for contemporary science and its closure principle: after all, the fact that sticking to the principle has so far been quite profitable doesn't show that it is *true!*' But this response is really not available. For to dismiss the principle – at least in its present application to human neuro-physiology – is not to reject an optional extra appended to contemporary physical theory: it is rather to reject something which lies at the very heart of that theory. Contemporary science is thoroughly wedded to two big ideas. First, that macro-phenomena such as the behaviour of human cells are the causal results of micro-phenomena (ultimately, the behaviour of the atoms which constitute the cells). Second, that the physical laws governing at least low-energy micro-phenomena at atomic level are now very well known, and leave no room at all for the possibility of immaterial causal influences. These two ideas together imply the closure principle (at least as applied to brain-functioning): so which is the Cartesian going to reject? Is he going to say that the physicists have got it horribly wrong about the physical laws governing (low energy) atomic events? Or is he going to say that the microbiolog-ists have got it wrong in thinking that the functioning of cells is to be explained in terms of the functioning of cell-constituents? Neither option has anything much to be said for it at all.

In short, the dualist is committed to rejecting what have, since Descartes's time, come to be held as utterly central scientific principles. He cannot really complain if the scientist laughs his armchair speculations out of court.

7   You will perhaps have noted that the objection raised in the last section is only to the idea that physical events can have immaterial *causes*. There is nothing there which damns the idea that physical events can have immaterial *effects*. We could consis-tently stick to the closure principle and hold that the physical world has (as it were) no causal input from outside, while asserting that it does have causal output affecting immaterial Minds. Noticing this point, the dualist might attempt a strategic retreat in the face of the problems just raised. Instead of claiming that there is two way causal interaction between Minds and bodies, he might concede

that the causal transactions here must all be one way, from bodies to Minds. On this view, happenings in Minds are a causal spin-off from the physical world but do not themselves have any physical upshots. So when, for example, Jill decides to raise her arm and her arm goes up, there is – contrary to appearances – no direct causal link between the decision and the action. Rather there is an event in Jill's brain which does all the causal work, i.e. it both causes an event in Jill's Mind (the conscious decision) and has further physical upshots (e.g. the arm rising). A dualism of this kind treats mental happenings as, so to speak, a side-show: they are phenomena which are tacked onto the physical world but can't affect the world. This rather bizarre view is standardly called *epiphenomenalism.*

The attractions of epiphenomenalism are very superficial indeed: the theory's only possible merit is that it avoids the Scientific Problem for interactionist dualism presented in the previous section (it is still vulnerable, of course, to all the difficulties raised in earlier sections). And it pays the price of being open to attack on a new front.

Suppose we ask the traditional dualist, perhaps Descartes himself, what grounds there are for thinking that anyone else has an immaterial Mind associated with her observable body. The reply would run roughly as follows: 'The hypothesis that there is a Cartesian Mind associated with Jill's body is required if we are to explain the intelligent behaviour which Jill manifests – this body is not a mere physical mechanism, but shows a complexity of response which can only be explained by supposing it to be animated by a rational soul'. Now, as our techniques for explaining complex human behaviour in neuro-physiological terms have increasingly improved, this line of reply has become correspondingly less plausible: but the point to note here is that the epiphenomenalist is in any case barred from offering any such reply. For *he* cannot claim to know that others have Minds because of the explanatory power of that hypothesis: *on his 'side-show' theory Minds play no part at all in explaining happenings in the observable physical world!* But if the assumption that other Minds exist has no explanatory force, then how can he justify this assumption? Even when he is talking to a fellow theorist who claims that she, at any rate, also has a Cartesian Mind, our epiphenomenalist could argue: 'These words on her lips are just sounds for which there can be a **purely physical explanation which traces back their production to** neural events (indeed *all* her observable behaviour – and I have nothing else to go on – can be causally accounted for in physical terms); so even the evidence of her words doesn't prove that Jill really has a Mind associated with her body'. And it will not help to say 'Well, I know in my own case that there is a Cartesian Mind associated with my body, hence there must by analogy be a Mind associated with all these other human bodies': for that is just a wildly irresponsible generalisation from one case. In brief, the epiphenomenalist – as well as facing the 'Many Minds' challenge and problems about evolution – is also devoid of any good reason for thinking that other people have Minds at all. Hardly an attractive position to end up in.

8   In summary, the interactionist version of the dualist, two-component, picture of the person faces the following difficulties (among others):

(a) there seems to be no way of demonstrating the truth of the standard 'One Mind' theory as against a rival 'Many Minds' theory, nor even of reaching the necessary understanding of what the difference between the truth of these rival theories could consist in;

(b) the dualist theory cannot readily accommodate the evolutionary facts;

(c) the nature of Mind/body interaction is necessarily a mystery;

(d) the claim that happenings in the Mind cause physical upshots runs counter to our best scientific theories.

If the dualist admits (d) and retreats to epiphenomenalism then he faces another difficulty,

(e) if Minds have no causal influence on bodies, then we have no reason for supposing that other bodies than our own actually have Minds associated with them.

Obviously, if the dualist retreats even further from interactionism – say by adopting the view which was in fact held by Leibniz, namely that Mind and body merely run in parallel with no causal transactions between them at all – then problem (e) just becomes more urgent.

All this adds up to a pretty damning indictment of dualism.

V

ASSESSING THE DUALIST THEORY

1   Dualism has not fared too well in our discussions! In Chapters II and III we argued that a number of initially tempting pro-dualist arguments fail to establish the existence of Cartesian Minds. And while, as we remarked before, this isn't yet to show that dualism is false, it severely diminishes the appeal of the Cartesian position. Then, in Chapter IV, we argued that dualism indeed gives a false account of the mind by showing that it faces what seem to be insuperable difficulties. We therefore reject dualism as false, and claim that we must look elsewhere for an adequate theory of the mind.

Now, despite all our arguments, it has to be admitted that there is still a minority of philosophers who remain in the dualist camp. And while some of them need not be taken very seriously – there are bad reasoners to be found in any camp – there are others who are well-versed in all the debates. This might seem to imply that our criticisms of dualism cannot be as powerful as we have presented them as being. In particular, if a competent thinker can grasp the anti-dualist arguments and still be a dualist, doesn't that show that the arguments must be straightforwardly invalid after all? Well, not necessarily so. And the reason why not lies in some extremely important considerations about the nature of theory assessment which it is well worth pausing to explain.

2   Suppose you are the adherent of some general theory – which can be a philosophical theory, or a theory from the physical sciences such as Newtonian mechanics, an economic theory like monetarism or more or less any other theory of sufficient breadth which you care to choose. And suppose that your favoured theory comes under attack. Then note that, strictly speaking, what really

comes under attack in nearly any instance is not the favoured theory taken in isolation but a complex *package* which includes the favoured theory as just one element. And it is always possible, in the face of such an attack, to preserve the favoured theory at the expense of some *other* element of the total package. If a given theory plus side assumptions leads to falsehood, you can always try blaming one of the side assumptions.

To illustrate the point, consider the following familiar example. In the eighteenth and nineteenth centuries, Newtonian physics was enormously successful in explaining the motion of the planets round the sun, and predicting their paths with great accuracy. But there remained small anomalies, unexplained deviations from the predicted paths. Yet physicists did not immediately reject Newtonian physics as being strictly false (even if a reasonable shot at the truth): and they were not irrational in continuing to regard their favoured theory as true. For the observed anomalies did not refute Newton. They caused trouble only for a very complex theory-package containing not only Newtonian physics but also side assumptions such as (i) that there were no additional, as yet unobserved, planets whose presence could gravitationally perturb the paths of the known planets, and (ii) that there were no further non-gravitational forces which also significantly affected the planets. And what physicists did, of course, was explore the possibility of retaining Newton's laws by rejecting (i) or (ii).

This policy was pursued with very considerable success. Thus, observed anomalies in the orbit of Uranus led, not to the overthrow of Newton, but to the postulation of a new planet whose presence was causing Uranus to deviate from its expected path: this hypothesis in turn led directly to the discovery of the planet Neptune in 1846. Anomalies in the orbit of Mercury proved more difficult to accommodate to Newtonian theory: but even so, nineteenth-century physicists were hardly being irrational in sticking with Newton. For one thing, they had nowhere else to go; for another, it didn't seem a bad bet to suppose that the anomalous behaviour of Mercury would also eventually be dealt with in some way compatible with their favoured theory (though, as it happens, Newton was eventually overtaken by Einstein's new Theory of Relativity partly because the latter could indeed account for some – though still not all – of the previously unexplained anomaly in Mercury's orbit).

There is a great deal to be learnt from reflecting on all this. But, for our present purposes, let's just emphasise again this crucial point: classical mechanics and gravitational theory cannot be directly refuted by any empirical observation – for it is only Newtonian theory *plus* various supplementary assumptions that can deliver definite predictions which are testable. And if these predictions fail, it is open to us to pin the blame on one of those supplementary assumptions rather than on the core theses of classical physics.

An exactly parallel point can be made about any other interesting theory. Take, as another example, recent disputes about monetarist economic theory. Here again we have a core of theory which only makes testable predictions about the real world when combined with a plethora of additional assumptions: and faced with an apparent disconfirmation of his favoured theory, the monetarist can always juggle with one of those side assumptions. Thus, an increase in the money supply is not followed by the predicted spurt of inflation, and the monetarist promptly explains this away – e.g. by challenging whether the measure of the money supply used in this apparent disconfirmation actually reflects the true money supply. Even the flat-earther, to take a third example, can save his theory if he is prepared to go to such lengths as rejecting the usual laws of optics and mechanics so that he can explain away the apparent refutations of his theory daily provided by the photographs from orbiting weather satellites.

In short, then, it is always possible to preserve a theory from attack by suitably adjusting one's supplementary assumptions. This simple logical point, however, immediately raises an extremely difficult problem: when is it *rational* to defend one's favoured theory from attack by adjusting one's other beliefs, and when is this sort of strategy irrational? As we noted a moment ago, nineteenth-century physicists manoeuvred in this way in order to be able to retain classical mechanics and gravitational theory despite the observational difficulties – and *that* was legitimate enough. But we surely want to say that the flat-earther's similar policy of juggling with his other beliefs in order to preserve his favoured theory is entirely disreputable. What distinguishes the physicist from the flat-earther?

One crucial difference is this: the physicists' project of protecting the core theses of Newtonian physics by developing new supplementary assumptions led repeatedly to the discovery of new facts. Thus, the attempt to explain away the anomalies in the orbit of Uranus by postulating the existence of a new planet was triumphantly vindicated by the observational astronomers' discovery of Neptune. The flat-earther, by contrast, can claim no such successes. He has to adjust the usual laws of mechanics and optics in order to explain how weather satellites can circle over a flat earth, sending back pictures as of a spherical globe. But he can find no independent corroboration for his new supplementary assumptions – on the contrary, without going into details, his revised optics and mechanics face their own problems. Indeed, he seems to be set on a downward path, which would force ever more radical revisions of our scientific beliefs, without any compensation by way of increased explanatory power or corroborated predictions of new facts. Let's say (following Lakatos 1970) that the flat-earther's attempt to preserve his favoured theory involves a *degenerating* pattern of problems and difficulties. The research programme of the classical physicist, on the other hand, was notably *progressive*, in the sense that the attempt to uphold Newton itself prompted the discovery of new facts and new explanatory theories.

Can we say that the project of protecting a favoured theory is rational while that project remains in a progressive phase (i.e. continues to prompt interesting new developments which can be independently corroborated), and that it is irrational to persist with the project when it enters into a degenerating phase? This would be pleasingly neat, but it is far too restrictive. For surely such a project might start off rather successfully, hit a temporary sticky patch, and then take off again with renewed vigour. We certainly don't want to prematurely damn a research programme as 'irrational' just because it has got bogged down in a degenerating phase, with more and more problems cropping up and no apparent way of dealing with them – for this unhappy state, even if it lasts a long time, *may* yet prove to be merely temporary. Indeed we should be rather glad that some people do keep obstinately working away at apparently hopeless projects; major scientific discoveries have been made in just this way. However, we might reasonably suggest that rationality *does* require that (A) one honestly faces up to the fact when one's project gets into a badly degenerating phase, (B) one doesn't fudge the score-line when one's own side is losing and (C) one can point to *some* positive feature of one's favoured theory (such as past success or remarkable structural elegance) which makes the theory still worth pursuing as against its rivals. It is because of failure on all three counts that the flat-earther can typically be accused of irrationality. (Whether the plight of the monetarist is more like that of the classical physicist or the flat-earther is not for us to judge!)

3   To return to Cartesian dualism: how do our very general remarks about rationality apply to this case?

Well, the central logical point clearly applies again. In other words, attacks on dualism do not strictly speaking directly engage the core thesis of dualism taken entirely by itself; rather they reveal internal difficulties in a more complex package of theories and supplementary assumptions. So, once again, it would be possible for someone to preserve his favoured core theory against attack by suitably adjusting his additional assumptions.

A key argument of the last chapter (IV.6), for example, showed that one cannot consistently hold (D) the core dualist thesis that minds are immaterial entities, together with (I) the interactionist thesis that mental events can cause and be caused by physical events, and the closure principle (P) that physical events do not have non-physical causes. One reaction to this argument is to insist, as we did, that (I) and (P) are so well-supported that (D) will have to be rejected; but a dualist could obstinately stick to his guns, and counter-claim that it is (P) or (I) that will have to go. Similarly with other anti-dualist arguments: for example, the dualist can side-step the evolution problem *if* he is prepared to accept the bizarre hypothesis that *everything* has an immaterial component.

So, the first and important point to make is this: someone could fully understand the logical force of our anti-dualist arguments yet still consistently be a Cartesian, *so long as he is prepared to pay the price of making suitable adjustments in his other beliefs.* To put it another way: any attack against dualism has got to start from *some* premises or other, and the dualist can always allow that his opponent's argument is valid (i.e. that the conclusion genuinely follows from the given premises) but then go on to reject one of the premises. Hence, as we claimed at the beginning of the chapter, the continued existence of dualist philosophers well-versed in the arguments is no evidence that our arguments must be straightforwardly invalid. The dissenting dualists may just be prepared to reject premises which we accept.

But this raises, of course, the further and more difficult question of how far it is rational for a latter-day dualist to pay the necessary price for preserving his theory. How far is it rational to seek to save the core of the Cartesian theory by repeatedly adjusting one's other beliefs – e.g. by rejecting the common-sense (I) or the scientists' (P)? Is this a respectable manoeuvre, as it was for nineteenth-century Newtonians? Or is the contemporary Cartesian altogether too like a flat-earther?

In our view the harsher second judgement is much nearer the mark. Certainly the dualist project is in a very badly degenerating phase: we have already noted numerous difficulties, and (as far as we can see) the manoeuvres which would be necessary to preserve the core thesis don't lead to any positive new insights or explanatory theories, but are quite consistently negative and purely defensive. For example, rejecting (P) would seem to lead to no interesting new discoveries: the *only* appeal of this move is that it protects dualism from falsification. And although sticking to a degenerating research project need not in itself be irrational, there does seem to be a further very uncomfortable resemblance between the dualist theory and the flat-earth theory – namely that it is by now quite unclear what the residual attraction of either theory is supposed to be which could make it worth continuing to explore.

Our own view, therefore, is that the Cartesian model of the mind is in a hopeless state. But this summing up involves an element of judgement and we don't need you to agree. It is enough for present purposes that you concede that the dualist faces some very tough problems indeed. That is more than sufficient reason to go on to explore alternatives to the dualist approach, as we shall do in the coming chapters.

Part II

TOWARDS A BETTER THEORY OF THE MIND

VI

AN ARISTOTELIAN FRAMEWORK

1   In Chapter I, we contrasted two conceptions of what it is to be a person. On the one hand, there is the two-component picture, the view that a person consists of a physical body and an immaterial Cartesian Mind. On the other hand, there is the naturalistic view which maintains that a person is an organism without any immaterial components or additions, and which regards the mind as being (in some sense which needs to be further explained) grounded in the structural complexity of our brains. Since the first, dualist, position has been shown to run into very serious problems, let's now consider the alternative. In the present chapter we will outline a naturalistic framework for understanding what it is to be a person, with a view to developing the framework in subsequent chapters. As we shall see, the basic approach is hardly new: indeed it can be traced back to Aristotle. Later, we will examine part of Aristotle's own discussion: but before doing that, it will be helpful to explore his kind of anti-dualist approach more informally.

Let's start by stepping back from the question about what it is to have a mind to a simpler question: what is the difference between animate and inanimate objects – what distinguishes amoeba, plants and animals from stones, lumps of iron and dead pieces of wood? To focus on a specific case, what is the difference between a living seed of corn and a lifeless pebble? To casual inspection, both look to be just hard little lumps of stuff: but there are of course crucial differences in their *potentialities*. The pebble necessarily stays inert in the ground, passively subject to the ravages of the elements, whereas the seed – given appropriate soil conditions – will germinate, grow and in time produce more seed-bearing corn. The seed can turn the elements in its environment to its own benefit for growth, and it eventually reproduces more of its own kind. Here, then, are two distinctive marks of life at its most primitive level: the potentialities for nutrition and reproduction.

We can go on to ask: in virtue of what does the seed have such potentialities, and the pebble lack them? Is it that the seed comprises, in addition to visible physical stuff, an invisible non-material constituent which the pebble does not have? Is that what the seed's life depends on? No one these days would say so. There is no question of our discovering an immaterial constituent in the course of investigating the biochemistry of the seed, nor is there the slightest inclination to hypothesise such a constituent when we try to understand the life cycle of corn. The potentialities of the seed are, we believe, a result of its complex physical structure.

We have just touched on two very different issues, either of which might be raised by the single question 'what is essential to life?' One issue is a *conceptual* one, concerning the analysis of the concept of being a living thing. What is required if a thing is to count as being animate? Or, as we might also put it, what is the definition of being alive? The second issue is a *scientific* one, concerning the make-up of living things and their inner workings: what is it about a thing's constitution that causally explains its distinctive form of life? Now, it is the conceptual question which is the main business of philosophers when they ask what it is for a thing to be alive. And the answer, we have suggested, is roughly this: a thing counts as being alive if it has certain potentialities, primarily those for nutrition and reproduction. The scientific question is the business of biologists – it is they who try to tell us about how seeds, for example, come to function as they do. The details of the biologists' story do not really matter for philosophy, except in this respect: in order to account scientifically for the potentialities of living things, it is *not* necessary to postulate any non-physical entities or processes. What makes a living thing alive is not an immaterial component or the presence of 'vital spirits', but the appropriate complexity of the organisation of its physical micro-components.

Now consider another question: among animate things, what distinguishes plants and lower organisms from animals? Taking this as a conceptual question about what counts as an animal – or *what it is to be* an animal – the answer would seem to run roughly as follows. The difference between animals and plants is again a difference in their potentialities or capacities, in what animals can do and plants cannot. Two capacities stand out. First, animals have the capacity for perception of their environment by sight, hearing and so forth. And second, they have the capacity for locomotion – movement from place to place. (This is crude, but it will do well enough for illustrative purposes.) If we go on to ask, in a scientific spirit, what causally explains the fact that some things have these capacities, then again the answer will be in terms of the special internal physical complexity of those organisms which are animals. We don't need to postulate any immaterial entities to do the explanatory work.

2   Once we are dealing with an organism which can move around in response to some perceptual contact with its environment, it doesn't seem to be a big step to take it to be acquiring beliefs as a result of its perceptions, and exhibiting desires which affect how it moves (e.g. it moves towards food because it wants to eat). Perhaps it isn't right to say that *all* animals have these psychological states; but when we are dealing with higher animals whose behavioural patterns are complex enough it is surely entirely natural to attribute to them beliefs and desires. And to have beliefs and desires is to have at least a simple mind. So – this suggests – the question of what it is to have a mind should be handled in a similar way to the question of what it is to be an animal. Something counts as an animal if it has the capacity for certain sorts of interaction with its environment: something counts as an-animal-with-a-mental-life if it has the capacity for some rather more complex sorts of interaction with its environment.

Note two key points about this suggestion. First, it is claimed that what counts as having a (simple) mind is having certain potentialities or capacities. Now, potentialities or capacities are not entities or things. The capacity to run a mile in four minutes is not an odd kind of entity, like an invisible third leg – and the capacity for belief and desire is likewise no kind of *thing* either. So this analysis of what it is to have a mind certainly doesn't start off by postulating any immaterial entities. Second, there is no obvious reason to suppose that a scientific account of what enables higher animals to have distinctively 'mental' capacities will need to mention anything other than (say) the complexities of mammalian neuro-physiology. So there seems to be no need to introduce talk of non-material entities or processes in order to do the scientific work.

Finally, then, let's turn from animal lives to human lives and ask: what is it to be a creature like us with our sort of mind? What is it to be a rational thinking being? Well, why shouldn't we try the same sort of answer again? Why not say that it is to be a creature with certain potentialities or capacities – and especially capacities for highly complex interaction with the environment? Of course, there are notable differences between our capacities and even those of the higher apes, just as there are important differences between their capacities and those of animals lower down the evolutionary tree. But that is no bar to giving an answer of the same general style: to be a creature like us is a matter of having the capacities for rational thought, for feeling, for perception of the environment, for action and so on. And again, having a collection of capacities is *not* a question of having a mysterious sort of component: rather, our human capacities depend only on our biological make-up.

Of course, Descartes wouldn't like that last claim at all. He would indeed emphasise the difference in capacities between us and other creatures. And he would allow that the capacities of lower animals could have their source in the physical make-up of those creatures, rather as the time-keeping property of a clock can be accounted for in terms of its inner mechanism. But rational capacities of the kind distinctive of human beings are, he would protest, a different case altogether: they would not be possible for us unless we had a non-mechanistic, non-material Mind (cf. Descartes *Writings* I: 139-141). However, to sum up points we have made before, Descartes's protest is not well-grounded. On the one hand, his hypothesis that there are immaterial Minds simply can't be developed to the point of adequately explaining the existence of rational capacities. Looked at as an explanatory theory of our capacities it is hopeless. On the other hand, all the advances in neurological and brain research since Descartes's time go to confirm the counter-suggestion that the potentialities of the central nervous system are tremendous, and in principle capable of explaining our distinctively human abilities.

3   The position we have reached is this: an analysis of what it is to have a mind should mention *capacities* rather than *entities*. And that points the direction for progress. To give a fuller account of the nature of the mind is to give a fuller account not of some special

sort of thing but of the capacities which constitute the mind. This thought will shape the rest of the book, and in later chapters we proceed to discuss in turn some of our characteristic mental capacities, and seek to give a reasonably unified account of their nature. But before getting down to details, it is well worth seeing how the ideas we have just been sketching emerge in the work of their most distinguished proponent, Aristotle. This should help to fix more clearly the important ideas which we have so far presented in a fairly free-wheeling way; it will also introduce some Aristotelian terminology which has become part of the standard working vocabulary of philosophy.

In Book I of his *De Anima* ('Concerning the Soul'), Aristotle reviews the opinions of his predecessors; then, at the beginning of Book II, he makes a fresh start at trying 'to determine what the soul is, and what would be its most comprehensive definition'. He begins with a terse general reminder to his reader about his crucial notions of 'Substance', 'matter' and 'form' (although it is not standard practice, we will capitalise the first of these terms in order to emphasise that it isn't being used in an everyday sense, but as a translation of special Aristotelian jargon). Aristotle presupposes that these ideas are already familiar: but we must obviously pause for explanations.

For our present purposes, a *Substance* can be taken to be a particular individual entity. Hence this particular woman, namely Jill, and that particular man, namely Jack, are both Substances. So too are Fido the dog, and also inanimate things such as this ball and that knife, this boat and that house. Now, with respect to any such Substance, we can ask two key questions – first *what is it made of?* and second *what makes it a thing of the kind it is, rather than another kind of thing?* Apply these two questions to the ball, for example. The answer to the first question will specify the *matter* which constitutes the ball – ivory, perhaps. The answer to the second question will specify the *form* of the ball – say, its spherical shape.

We should immediately note two points arising from these answers. First, while ivory might be said to be a 'substance' in the ordinary English sense of the word, it is *not* a Substance in Aristotle's primary sense – ivory is not a particular individual thing but rather a kind of stuff or matter. This same matter could have been made into many different Substances – a ball, a statuette or a piano key: which kind of Substance we actually have will depend on the form the matter takes. Second, our elementary example might encourage the simple-minded thought that the form of a thing in Aristotle's sense is just its form or shape in a straightforward geometrical sense. But not so. A thing's form is what we describe when we answer the question 'what is it to be a thing of that kind?' or 'what makes something *count* as being a so-and-so (person, dog, knife, house or whatever)?' And this may obviously involve something a lot more complex than the thing's shape. Consider the knife. Its matter, i.e. what it is made of, is perhaps steel and wood. Its form, i.e. that in virtue of which it is a knife rather than some other kind of thing, is something to do with its usefulness in certain cutting tasks. And while this form puts some constraint on the possible shapes that knives can have, it remains true that things of various shapes can all be knives, and that other things of rather similar shapes but which can't cut will not be knives. To take another example, consider the house: its form, the 'what it is to be a house', is not simply a question of its shape but (again putting it roughly) something to do with its aptness for providing human habitation.

We will see shortly how Aristotle intends to apply the matter/form distinction to our first examples of Substances, i.e. Jack and Jill. But let's stick for a moment with simpler cases, and use them to illustrate one further crucial point. While we might speak of a Substance as being in some sense a compound or product of matter and form, it would be a bad mistake to think of these two as somehow being simply *parts* or *components* of the whole. Consider the humble cheese sandwich. Its matter is bread and cheese; but not any arbitrary arrangement of this matter constitutes a sandwich. Diced bread and cheese mixed in a bowl may be equally nutritious, but most of us prefer to eat the stuff when arranged in neat slices with the cheese between the bread: that is, we want the matter to have a certain form. Now, if we ask for a cheese sandwich and get the diced ingredients, what is missing isn't a further component part or ingredient. Imposing the form of a sandwich on the available bread and cheese is a question of arranging the materials in a certain way, not a question of adding a new ingredient rather as one might add pickles. Likewise, making a knife out of suitable matter (wood and steel) obviously doesn't require adding in more stuff of a mysterious kind: what's needed is not a new ingredient or component but an appropriate organisation of the given matter.

Putting these points together, we can sum up Aristotle's view roughly as follows. A Substance is an enduring entity which is, in a sense, a compound of matter and form (though these two are not *parts* of the Substance). Its matter is what the Substance is made of, its form is what is specified by an answer to the question 'what is it to be that kind of thing?' The matter is, we might say, potentially the matter of many different Substances; the form determines what sort of Substance the matter constitutes in actuality.

4   In his discussion of the mind or soul in *De Anima*, Aristotle also uses a second distinction alongside the matter/form distinction – a distinction that (very cryptically) emerges in the following remark:

> Matter is potentiality, form actuality; and the latter in two senses, related to one another as e.g. knowledge to the exercise of knowledge.
>
> (412a9-11)

The first half of this we have just explained: but what on earth are we to make of the rest? Well, consider Jill who is learning Welsh: if she continues with her lessons, so that she comes to know Welsh, then she becomes in one sense an *actual* Welsh-speaker. In this first sense, she will be a Welsh-speaker even when she is silent and not actively exercising her capacity to speak the language. But we might say that there is a second sense in which she is actually a Welsh-speaker only when she is actively engaged in exercising her linguistic knowledge, and talking Welsh. These two ways in which Jill could be an actual Welsh-speaker are, to echo Aristotle's own words, related to each other as (the mere possession of) linguistic knowledge to its active exercise. So Aristotle's distinction here between the two kinds of 'actuality' is the perfectly ordinary distinction between a capacity and its active use – it is evidently this familiar distinction which he wants to illustrate and to use in elucidating the notion of form.

Oversimplifying somewhat, let's consider the knife again: when we asked what it is to be a thing of that kind, i.e. when we enquired after its form, the answer referred to its characteristic use in cutting. We can now ask more specifically whether the form is its *capacity* to cut or the *actual activity* of cutting. In this case, the first answer seems right, for a knife is still a knife when lying unused in the kitchen drawer.

With these preliminary general remarks about Substance – which can only hint at the complex subtleties of Aristotle's discussions – we can now turn to his account of the soul.

5   We will follow standard convention in translating the Greek word *psyche* – familiar to us as the root of words like 'psychological' – by the English 'soul'. This is potentially misleading, for the sense of the English word is coloured by certain theological usages with decidedly dualistic connotations. For Aristotle, however, a creature's *psyche* is simply what determines it to have the sort of life characteristic of creatures of that kind; for him there would be nothing at all controversial in talking of a dog's having a *psyche*, whereas for most of us talk of Fido's *soul* seems distinctly tendentious. It is therefore worth remembering in what follows that the less loaded word 'mind' – though still far from ideal – will sometimes serve as an alternative translation.

Aristotle notes that 'bodies and especially natural bodies are reckoned to be Substances'. In particular,

> every natural body which has life in it is a Substance ... But since it is a body of such a kind, viz. having life, the body cannot be soul; the body is the subject or matter, not what is attributed to it. Hence the soul must be ... the form of a natural body having life potentially within it.
>
> (412a15-21)

This is extremely compressed – and indeed, *De Anima* has more of the character of lecture notes than of a discursive text: but the underlying line of thought can be teased out easily enough. Life is a *property* we attribute to bodies; it would therefore be nonsense to say that life is itself a body, or any other kind of entity. But to have a soul of a certain kind just is to have a life of a corresponding kind. Hence it would again be nonsense to say that the soul is a body (or any other kind of entity). The soul is rather what makes a body a living creature of the kind it is – that is, the soul (or perhaps better, *having* such a soul) is the 'what it is to be what it is' or form of a living creature.

Now, as an argument, this might be challenged: the dualist, for example, will be chary of accepting too quickly the premise that having a mind or soul is simply having a life of a certain kind. But let's take Aristotle's remarks here not as an argument-sketch but simply as an outline statement of a possible position, and examine the way he develops the position.

Aristotle's first move is to connect his thesis that soul is form with his earlier cryptic remark about two sorts of 'actuality':

> But form is actuality, and thus soul is the actuality of the kind of body just described [i.e. a natural body having life]. Now we speak of actuality in two ways – cf. again the possession of knowledge and its actual exercise. It is obvious that the soul is actuality in the first sense, viz. that of knowledge as possessed, for both sleeping and waking presuppose the existence of soul. ... So the soul is the first kind of actuality of a natural body having life potentially in it.   (412a21-28)

In other words, having a soul is to be thought of on the model of having the *capacity* for the characteristic activities essential for a certain kind of life – for one still has a mind or soul even while asleep and not actually exercising one's capacities.

> It has now been said in general what the soul is: it is ...a thing's defining essence, the 'what it is to be what it is' of a body of the kind described [i.e. a natural body having life]. Now, suppose that some instrument, such as an axe, were a *natural* body; its essence would be 'what it is to be an axe', and this would be its soul. If this were removed from it, it would cease to be an axe, except in name.   (412b10-15)

The form of an axe is its aptness for a certain kind of cutting: if we pretend for a moment that an axe is a living thing whose form is its *psyche*, then its soul will be its capacity to cut (a capacity it has in virtue of the way its matter is arranged): if this capacity is lost – say, the axe loses its edge and becomes purely ornamental – then although we might still *call* it an axe, it is no longer really one in the full sense.

> But as it is, it is just an axe; the soul is not the 'what it is to be what it is' or defining essence of *that* sort of body, but of a certain kind of *natural* body, viz. one having *in itself* a source of movement and rest.
> (412b15-17)

Aristotle is of course not assimilating people to axes! – all he is doing is making the logical point that the relation of a soul to the living thing is like the relation of the capacity for cutting to the axe: i.e. it is a case of the form/Substance relation (and not, for example, the component/whole relation). He continues

> Suppose that the eye were an animal; [the capacity for] sight would be its soul, for sight is the ... defining essence of the eye. The eye is matter

for sight; when seeing is removed the eye is no longer an eye except in name – it is no more a real eye than the eye of a statue or of a painted figure.   (412b18-22)

Of course, the supposition that the eye has a 'soul' is again a mere expository pretence; it is only whole living things which, as it were, work under their own steam that strictly speaking have forms which are souls. Aristotle's concern here is again merely to illustrate how a thing's form can relate to its capacities. The 'what it is to be an eye' is a question of that organ's role in the process of sight – and while an eye remains an eye when closed in sleep and not seeing, it ceases to be fully an eye if the capacity for seeing is lost.

In summary, then:

> While the waking state [when there is mental activity] is actuality in a sense corresponding to the cutting [of the axe] and the seeing [of the eye], the soul is actuality in a sense corresponding to [the capacity for] sight and the power in the tool.   (412b27-413a1)

So, in Aristotle's terms, the 'natural body' Fido is a Substance. His matter is, shall we say, flesh and bone. His form is his *psyche*, which stands to his waking canine activities rather as the capacity for cutting stands to the activity of cutting: so, roughly, his *psyche* is his capacity for a characteristically doggy life (a capacity he has in virtue of the arrangement of his constituent matter). Likewise Jill is a Substance: her form too is her soul, and in this case her soul is roughly her capacity (or interrelated family of capacities) for the sorts of activity, and especially mental activity, which make her a rational human person.

6   There is a very great deal more that could be said about Aristotle's theory of the soul. His views are in fact less clear-cut and more complex than our account suggests. Still, brief though our discussion has been, we have said enough for our purposes in this book. We have shown that the anti-Cartesian position we outlined earlier in the chapter has clear Aristotelian roots. Aristotle presents – in terms of his form/matter distinction – a version of the distinction which we earlier marked as that between the conceptual question 'what is it to be a person?', and the scientific question 'what are people made of (corporeal stuff or immaterial stuff)?' He also articulates the key idea that having a soul or mind is a question

of one's capacities. From the perspective of this Aristotelian framework, the rival Cartesian supposition that the mind is a component of a person is diagnosed as a simple fallacy of the kind we remarked on in §4, i.e the fallacy of treating something's form as one of its constituents. If certain matter is to constitute a person, what is required is not the admixture of some quantity of extra non-physical stuff, but that the physical materials be so arranged as to give us a creature capable of perceiving and acting, thinking and feeling.

The Aristotelian approach has considerable merits: in particular, it has the very considerable virtue of successfully avoiding the difficulties which plagued the Cartesian. In Chapter IV we presented three main lines of attack against the dualist position – the counting problem, the evolution problem, and the interaction problem. The first of these evidently presents no difficulty for the Aristotelian. The question 'how many minds associated with this body?' is, for him, no more problematic than the question 'how many capacities for cutting associated with this axe?' If the axe can cut then it has the capacity to cut, and if it can't then it hasn't: and the suggestion that it might have seventeen distinct but qualitatively identical capacities to cut is simply nonsense. Similarly, for the Aristotelian, if a creature exhibits the characteristic capacities of a rational being, then it has a rational soul, and if it doesn't then it hasn't: and the suggestion that it might have seventeen distinct but qualitatively identical souls is simply nonsense (just as it is nonsense to say that someone has seventeen distinct but qualitatively identical builds – see IV.2). To repeat, the problematic counting question for minds can only arise if you take the dualist view that the mind is a genuine *entity* in its own right, and is thus quite unlike an Aristotelian *form*.

Consider next the evolution problem. As evolution progresses, new and more complex behavioural capacities emerge: in other words, beings with more complex forms develop. Aristotle himself would reserve talk of souls for creatures which have within them 'a source of movement'; but such creatures are not thereby distinguished from lower organisms by being assigned some extra non-physical component – the differences are just differences in complexity of form (to say this is in no way to diminish the differences). So the distinction between creatures with a *psyche* and lower organisms need not be thought of as involving a radical break on the evolutionary curve. Unlike the Cartesian, the Aristotelian is not required to impose a black/white distinction on the graduated evolutionary facts.

Thirdly, the interaction problem can also be side-stepped by our Aristotelian: since he does not postulate the existence of any mysterious non-physical entities, he isn't faced with any puzzles about how such things can interact with the physical world. For him, just as the axe's capacity to cut is dependent on the arrangement of the axe's matter, so also the mental capacities constitutive of the soul are dependent on the immensely more complex structural arrangements of brain-matter. When these mental capacities (e.g. for thought or perception) are exercised, this involves no changes in any stuff but physical brain-stuff. We might overhastily put this point by saying that mental happenings just *are* a certain sort of physical happening, namely occurrences in the brain: and, put like that, there is obviously no intrinsic mystery about how mental events can cause and be caused by other physical events. We shall see in later chapters how to put this point less crudely.

In summary, the Cartesian has grave difficulties in explaining the relationship between physical body and immaterial Mind; for the Aristotelian, the problem evaporates. To borrow one of Aristotle's own examples, if mind or soul is form, then there is ultimately no more a problem about the relation of physical stuff to minds than there is a problem about the relation between 'the wax and the shape given it by the stamp'. Both are simply cases of the relation between the matter of a thing and the form which the matter takes.

7   The dualist theory of what it is to be a person was first presented in Chapter 1 in a very schematic way; and the theory started to fall apart when we later pressed for a more detailed version which could tell us more about how Cartesian Minds are supposed to function. Our new anti-dualist picture has been introduced in an equally schematic way: so we now need to go on to develop a systematic account of the capacities which supposedly constitute the mind. To do this is obviously a major task requiring careful analysis of the capacities in question: we will make a start on the necessary investigations in the next chapter, and they will occupy us for the rest of the book.

But first, let's briefly sum up the significance of the move from a Cartesian to an Aristotelian approach. The Cartesian takes the question 'what is it to have a mind?' as asking about the nature of a special sort of *thing*. And if you assume the mind to be some kind of entity it is easy enough to slide into thinking of it as being a non-bodily, non-spatial, immaterial Mind. Taking this line would fix an agenda for further enquiry. We would urgently need to know more about the nature of Minds; e.g. are they made of Mind-stuff? how are they created? can they perish? can they be located? how are qualitatively similar ones distinguished? We would want to know how the states of Minds which constitute – say – deciding to do something can result in bodily activity. We would want to know if Minds can hop from body to body. And so on. As we saw in Part I, the prospect of getting clear enough about dualism to answer such questions is very dim indeed. The Aristotelian, by contrast, will say that these enquiries all get off on the wrong foot. The question 'what is it to have a mind?' is not a question about a special kind of entity, any more than is the question 'what is life?' To have a mind is not like having a heart, it isn't to have a special sort of component or constituent: rather, it is to have a set of capacities, such as those for perception and action, belief and sensation. Taking this line sets a rather different agenda for discussion; the puzzles about Minds we just raised will be crossed off, and top of the list will now be questions about the nature of those various mental capacities. What is it to perceive or to act? What are belief and desire? What is involved in feeling sensations like pain? And what is involved in conscious thought? (Of course, we will need to confirm that there is no reason for saying that creatures with such capacities must be made of more than physical stuff – for we want to make good our repeated suggestion that it is possible for a purely corporeal being to have 'mental' capacities. But the question about the matter of a person, which the Cartesian treated as absolutely fundamental, is no longer the pivotal issue.)

The move from Descartes to Aristotle, as we said, changes the agenda for discussion; and we will be following this new agenda for the remainder of the book. In a very broad sense, therefore, we will be working within an Aristotelian framework. However, to avoid misunderstanding, we should stress straight away that some of our detailed discussions of the various capacities which constitute the mind will not themselves be notably Aristotelian: we will not, for example, be examining Aristotle's theory of perception. In other words, while our new set of problems is broadly Aristotelian, our suggested answers will not always owe very much to Aristotle.

Where should we start the discussion of our 'mental' capacities? Given that our ultimate concern is to get clear about the nature of human mental abilities, it might seem natural to start by investigating the most distinctively human ability, namely our capacity for rational conscious thought and deliberation. Common sense allows that dogs and apes perceive the world around them and have beliefs about what they see. We are also normally prepared to credit such animals with at least basic desires for food and sex, and with feelings of pain and other sensations. On the other hand, we are reluctant to suppose that dogs or even apes can reflectively ponder their situation or reach a conclusion by consciously weighing the reasons for and against it. So, it is indeed tempting to suggest that we humans are distinguished from the lower animals by our capacity for deliberative thought. Should we therefore begin our enquiry by concentrating on the nature of thought?

A little reflection suggests that this would not be the best starting-point after all. It is plausible to suppose that if we are to understand the nature of rational thought we must understand what such thought is *for*. And, while some thinking is carried on quite for its own sake, it seems to be characteristic of much rational thought that it aims to process the information we pick up by perception in order ultimately to guide our actions. In other words, thought typically mediates between perceptual input and behavioural output. If this is right then, in order to understand the nature of thought, we should set out with some understanding of the fundamental animal capacities for perception and action which thought interconnects. This suggestion will therefore shape our discussion over the coming chapters. We will begin by enquiring what it is to perceive (Chapters VII and VIII) and to act (Chapter IX). This will lead us into a discussion of what it is for humans and other animals to have beliefs and desires (Chapters X to XII). Only then will we be in a position to move on to discuss the characteristically human capacity for deliberative thought.

VII

PERCEPTION AND SENSE-DATA

1   What is it to perceive? Consider the claims 'Jack sees the cat', 'Jill hears the bell'; what must be the case if such claims are to be true? The following seems essentially right: if Jack is to count as really seeing a cat, then there must be a cat in front of him, and the presence of the cat must be making a difference to Jack. If things would not look any different to Jack even if the cat were not present, then he can hardly count as seeing the beast in front of him. To see the cat, Jack must be – so to speak – visually locked onto it. Similarly, for it to be the case that Jill hears the bell, then the bell must be causally responsible for her auditory state. If things would not sound any different to Jill even if the bell were left untouched or were completely absent then she cannot count as really hearing it. To hear something involves being auditorily locked onto it.

These remarks give us the beginning of a story about what is involved in genuine cases of perception (as contrasted, perhaps, with cases of mere hallucination or experiences in dreams). If Jack is genuinely to see the cat, the cat must causally affect the way things look to him, i.e. the cat must cause Jack to have certain visual experiences. Likewise, if Jill is to count as hearing the bell, then the bell must affect the way things sound to her, i.e. it must cause Jill to have certain auditory experiences. We might add that if Jane is to taste the cheese, then the cheese must cause her to have certain taste experiences. And so on through the other senses.

Generalising, we can say that if we are to perceive something then it must cause us to have perceptual experiences. This gives us a necessary condition for perception; but it isn't a sufficient condition. If a cat causes Jack to have certain visual experiences, it does not automatically follow that he is seeing the cat. There could be abnormal situations in which the presence of a cat causes Jack's visual system to blow a fuse and so triggers off a random visual hallucination (perhaps even a hallucination of a cat!) These would not be cases where Jack genuinely sees the cat even though the cat is responsible for his experiences. Genuine cases of seeing a cat require us to have visual experiences caused in near enough the *normal* kind of way by a cat. Now, there is an interestingly complex issue lurking here; how do we distinguish in general between normal cases and deviant ones? But we need not pause over this issue. All we need now is the thought that perceiving something involves having perceptual experiences caused in the right kind of way by the thing in question (however we might further analyse 'the right way'). This view forms the core of what might naturally be called a *causal theory of perception*. But, of course, it is only as clear as the notion of a perceptual experience. So our next task is to investigate this key notion.

2   The view we have just sketched treats seeing, for example, as a causal process: at the beginning of the causal chain there is the object seen, and at the end of the chain there is (we are inclined to say) a visual experience. Presumably it is the business of science to tell us more about what fills the gap between the beginning and end of the chain: we are all familiar with at least some of the story about how objects reflect light which enters the eye to cause changes in the retina and so forth. Our immediate worry, however, is about the alleged end effect of the causal chain, the visual experience. What exactly *are* visual experiences?

Can we turn to the scientist to get an answer to our question? Well, the scientist can tell us a lot about how light activates the nerve cells in the retina in such a way as to cause nerve impulses to be sent up the optic nerve through to a certain area in the cortex of the brain. And he can tell us how neurones in the visual cortex function. But all this somehow appears curiously beside the point. As we expand this physiological story, we get to learn more and more about the fine detail of the physical processes which in some sense underlie our perceptual capacities; but at no point in this physical story do we seem to get a firm hold on those elusive 'experiences'. At least at first sight, it would seem quite unilluminating to say of some neural occurrence 'that is the experience', for at the moment we have no understanding of how that could possibly be true. So, to repeat our question, what *is* involved in a visual experience?

At this point, it is very tempting to suppose that what we need to do is to 'introspect', to take an internal look at what is going on in our own minds when we see something. Locke put it this way:

> *What perception is*, every one will know better by reflecting on what he does himself, when he sees, ... than by any discourse of mine. Whoever reflects on what passes in his own mind cannot miss it.   (*Essay*: II.ix.2)

So what do we find when we introspect? A major tradition in British philosophy offered roughly the following answer: when we examine what is going on in visual experience we find that we have before the mind's eye a special sort of item, a (visual) 'impression' or 'idea' or 'percept'. The terminology varies but the guiding conception remains the same. Having a visual experience involves an inner awareness of something in one's own mind, which might perhaps be thought of – and often *has* been thought of – as a mental picture. Concentrate on your experience as you look around you and (so the story goes) you find that what you are directly aware of are coloured images in your visual field. These images are mental items in the strong sense that they only exist while you are aware of them; they have no independent existence outside the mind. As you read this book, you are aware of a black and white pattern in your visual field: press one eyeball and the pattern is duplicated, shut your eyes and this pattern disappears to be replaced by a more uniform and (almost) dark field. But of course these changes in your visual imagery do not imply that there has been any change in the book: the changes are alterations in the impressions which are internal to your mind. Again, while such impressions or images in your visual field are spatially arranged – which is just to say that one image can be to the left or right, above or below another image in your field – they are not to be found anywhere in physical space. In summary, visual experience on this view involves awareness of some sort of inner object (or objects) in your own mind.

We will call this type of account of visual experience an *inner object* theory. There can be analogous theories for other kinds of experience: it might be argued, for example, that hearing involves the awareness of auditory impressions, and touch the awareness of tactile impressions – where these impressions are again to be regarded as inner objects in our own minds. However, for the sake of brevity, we will concentrate in this chapter entirely on the case of vision (where indeed the inner object theory of experience has traditionally been thought to be on its strongest ground).

3   You can without any inconsistency accept a causal theory of perception while rejecting the inner object theory of experience. For you can maintain that seeing an ordinary physical object requires it to cause a visual experience without thereby committing yourself to any particular theory of the nature of experience. But although the two theories are quite independent, they have often been held together. If you do put the theories together, then you are going to say this: Jack sees the cat only if the cat causes Jack to have certain visual experiences, i.e. only if the cat causes Jack to be aware of certain 'impressions' or 'ideas' in his own mind. In other words, on the combined theory, seeing a cat involves being aware of something *other* than a cat, namely some mental impressions (or whatever) which in some sense represent the cat: we perceive a cat via an intermediary representation of the cat. Not surprisingly, this popular combination of a causal analysis of seeing with an inner object account of visual experience is standardly called *the representative theory* of (visual) perception.

An analogy might help. The idea is roughly that your eye operates as a television camera, sending signals via the optic nerve to the brain. And then pictures are produced on a mental television screen in front of the mind's eye. What you are immediately aware of are the inner images on the mental screen: and normally, as with a normally functioning television system, these represent how things are in the physical world.

This representative theory immediately raises, in a virulent form, the sort of sceptical worries that Descartes battled with. If, strictly speaking, what we are directly aware of in visual experiences are ideas or impressions in our own mind (and similarly for the other senses) how can we possibly prove that there really is a physical world outside the mind for our experiences to represent? How can we know anything about the world beyond the realm of our own ideas? How can we show that when we think we are seeing a cat (i.e. having impressions of a cat caused by a cat) we really are seeing a cat, as against having a play of impressions brought about by an evil demon? This sort of sceptical problem, which held British philosophers in thrall for more than two centuries, is evidently particularly pressing given the representative theory of perception. But this theory is only as good as the inner object theory of experience which is an essential part of it. So should we accept the inner object theory?

Our discussion will be structured as follows. In the next section,

§4, we will look at a number of passages in which some major philosophers expound versions of the inner object theory. This will serve both to clarify the theory and to make good our claim that it has been highly popular at least among British philosophers. In §5 to §7, which could perhaps be omitted on a first reading, we outline and assess three lines of argument which might be offered in support of the inner object theory. Finally, in §8, we give a powerful argument against the theory, and this clears the way for the very different account of perceptual experience to be presented in the next chapter.

4   Consider first the following remarks from Locke's *Essay concerning Human Understanding:*

> wherever there is sense *or* perception, there some *idea* is actually produced, and present in the understanding.   (II.ix.4)

> It is evident the mind knows not things immediately, but only by the intervention of the *ideas* it has of them ... The mind ... perceives nothing but its own ideas.   (IV.iv.3)

> It is therefore the actual receiving of *ideas* from without that gives us notice of the *existence* of other things and makes us know that something does exist at that time without us which causes that *idea* in us.   (IV.xi.2)

These passages suggest very strongly that Locke held a general representative theory for all kinds of perception. So when Jack sees a cat, for example, some ideas are causally produced in his mind; and strictly speaking it is these ideas which Jack is immediately aware of. Likewise, when he judges something to be white, this is because it causally produces in him a certain idea:

> whilst 1 write this, I have, by the paper affecting my eyes, that *idea* produced in my mind which ... I call *white*.   (IV.xi.2)

And how does Locke regard the idea whose presence in the mind is distinctive of visual experience? Well, on one occasion where he is attending to what specifically occurs in the case of visual perception, Locke writes as follows:

> When we set before our eyes a round globe of any uniform colour ... it is certain that the *idea* thereby imprinted in our mind is of a flat circle,

variously shadowed ... the *idea* we receive from thence is only a plane variously coloured, as is evident in painting. (II.ix.8)

This seems to imply that Locke took visual experiences to involve awareness of an arrangement of coloured impressions in a two-dimensional visual field. In summary, then, Locke appears to accept just the sort of inner object theory of visual experience that we sketched in §2.

Now, it has to be said that there is a good deal of scholarly dispute about whether the passages we have quoted from Locke mean what they certainly appear to mean. It is in fact arguable that Locke did *not* hold an inner object theory of experience and consequently was not a devotee of the representative theory of perception. Fortunately, we do not need to delve into the scholarly debate here. For whether or not Locke himself really held the combination of views we have just imputed to him, it is quite certain that many of his philosophical successors read him as expounding those views. And so, whatever his own intentions, Locke's work placed the representative theory firmly on the agenda for philosophical discussion.

Berkeley, for one, plainly thought that Locke was committed to a representative theory of perception. Towards the end of the first of Berkeley's *Three Dialogues*, the character who represents the Lockean position is given to say:

> To speak the truth ... I think there are two kinds of objects, the one perceived immediately, which are likewise called *ideas*; the other are real things or external objects perceived by the mediation of ideas, which are their images and representations. Now I own, ideas do not exist without the mind; but the latter sort of objects do. (*Works*: 160)

But Berkeley himself rejected this, and attacked the combination of a straightforward causal theory of perception with an inner object theory of experience. Interestingly enough, Berkeley's quarrel was only with the first of these two theories: he held that ideas are imprinted on our mind, not by corporeal things, but by God. He was, however, quite happy with the second part of the representationalist's position, and enthusiastically embraces the notion that in visual experience one is aware of 'ideas' in the mind. He asks

> For ... what do we perceive besides our own ideas or sensations ...?
> (*Works*: 78)

evidently expecting the answer 'nothing'. And early in the *Three Dialogues*, the character who speaks for Berkeley challenges

> You will farther inform me, whether we immediately perceive by sight any thing beside light, and colours, and figures,

and receives the reply 'we do not' (*Works*: 138). Putting these two thoughts together: what we are aware of in visual experience are our own ideas, 'colours and figures' before the mind.

The same view of experience is shared by Hume: when he is writing about the senses he remarks

> philosophy informs us that everything which appears to the mind is nothing but a perception, and is interrupted and dependent on the mind.

And such perceptions or impressions

> are internal and perishing existences.   (*Treatise*: I.iv.2)

So Hume again accepts the conception of experience as awareness of a fleeting inner object. Writing of his distinguished predecessors, Thomas Reid felt he could sum up the common tendency of their thinking as follows:

> all the systems of perception that have been invented ... suppose that we perceive not external objects immediately, and that the immediate objects of perception are only certain shadows of the external objects. These shadows or images, which we immediately perceive ... since the time of Descartes have commonly been called *ideas*, and by Hume, *impressions*.   (*Intellectual Powers*: II.vi)

Reid considerably exaggerates when he says that '*all* the systems of perception' involve, to use our terminology, an inner object theory of experience; but there can be little doubt about the past popularity of the theory.

This popularity lasted well into the present century. Thus G. E. Moore could still claim in lectures given in 1910 that 'an overwhelming majority of philosophers' have held that what we are immediately aware of in perception are inner objects in our own minds (Moore 1953: 40). And while this view can no longer be said to command anywhere near the same degree of support, it still has its vigorous defenders (e.g. Jackson 1977), who continue to argue the now familiar conclusions that whenever seeing occurs there is a coloured patch which is the immediate object of perception and that this object which we are immediately aware of is a *mental* object.

We can take it, then, that the inner object theory of experience has proved extremely popular. Let's now turn to ask what *arguments* can be presented in its favour.

5   First a brief remark about terminology. As we have already noted, philosophers have used a variety of labels to refer to the inner objects supposedly involved in experience. But in this century, the term used by Moore – namely *sense-datum* (plural: sense-data) – has become fairly standard. This bit of jargon has the considerable advantage of lacking the potentially misleading everyday associations of Locke's 'idea' or Hume's 'impression', so it will occasionally be useful to adopt the jargon here. But, at least in our hands, this term is to be read as no more than a shorthand way of referring to inner objects of the sort supposedly involved in experience according to many traditional views. The new terminology does not herald a new theory.

We will discuss three types of argument for an inner object theory which have been offered by its defenders (for the sake of brevity, we continue to concentrate on the visual case). For ease of reference these can be called, respectively, 'arguments from science', 'arguments from the relativity of perception' and 'the argument from hallucinations'. We will consider them in turn.

We begin, then, with the *arguments from science*. And we can immediately set aside the entirely confused idea that science itself warrants our earlier television analogy. Science indeed tells us that perception is a causal process: but it most certainly does not tell us that what occurs at the end of the process is the awareness of images on an internal screen. As far as neuro-physiology is concerned, the television analogy is only half accurate, and shouldn't be pressed too far. The eye may be a bit like a television camera; but the brain doesn't contain anything in the slightest like a television screen displaying images!

However, there are other, less naive, ways of appealing to science in the hope of establishing an inner object theory of experience. For example, it is known that light takes time to travel from an object to a perceiver; so the following argument step might seem tempting:

If you are seeing the sun, then what you are aware of in your visual field exists right now, at the moment of perception. But the phase of the sun's surface that you are seeing does *not* exist now, but existed about eight minutes ago. More dramatically, you may see a distant star that has by now gone out of existence entirely. Hence what you are aware of must be a currently existing sense-datum, as distinct from the past phase of the sun or star.

What are we to make of this argument? Well, it is true that, when you see the sun, the visual experience occurs at the end of a causal process which stretches over about eight minutes. And if you assume that seeing must always involve – as it were – simultaneous and direct contact with some object or other, then this object would have to be distinct from the sun, which is at the far end of the causal process. But why accept the assumption? After all, in the auditory case we are familiar enough with the fact that we can hear the distant starting-gun firing some appreciable time after the event. In other words, we can hear things as they were a few moments ago. And now we know the more esoteric facts about the finite velocity of light, why not similarly say that – in astronomical cases – we see things as they were some time ago? (This maybe involves a marginal revision of pre-scientific common sense, but it seems preferable to conceding the conclusion that what we are aware of is a *different* object from the sun, an inner object brought into existence at the time of seeing.)

Here is another argument from science:

According to contemporary physics, a table is constituted of an aggregate of atoms arranged into molecular structures, with each atom in turn consisting of a swarm of electrons buzzing around a nucleus. The fundamental building blocks of the atoms have properties such as mass, electric charge and 'spin' – but they certainly are not deemed to be coloured (in any ordinary sense of the term). The table, therefore, is a collection of colourless particles milling about in largely empty space. Now, such a collection may take up a certain amount of space or have a particular overall mass; so the scientific picture will allow us to talk as we ordinarily do about the size or weight of the table. But a collection of colourless particles can have no real colour in itself; any appearance of colour must be the result of the way the colourless table affects our perceptual equipment. So we must conclude that the table is in itself colourless. However, what we are immediately aware of in visual experience plainly *is* coloured; at any given moment when we look at the table our visual field is replete with patches of various particular colours. So what we are immediately aware of cannot be the colourless table, but must be something else instead – a coloured sense-datum, or internal representation of a table.

This argument moves from the agreed premise that the atomic constituents of a table are colourless to the contentious conclusion that the table itself lacks colour. But what can justify this inference? At first sight, it seems that the argument depends on the principle that if the constituents of an object lack a certain property, then the object itself cannot have the property either. Yet this principle clearly doesn't apply to all properties: imagine someone using the principle to 'prove' that, since you cannot swim in a water molecule, and water is comprised of water molecules, you cannot swim in water! So, the stated argument from science apparently stands convicted of resting on a quite absurd principle.

However, a defender of the argument might well protest: 'Of course I wasn't relying on the absurd principle that you just imputed to me. I can understand as well as the next person how a mass of water molecules can come to have properties lacked by the individual molecules. I just have a *special* problem in understanding how something made of colourless atoms can really be coloured. In particular, I see the table as uniformly brown all over – i.e. as being coloured brown at every point of its surface. Yet according to the scientific picture, the surface of the table is really a gappy network of colourless particles. So it is false that the surface is coloured at every point. Hence the uniform colour must be a property of the appearance or sense-datum which the table presents to my mind, rather than a property of the table itself. To repeat, I am not appealing to the principle which you rightly say is absurd: my argument springs from the contrast between the granular gappiness of the table's surface as revealed by physics and the uniform appearance it presents to the gaze.'

This slightly more sophisticated version of the argument is still a failure. Let's agree that, if we take a small enough region of the table's surface (containing just the odd molecule or two), then it will make little sense to suppose that it is coloured. So we can agree that very small regions of the table are not brown. But why should it be thought to follow that the table itself isn't, in the ordinary sense, uniformly brown – and hence that the colour belongs not to the table but to its appearance? This move rests on the following assumption:

> The everyday claim 'The table is uniformly brown all over' commits you to holding that every region on the table's surface is brown, no matter how small a region we choose.

And why on earth should we accept that? The everyday claim surely commits you, at most, to holding that any patch of the surface *large enough to be seen* is brown. What happens at the microscopic level is beside the point, and hence arguments from science which spring from considerations about the microscopic details are doomed to fail.

6   We next discuss *arguments from the relativity of perception.* These start from the familiar observation that how things look to us is heavily dependent on the lighting, our angle of vision or whether we are wearing spectacles. In other words, at least some of the properties that things appear to have are relative to the conditions under which they are seen. It is then argued that what we are immediately aware of in perception must be the fluctuating appearances rather than the stable objects themselves.

Consider again colour properties in particular. Bertrand Russell argues:

> It is evident ... that there is no colour which pre-eminently appears to be *the* colour of the table, or even of any one particular part of the table – it appears to be of different colours from different points of view, and there is no reason for regarding some of these as more really its colour than others. And we know that even from a given point of view the colour will seem different by artificial light, or to a colour-blind man, or to a man wearing blue spectacles, while in the dark there will be no colour at all, though to touch and hearing the table will be unchanged. Thus colour is not something which is inherent in the table, but something depending upon the table and the spectator and the way the light falls on the table. When, in ordinary life, we speak of *the* colour of the table, we only mean the sort of colour which it will seem to have to a normal spectator from an ordinary point of view under usual conditions of light. But the other colours which appear under other conditions have just as good a right to be considered real; and therefore, to avoid favouritism, we are compelled to deny that, in itself, the table has any one particular colour. (1912: 2-3)

So, the argument goes, the physical table strictly speaking has no particular colour: apparent colour fluctuates too much to belong to the table itself. On the other hand, what we are immediately aware of in visual experience plainly is coloured in some definite way. What we are aware of is coloured; tables strictly speaking are not – hence what we are immediately aware of are not the tables themselves but coloured 'ideas' or 'sense-data' which represent the tables.

Here is another argument from the relativity of perception, couched this time in terms of shape rather than colour. Consider the case of viewing a round penny from different angles. The penny's apparent shape (the one that we would have to reproduce on the canvas if we were to paint an accurate picture of the way the penny looks to us) changes with our point of view. Face on, the penny's apparent shape is circular; from an oblique angle it is an ellipse whose eccentricity varies as the angle of vision varies. In short, while the penny itself of course retains a constant real shape, its appearance – i.e. what we are directly aware of in our visual field – constantly changes in shape as we move around the penny. Hence, what we are directly aware of cannot be the penny but must be something else – a sequence of varying sense-data.

We must grant Russell, of course, that the way a table looks will vary with our angle of sight, the lighting conditions and so on. But why should this utterly familiar fact make us agree that colour is not something which is inherent in the table? It seems as if Russell thinks that the odd look of a red object under abnormal viewing conditions should shake our confidence that the object really is red. But who doubts that London buses are red just because the way they look under sodium street lights is different from the way they look in the sunshine?

When we examine the details of Russell's argument, it becomes clear that in formulating the argument he has already assumed an inner object theory of experience. No wonder that he thinks he can reach the desired conclusion! For consider his absolutely crucial claim that when we observe something under non-standard conditions 'the colours which appear have just as good a right to be considered real'. What can this mean? When we see the bus under the sodium light it looks a nasty khaki colour; in what sense, though, could we consider this khaki colour to be 'real'? True, the bus really does look khaki in these conditions – but this claim is ordinarily taken to be quite compatible with saying that the bus is in fact really red, and looks khaki under sodium lights *because* it is red. What Russell seems to be assuming is the contentious thesis that when the bus looks khaki the colour is real *because something really is khaki* – not the bus itself, of course, but our visual sense-datum. Given this sort of inner object theory of experience according to which colour is strictly speaking a property of sense-data, then it would be true that the khaki was just as 'real' as the red we see when we observe the bus under normal conditions. In both cases the colours would really belong to a real sense-datum, and it would indeed be 'favouritism' to say that one is more real than the other or that one more truly 'belongs' to the bus than the other. So, from the perspective of an inner object theory, Russell's remarks begin to make good sense. But what they cannot do is provide us with an independent argument for adopting that perspective in the first place.

Russell's colour argument ambitiously tries to show that tables are not really coloured at all. The elliptical penny argument is more modest, and sensibly doesn't try to show that pennies really have no shape. But it fares no better. Of course, the way that a penny looks changes with our point of view, in the sense that the shape we would have to reproduce in an accurate picture of the scene with the penny will depend on our angle of vision. We can if we like say that, when seen from an oblique angle, the penny's apparent shape (in some such sense) is elliptical. Or, much more misleadingly, we might say that the penny then 'has an elliptical appearance'. However, this *is* a misleading way of putting it, as it might suggest that when we look at the penny there really is some inner elliptical object which we see, namely an 'appearance'. And this does not follow – any more than it follows from the fact that the bus appears khaki that there really is an inner khaki object which we see. As we shall see in the next chapter, a theory of perception which postulates sense-data is not the only one which can deal with the evident facts that things look different from different angles and in different lighting conditions. And so the evident facts cannot be invoked as demonstrating the existence of sense-data.

7   The third sort of argument, exemplified by the *argument from hallucinations*, tries to beef up the appeal to introspection with which we first introduced the inner object theory. The

suggestion was that introspection reveals that in perception we are aware of inner objects in our own minds. To this suggestion, the obvious first reply is a brusque 'Nonsense – when I visually experience a cat I am aware of the *cat*, not of something else!' But to this reply, the defender of the inner object theory will retort that we are forgetting that one can have an experience as of a cat without there actually being a cat present: and so experience cannot always be a matter of awareness of objects outside the mind.

Consider the well-worn example of Macbeth and his hallucination of a dagger. Quite clearly, Macbeth did not genuinely see a dagger because, by hypothesis, there simply was no dagger there for him to see! On the other hand, we surely want to say that Macbeth was aware of *something* – his visual field was not a complete blank since he 'saw' a dagger. So, the argument continues, what Macbeth was visually aware of was not a physical object but rather something that only he could sense, something in his own deranged mind. In short, what Macbeth was aware of was an inner object – a sense-datum. But now compare Macbeth's delusory experience with a normal case of genuinely seeing a dagger. As far as the inner quality of the experiences is concerned, these two cases could be exactly alike. Indeed, it is precisely because the intrinsic quality of the experiences can be the same that delusions are possible; i.e. it is because a hallucination and a case of real seeing can seem exactly alike 'from the inside' that it is possible to mistake the one for the other. But if the visual experience in the case of really seeing a dagger could be exactly the same as the experience in the case of hallucinating one, then it is natural to suppose that the account of what is experientially involved in the two cases should be the same. And since in the hallucination the experience obviously consists of awareness of an inner object, an idea or sense-datum, the same must be true of the experience in the case of genuine seeing. In the hallucination the sense-datum has an internal origin, while in the other case the sense-datum is caused by a real dagger (or a real cat, or whatever); but either way the experience involves awareness of an inner mental object, a sense-datum.

This argument is certainly more attractive than its predecessors; but once more it is a failure. Consider Macbeth again: it seems to him just as if he is seeing a bloody dagger; so he is certainly having a visual experience. But the argument from hallucinations requires us to agree with the crucial claim that Macbeth is then aware of some *thing* which really exists, an inner object. If we accept that this is the right account of hallucinatory experience then the rest of the argument runs smoothly enough. For it is natural to suppose that there is something in common between seeing a dagger and vividly hallucinating a dagger, namely having a visual experience as of a dagger. And if this visual experience in the hallucinatory case involves awareness of an inner object, then it is indeed very tempting to conclude that the same visual experience occurring in the case of genuinely seeing a dagger will also involve awareness of an inner object. Everything depends, therefore, on that quite crucial step of claiming that in hallucinating a dagger Macbeth is aware of some inner thing. But why should we accept the move from the premise that it *seems* to Macbeth that he is seeing a dagger to the conclusion that Macbeth *really is* visually aware of an object (a sense-datum) in his own mind? The argument from hallucinations offers no justification for this essential move: so the whole argument which turns on this inference is quite inconclusive.

A defender of the argument might reply in the following vein: 'Well, what is it to have a visual experience of a dagger in the absence of a real dagger if not to be aware of an inner representation of a dagger? At least my position embodies *one* account of what it is to have such an experience. Until you propose a rival account, the complaint that I have just assumed my account to be true is rather hollow. After all, any argument has to start somewhere; and mine starts with what seems to me the evident truth that Macbeth had something before his mental gaze when he hallucinated, namely some 'ideas', 'impressions' or 'sense-data' – call them what you will. In the absence of a rival story, why *shouldn't* I start off with the assumption?'

This counter-challenge is fair enough; but it can be met. And in the next chapter we will sketch the outlines of the desired rival account of experience, which will show why the possibility of hallucinating a bloody dagger does not force us to admit the existence of coloured inner objects.

8   We have now examined three types of argument for an inner object theory of visual experience. These discussions have left some unfinished business to be taken up again in the next chapter. But we can say that, so far, the existence of sense-data is non-proven. Still, the weakness of a handful of arguments for a theory does not by

itself demonstrate the falsity of the theory. So can we mount a successful attack against the inner object theory?

We might argue that the theory is, in a sense, dualistic and is objectionable for just that reason. Call Descartes's theory that the mind is itself a special sort of immaterial entity 'dualist in the narrow sense'. And call any theory which isn't necessarily committed to Cartesian Minds but which still maintains that certain mental phenomena have to be explained by reference to some special class of non-physical entities 'dualist in the broad sense'. The inner object theory of experience is naturally construed as being dualist in the broad sense – for ideas or impressions or sense-data certainly don't seem to be physical things. And the theory therefore appears to inherit some of the difficulties which beset dualism in the narrow sense. In particular, just as Descartes has a problem accounting for the causal interaction between immaterial Minds and bodies, so the inner object theorist is going to have an analogous problem accounting for the causal relations which there must surely be between sense-data and the physical objects which they represent. However, we will not press this difficulty here.

We will concentrate instead on another difficulty, one that might well have seemed pressing at the very outset. For we started by wondering what is involved in seeing a physical object, and arrived at the suggestion that it involves being aware of a sense-datum produced in the mind by the object. This talk of awareness of an inner object makes it sound as if there were a mental screen with images projected onto it which are seen by us with an inward gaze. In other words, we see the world outside by 'immediately perceiving' inner pictures of it. (On this view, as we said before, it is as if the eye works like a television camera, sending images to be reproduced on a mental screen.) *But if there is a problem in understanding what it is to see an outer physical object, then there is going to be exactly the same problem in understanding what it is to 'see' an inner mental object.* If there is a puzzle about what is involved in seeing a real physical picture then there is equally a puzzle about what is involved in 'seeing' an inner mental picture. Indeed, such understanding as we have of the nature of the supposed inner transaction would have to be modelled on our prior understanding of seeing in the ordinary sense, rather than vice versa. So the invocation of inner seeings of inner objects is hardly a helpful move if we are worried about the general concept of seeing, and moving from talk of inner seeings to more guarded talk of 'awareness' simply disguises the problem.

Since we are trying to analyse seeing in terms of having visual experiences, it would be hopelessly circular to try to explain what it is to have a visual experience as of a cat (for example) in terms of seeing a cat. The point we are now making is that it is no more helpful to try to explain what it is to have the visual experience in terms of 'seeing' or 'being aware of' an inner cat-representation. This point is extremely important, so it will bear the most emphatic repetition. The inner object theory of experience attempts to tell us what goes on at the end of the causal chain involved in perceiving an object. However, the theory circles around to characterise experience in perceptual terms again: it refers to *awareness* or *immediate perception* of an inner object. But then why shouldn't we ask what is involved in perceiving an inner object? Isn't this just as troublesome a notion as the original one of perceiving an object outside us? Is what is involved in Macbeth's perceiving a sense-datum of a dagger any more obvious than what is involved in really seeing a dagger? You might think that once we get down to the level of sense-data or images in the mind, our problems are at an end: but this is a bad mistake. To quote Dennett:

> Consider how images *work*. It is one thing just to be an image – e.g., a reflection in a pool in the wilderness – and another to function as an image, to be taken as an image, to be used as an image. For an image to work as an image there must be a person (or an analogue of a person) to see or observe it, to recognise or ascertain the qualities in virtue of which it is an image of something. Imagine a fool putting a television camera on his car and connecting it to a small receiver under the bonnet so the engine could 'see where it is going'. The madness in this is that although an image has been provided, no provision has been made for anyone or anything analogous to a perceiver to watch the image. This makes it clear that if an image is to function as an element in *perception*, it will have to function as the raw material and not the end product, for if we suppose that the product of the perceptual process is an image, we shall have to design a perceiver-analogue to sit in front of the image and yet another to sit in front of the image which is the end product of perception in the perceiver-analogue and so forth *ad infinitum*.
>
> (1969: 134)

In short, images need perceivers who stand in a perceptual relation to the images – so we are still left with the *whole* question of the nature of the relation between a perceiver and what he perceives (mental image, physical picture or whatever).

To all this the inner object theorist might retort that we have been unfair. Sense-data – he might protest – are not to be thought of as literally being images or pictures, and the awareness we have of sense-data is not to be thought of on a perceptual model. By insisting on the differences between sense-data and images or pictures, and between inner awareness and perception, our theorist can escape the criticism of circularity. But the price that he pays for his escape is too high: for by emphasising those differences he levers us away from those models and metaphors which enabled us to give at least *some* content, however obscure, to the theory. We can perhaps make a shot at understanding the idea of inner observation of inner pictures: but if the theorist stresses the *differences* between observation and 'awareness', between pictures and sense-data, then we loose any firm grip on what he is saying, and his theory becomes quite uselessly empty. The inner object theory of visual experience loses its last shreds of plausibility.

VIII

PERCEPTION AND
THE ACQUISITION OF BELIEFS

1   Let's resume our discussion by returning to basics and reminding ourselves of two truisms about perception. First, it is through perception that we discern the whereabouts of objects in the world around us, discover the properties of these objects (such as their colours and shapes) and learn about their movements and the way they change. Second, it is only possible for us to acquire information about our environment in this way because we are equipped with sense organs which are sensitive to a variety of stimuli, such as light and sound; the causal mechanisms involved in these organs must be in good working order if we are to perceive the world.

The second truism strongly suggests that any sound theory of perception is bound to be, at least in part, a *causal* theory; and early in the last chapter we began sketching such a theory. But we saw that a problem arose over the end effect of the causal transaction which constitutes perception: what *sort* of effect has to be produced in us if, for instance, we are to count as seeing a cat? We have so far examined one response to this question – a response which supposed that seeing a cat requires having in mind a representation or idea or sense-datum of a cat (i.e. something like a mental picture of a cat). The root assumption behind this answer seems to be that the world can only impress itself upon us in perception by producing a likeness of itself in our minds, rather in the way that a scene produces a likeness of itself on the film in a camera. And, as we saw, the prime difficulty with this assumption is that it reduplicates the problem we are trying to solve. If there is a philosophical problem about the ordinary perception of outer objects then there can be no less of a problem about the postulated inner perception of inner objects. So, if we are to maintain a broadly causal theory of perception, we need a better account of the end effect of the perceptual process.

At this point we might try to take a lead from the first of our two truisms above. Perception, we noted, is the major route by which we acquire information; it is the primary means by which we come to form new beliefs about how things stand with the world. So perhaps we should say the end effect of the perceptual process is exactly that – the acquisition of beliefs. In other words, what is essential to perception is not the receiving of, say, pictorial representations before the mind's eye but the receiving of information. It is this idea which we will be exploring in the present chapter.

2   Suppose that you are led into an unfamiliar room which is in pitch darkness, and seated in a chair. The first thing that happens is that you hear a dog bark outside; and one obvious change that is produced in you is that your beliefs alter as you come to believe there is a dog barking. When silence returns, your beliefs will of course change again, for you will then no longer believe there is a dog currently barking outside. Suppose next that you run your hand over the chair you are sitting on, and feel its velvet seat and wooden arms; then again your beliefs will change as you acquire information about the texture, softness and felt temperature of its surfaces. And then finally the light is suddenly switched on. Assuming that you have normal eyesight, you come to see the room around you – the table to your left with its vase of flowers, the piano to your right, the window in front of you. Again a crucial change that is produced in you when you come to see these things is that you now believe (as you didn't when the room was still in darkness) that the table is over to your left, there is a vase of flowers on it, that the vase is blue, that it is smaller than the table, and so on. The visual perception in this case – like the earlier auditory and tactile perceptions – seems inseparable from the acquisition of a great number of beliefs about your environment.

Of course, the beliefs you pick up in perception are mostly of the unreflective kind which it is appropriate to ascribe to small children and animals as well as to adult perceivers. These beliefs will not normally be verbalised, and you might not be able to put them into words even if you wanted to. Take the case where you can visually discriminate two very similar shades of red, and successfully sort things of these shades into two piles. Your sorting behaviour shows that you have visually registered information about the objects before you, but you would probably be very hard pressed to verbalise this information, given that you have no names for precisely those shades. A related point is that the beliefs acquired in perception will not normally be consciously entertained or dwelt upon: but then the same is true of the great bulk of your beliefs at any given time. For example, a few moments ago you doubtless believed, as you still believe, that you are not stark naked: but only now have you come to consciously entertain that thought.

Can we say, then, that perception consists in the acquisition of beliefs as a result of some interaction with the world? Well, not any interaction will do, of course. Suppose a drug is slipped into your coffee, and as a result of drinking the stuff (which presumably counts as some kind of interaction with the world) you come to believe that you are flying. This case of belief-acquisition is evidently non-perceptual! Genuine cases of perception must involve the use of some more trustworthy means of acquiring beliefs: a mechanism for producing beliefs which pretty consistently engenders *false* beliefs wouldn't be a perceptual mechanism at all, but only a way of producing dreams or hallucinations – for perception, you must be fairly reliably 'locked onto' the world. So, for example, seeing a cat should typically involve acquiring the belief that there is a cat there (along with many other beliefs): or at least – since you can see a cat and mistake it in the gloom for a small dog – seeing a cat should involve coming to believe that there is something at least approximately cat-like present. If your beliefs were wildly erroneous, if you thought that what was in front of you was a small, very shiny, metallic cube with the number eight printed in bright red on the side, then you could hardly count as seeing the cat (perhaps you just had a hallucination triggered by the presence of the cat). It is, as they say, a nice question just how mistaken your beliefs can be before it ceases to count as a case of seeing.

Let's therefore say, as a second shot, that perception consists in the acquisition of beliefs via receptors which provide a sufficiently reliable information-transmitting interface between the believer and the world. And we should add, in order to deal with the cases where your perceptual mechanisms blow a fuse and go completely haywire (cf. VII.1), that the mechanisms involved should be functioning normally. So, in ordinary English, perception involves acquiring beliefs in the normal kind of way via one's sense organs.

3   Suppose you read a lengthy and vivid description of Jill: you do not thereby perceive Jill, yet you do acquire many beliefs about her by using your eyes. How can our sketched theory cope with this common sort of case?

To perceive, it is being suggested, is to directly acquire certain beliefs; but obviously, by means of acquiring these first beliefs you may very well come to have many additional derived beliefs. For example, you visually acquire beliefs about what is written on a piece of paper: since you understand the words, your first beliefs immediately lead you to acquire some further beliefs which are about Jill, and from these you may perhaps deduce yet more beliefs about her. However, if you are to count as seeing Jill, it is not enough to come by such *derived* beliefs about her, even if what starts the process off is visual. Seeing Jill would require her to be more directly involved in causing the *initial* set of beliefs in the perceptual situation (i.e. the beliefs which form the basis of any additional derived beliefs). And these initial beliefs would have to be appropriately about her and not about (say) writing on paper.

This distinction between initial and derived beliefs enables us also to say something about the differences between the senses. Suppose first that you look at the electric fire element, and visually acquire the belief that it is glowing red: in this case you will thereby arrive at the derived belief that the element is hot. Now suppose alternatively that your eyes had been shut, and you had held out your hand instead. By your temperature sense (part of the complex we call 'touch') you would have acquired straight off the initial belief that the element is hot, and this time it would have been the colour belief that was derived. And the point generalises: sight initially produces – among other things – colour beliefs but not temperature beliefs, whereas with touch it is the other way about. More generally still, the various senses are distinguished by the types of information they initially register. We can say that sight, for example, is a sense which initially produces, among other beliefs, beliefs about the colours of objects (taking 'colour' broadly to include achromatic shades). Similarly for the other senses.

4   We have given a sketchy outline of what we can call the belief-acquisition theory of perception. It falls into two parts: the first part introduces a causal requirement (*very* roughly, to perceive

an object one must be causally affected by it in the appropriate way), the other part specifies the sort of effect involved in perception. The causal requirement is not new, for it was of course an essential part of the representative theory of perception which we discussed in the last chapter. But the two theories divide sharply on the question of the effect produced in perception: the present theory holds that it is not an image or a likeness of the object perceived, but rather a belief or set of beliefs which is (in some sense) about that object.

Now, does all this really point the way to an adequate theory of perception? You might still be able to think of a number of objections, and certainly we have left the story vague in various respects. But perhaps the most obvious problem is that we seem in some way to be leaving out what is essential to perception, namely its experiential or phenomenological character. 'Surely', you might say, 'there is something experiential involved in seeing a point of light: but there needn't be anything experiential involved in acquiring the belief that there is a light there. So the theory that perception is just belief-acquisition throws out the experiential baby along with the bath-water!' This is an extremely serious accusation, to which we will be returning later (§8). However, let's temporarily suppress our worries on this and other points, and pause to note some of the theory's attractive features; for these suggest that – despite the initial difficulties – it may still be well worth developing.

The first and biggest advantage which the belief-acquisition theory has over the representative theory is that it does not immediately threaten to be circular. Instead of trying to explain the perception of outer things in terms of some kind of perception of inner things, it speaks instead in terms of the acquiring of beliefs. And having a belief is not a matter of seeing or perceiving something on a screen inside the head, nor is it essentially a matter of having images in the mind, nor does it necessarily involve anything else of a perceptual kind. This negative point should perhaps be obvious enough. But we will in any case return to discuss this point in Chapter X.

A second consideration in favour of the belief-acquisition theory (at least as against the representative theory) emerges if we reflect on how we get to know whether someone else can see or hear. Consider, for example, the mother's happy assumption that her child is sighted and not blind. Her knowledge is evidently based on her observation that the child can get around the world by using its eyes and is able to tell how things are just by looking. And on the belief-acquisition theory this evidence is indeed exactly what is needed to prove that the child can see: for on this theory to see *is* to pick up information by using one's eyes, and therefore evidence that the child can acquire information in this way is the most direct evidence we could possibly have that it is sighted. On the other hand, according to the representative theory, in order to show that someone is sighted we would need evidence that he has internal visual representations before his mind's eye – and how could we get such evidence? The mother cannot 'get inside' her child's mind to discover whether there are visual representations to be found there. To repeat, all she has to go on are her observations of how her child manages to get around the world; and why should we suppose that these observations prove that the child is not only acquiring beliefs but is also aware of visual sense-data? What could justify the move from 'my child acquires beliefs by using his eyes' to 'my child is aware of pictures on an internal mental screen'?

A third advantage of the belief-acquisition theory is its ability to deal very smoothly with an important general fact about perception – namely that our experiences are in part a function of our capacities for understanding and our background beliefs (e.g. our expectations about what we are going to see). There is a wealth of empirical investigation into the psychology of perception which shows this: but we can illustrate the key point here without reference to any esoteric experiment. Just recall the experience of looking at a child's puzzle picture, trying to find what is hidden in the leaves of a tree. Suddenly, the lines – as it were – assemble themselves into a recognisable face *and the picture now looks different.* The way the picture now looks is evidently a function of one's capacity to understand line-drawings; if one couldn't understand the lines as outlining a face, one couldn't see the picture like that. Or compare how things sound to the child who first hears a record of (say) the sextet in *Don Giovanni* with the experience of its mother who, we shall suppose, is a distinguished opera singer and can therefore bring to bear a much richer understanding of music. As they sit together, the sound-waves reaching their ears are no doubt much the same: but their auditory experiences (i.e. the ways they hear the music) are quite different. It would be sheer dogma to insist that their auditory perceptions are the same; what is to the child fairly undifferentiated noise and muddle is heard by the mother as a complex structure of sound. And to hear the sound as structured is to hear it differently, just as to see the lines as a face is to see them differently.

In short, then, our capacities for understanding and the stock of knowledge we have at our disposal can affect the ways we see or hear. Now, the belief-acquisition theory has no difficulty at all in accommodating this point: if perception *is* belief-acquisition then it will be no surprise to learn that the precise beliefs acquired in a perceptual situation will be in part a function of our capacities for understanding and our prior beliefs. On the other hand, the representative theory has traditionally encouraged the myth that in perception we are directly aware of raw, unprocessed sense-data – and any subsequent interpretation of the images before the mind's eye is the quite independent work of the understanding. According to this myth, what we *experience* in the puzzle picture case should stay constant even while our *understanding* of what we see changes. The resourceful representationalist could try rejecting this extreme version of his theory and – in order to deal with the experiential facts – allow that our understanding can affect the inner objects we are aware of (cf. Locke *Essay*: II.ix.8); but on his view there will certainly be a puzzle about *why* that should be so.

In summary: the belief-acquisition theory of perception has the considerable merits of being non-circular and of not making any mystery of the fact (as it certainly seems to be) that we can get to know that other people are perceivers like ourselves. Further, the theory easily accommodates the fact that perception is a function of prior beliefs and capacities for understanding. So what are the snags?

5   First, a few problems that require (at most) some relatively minor adjustments to the theory.

We have already said that the beliefs picked up in perception are mostly of a relatively unreflective and unsophisticated kind. But now consider the case of the frog, for instance. Presumably we are all quite ready to say that frogs see the flies they catch; but many may well hesitate to speak of frogs as acquiring any *beliefs* about flies at all. So how can seeing in general be a matter of acquiring beliefs?

One possible riposte to this line of criticism would be to insist that frogs *do* have beliefs: but we can afford to be more conciliatory. Let's grant that the everyday notion of belief is often used to signify states of mind arrived at by conscious deliberation or reflection (as when we speak of Jack's religious beliefs or Jill's political beliefs). And while we may stretch the term to cover less reflective human thoughts, as we move down from human cases there soon comes a point where we can no longer ascribe beliefs in anything like such a rich, full-blooded sense. In particular, then, we may well feel that it is a bit misleading to talk in an unqualified way of frogs having beliefs about flies. However, we might more happily say that the frog 'takes it that' there is a fly in front of it. And we are even happier to speak of the frog as acquiring information about its environment by using its eyes. So what we need in the theory of perception is perhaps not the idea of belief-acquisition (properly so called) but a somewhat thinned-down notion of the acquisition of belief-like states of mind which register information.

We will touch on this point again in XII.3, where we shall see that there are some other reasons for wanting to operate with a thinned-down notion of this general kind. But it won't do too much harm to continue speaking loosely of acquiring beliefs in perception, when we should strictly be more cautious and speak of coming to take-it-that or of acquiring information-registering states.

This general point about the contrast between a narrow everyday sense of 'belief' and our current catch-all sense can also help us out with another possible problem. It might be objected that perception is a passive state; seeing a cat, for example, is something that *happens* to you. But belief-acquisition (the argument continues) is a more voluntary state, involving the will. So passive perception cannot be equated with belief-acquisition. Here again, we can afford to be conciliatory, and to allow that there may possibly be some element of will involved in the formation of (say) sophisticated political or religious beliefs. However, such cases apart, it still remains plainly true that most beliefs – in our currently operative broad sense – are *not* subject to the will. Thus, your current belief that there is a book in front of you is not something that you *decided* to believe. In the general case, as Hume put it, belief

> depends not on the will, but must arise from certain determinate causes
> and principles, of which we are not masters.   (*Treatise*: Appendix)

There is thus no obstacle to equating perception with the acquisition of lower-level, involuntary beliefs.

A third line of objection to our sketched theory might run as follows:

> Suppose that you are steadily looking at a completely static scene. Then after a little time you will still be seeing that scene, but will no longer be acquiring any new beliefs. So seeing can't be belief-acquisition.

But is this right? Shouldn't we perhaps insist that one is in fact acquiring new beliefs even when regarding a static scene? For example, when you first set eyes on the scene, you initially acquired beliefs such as that there was *then* a cat asleep in front of you: as you continue to look at the scene, your beliefs are updated, so that you come to believe that there is a cat there *now*. Your perceptual beliefs have a changing time reference, and so we can say that strictly speaking you are continuously acquiring new beliefs. Alternatively (though this is really little more than a verbal variant of the same idea), we could more casually say that someone who believes over a period of time that there is a cat currently in front of him has the same belief throughout; and in perception this belief is *causally kept in being* – for of course the belief will evaporate when the cat is seen to stalk away. Taking this second line would lead us to say that perceiving an object involves that object's causing or causally sustaining appropriate beliefs.

6   Now to turn to a much more serious problem. We have said that perception involves belief-acquisition. But can't you see something without 'believing your eyes', as the phrase has it?

Consider this slightly esoteric case, which brings out the point forcefully. Suppose you are the subject of a neuro-physiological investigation and the experimenter explains that he will be implanting an electrode in your skull and passing a weak electrical impulse into a certain part of the visual cortex. He tells you that when this happens you should *seem* to see a flash of light, and he emphasises that there will not actually be a flash at all; it is simply that you will get that impression. And let us suppose you believe him. Then, when the impulse is given you will get a hallucinatory experience as of seeing a flash of light, but you will of course not come to believe that there *really* is a flash of light, nor will you acquire any similar beliefs. So your having the visual experience in this case cannot be simply a matter of acquiring appropriate beliefs. But now suppose that at one stage in the experiment no electrical impulse is given, but instead a *real* flash of light is produced, and you see it in the normal way. Yet, because of what you have been told by the experimenter, you will still not come to believe that a flash of light appeared! So, again, there seems to be visual experience – indeed this time a genuine case of perception – but without the sort of acquisition of beliefs posited by the belief-acquisition theory.

In short, then, you can see without believing your eyes. Or to put it another way, the change produced in you when you perceive may not involve any relevant changes in your beliefs about the thing perceived. The belief-acquisition theory of perception, in its present form, is therefore straightforwardly false.

The obvious move to make in response to the case of the deceiving neurologist is that proposed by David Armstrong, a notable contemporary defender of the belief-acquisition theory. He writes that, in cases where perception occurs without the relevant beliefs,

> there may still be an inclination to 'believe our senses'. If a thing looks to be a certain way, although we know on independent grounds that it cannot actually be that way, we may still half-believe, or be inclined to believe, that it is as it looks. ... [And in] cases of perception without belief and even without inclination to believe, it is still possible to formulate a true counter-factual statement of the form 'But for the fact that the perceiver had other, independent, beliefs about the world, he would have acquired certain beliefs – the beliefs corresponding to the content of his perception.' We do not believe that our mirror-double stands before us *only* because we have a great deal of other knowledge about the world which contradicts the belief that there is anything like the object we seem to see behind the surface of the glass. (1968: 221-2)

This, we will now argue, points the way to an improved belief-acquisition theory.

It will be useful to introduce a bit of technical jargon here. Let us say that someone has a *propensity* to be φ if he is in such a state that he will be φ unless some special blocking factors intervene. Jack has a propensity to put on weight, meaning that he does so unless he takes definite countermeasures. Jill has no such propensity; however, she does have an unfortunate propensity to suffer from hay-fever, meaning that she gets hay-fever in season unless she is taking appropriate drugs. In the same sense, then, we can say that a person has a propensity to have a certain belief if he is in such a state that he will hold the belief unless it is blocked by some special factors such as countervailing beliefs. And using this jargon we can now sum up Armstrong's suggestion as follows: we should modify the belief-acquisition theory so that it says that perception involves (at least) the acquiring of various *propensities* to have appropriate beliefs. In other words, the change produced in you in perception may not be a change in your beliefs, but only a change in your propensities to believe various things about your environment. To return to our example above: in the case where you genuinely saw a flash of light without acquiring any such belief, you did at least have a propensity to believe that you were seeing a flash – for you were in a state such that you would have believed that there was a flash, but for what the experimenter said.

According to Armstrong, then, we should say that perception involves (not necessarily the acquisition of new beliefs but) the acquisition of propensities to believe. This is a substantial revision of the original theory: however, it is easily checked that the revised version still retains the attractive features of the cruder version as outlined in §3.

7   The essential idea of the revised version of the belief-acquisition theory is this. To be a perceiver is to acquire beliefs via organs which are causally sensitive to the environment. But not every perceptual encounter need produce appropriate beliefs: to be a perceiver it is enough that the stimulation of your sensory receptors produces correlated internal states which in turn *normally* affect your beliefs in such a way that the acquired beliefs are broadly speaking true to the world around you. However, there can be cases where light hitting your retina, for example, produces the usual internal state but, for one countervailing reason or another, appropriate beliefs do not follow. These would be the cases where there is seeing without belief, or with the wrong beliefs: there is production of the right internal state – a state which *normally* leads on to appropriate beliefs – but the normal upshot is blocked. Or in the terminology we introduced in the last section, there is production of a *propensity* to have certain beliefs, but without the beliefs actually ensuing.

We can now use this theory to redeem some undertakings we made in the last chapter. In VII.7 we promised to show that the possibility of hallucinating a bloody dagger does not force us to admit the existence of the coloured inner objects postulated by the representationalist. And indeed, the rival belief-acquisition theory of perception in its latest form can easily cope with this sort of case. Hallucinating a dagger, we might naturally say, is like genuinely perceiving a dagger because it too involves acquiring at least a *propensity* to such beliefs as that there is a red, bloody dagger in front of you; for things are such that you will believe that there is a dagger there, unless you have some countervailing beliefs. What makes the case a hallucination is that this propensity is not produced by the normal causal antecedents of genuine perception, but by some malfunction of the perceptual system. Whether you *actually* come to believe, in the hallucinatory case, that there is really a dagger there will obviously depend on your other beliefs.

Consider next the case where the red bus looks khaki under sodium lights (see VII.6). We can now deal with this case without supposing that the khaki colour really belongs to some inner object or sense-datum. On our theory, what happens is this: when the bus looks khaki, you are acquiring the propensity to believe that there is a khaki bus in front of you. No doubt, once you are familiar with the effect of sodium lights, you don't have any serious inclination to think that there really is something khaki there, in front of your eyes: indeed you will probably judge what you see to be red. Still, if you *didn't* have some appropriate countervailing beliefs, you *would* believe that something khaki was there, and this propensity accounts for the inclination to say that the bus looks khaki.

Finally, to gather up one more loose end from VII.6, the belief-acquisition theory can also deal with the 'elliptical penny' case. Of course, when we see the penny from an oblique angle we do not normally come to believe that there is something elliptical in front of us, for we are familiar with the way that circular things look from various directions – we typically come to believe that there is a circular thing there set at an angle! The sense in which the penny 'has an elliptical appearance' (and a different appearance from different angles) is captured roughly as follows: if we didn't know that the thing in front of us was set at an angle, and assumed that we were seeing it face on, then we *would* believe that it was elliptical (and believe it elliptical to varying degrees depending on our angle of vision).

8   We now return, and not before time, to discuss what many people would hold to be the most obvious and decisive kind of objection to the belief-acquisition theory – namely the thought that the theory leaves out exactly what is most important about perception, its experiential character.

When we first sketched a causal account of perception in the last chapter, we said that the natural way of characterising the end effect of the perceptual process is as *the having of perceptual experiences*. We went on to discuss at length, and then reject, one account of the nature of such experiences: but we didn't reject the initial thought that perception involves the causation of experiences, properly understood. In the present chapter, however, we have used the word 'experience' much less often, and have characterised perception as the production of a state which, if there are no countervailing factors, results in appropriate beliefs. In a phrase, the end effect of the perceptual process is *the acquisition of propensities to believe*. Now, if our later remarks are to be consistent with our plausible first thought, this must be because we hold that the having of perceptual experiences just is one and the same thing as the acquisition of propensities to believe of the appropriate kind. But this implication of our discussions, frankly presented, will strike many as quite preposterous.

'This equation can't be right', the protest runs. 'Perceptual experiences have a particular intrinsic phenomenological quality. Blind people apart, we all know what it is like, experientially speaking, to have visual experiences. Likewise for the other senses. But there need never be anything experiential involved in acquiring beliefs or propensities to believe. We can surely imagine a creature – and maybe even a machine – which acquires beliefs in various causal ways without having any genuine experiences at all. In short, experiences can be entirely absent while any particular beliefs or propensities to believe are acquired. A theory of perception that speaks only of belief-acquisitions must therefore inevitably fail to capture the intrinsic nature of perceptual experience.'

But despite the vigour with which such protests are often pressed, it is not at all clear what weight we should give them. There are serious problems about how to understand such phrases as 'knowing what it is like to have visual experiences'; and one useful way of approaching the issue raised by our imagined protestor would be to examine critically the use made of such puzzling notions. We will return to this issue in XV.7, but here our tactics will be different: for the sake of argument, we will go along with this way of talking, we will assume that there is some good sense to be made of it, and argue that even with this concession we are not obviously forced to accept the protestor's conclusion.

Consider again the protestor's blanket assertion that there need never be anything experiential involved in acquiring propensities to believe – call this claim (E). Why shouldn't we agree that this applies in some cases, but then go on to counter-claim that in some other cases, and in particular in those cases involved in perception, there *is* something which it is like to acquire the appropriate propensities? The protestor's bald generalisation gets much of its appeal from being confused with a couple of neighbouring points: but we can acknowledge the truth in these points without being forced to assent to the disputed claim (E).

The first neighbouring truth is this: there is usually nothing that it is like to *possess* any given belief. Consider your perceptually acquired standing belief that blood is red. While there is perhaps something which it is like to be actively entertaining that thought, the rest of the time there is nothing of a broadly experiential kind associated distinctively with the possession of that belief. Five minutes ago, you no doubt believed that blood is red: but you weren't then *experiencing* anything relevant. However, this observation causes no difficulty at all for the belief-acquisition theory of perception. For it does not follow from the fact that there is nothing which it is like to *have* some particular belief that there will be nothing which it is like to *acquire* such a belief (or a propensity to have the belief). Acquisition is an event which initiates a state; and what is true of the ensuing state will not necessarily be true of the initiating event. The state of being on a moving train may be unexciting; it doesn't follow that the initiating event of jumping on the moving train was unexciting! Similarly, having a belief may involve nothing experiential; but that doesn't mean that picking up the belief must have been non-experiential.

Still – and this is the second point which might be thought to lend plausibility to our protestor's generalisation (E) – there surely *could* be cases where one acquires beliefs via a sense-organ but without having conscious experiences. Let's take an admittedly extreme case to illustrate the point (the example is from Craig 1976). You are out in the country in the dead of night, your visual field seems uniformly pitch dark, and yet you suddenly find yourself inclined to believe that there is a light emanating from a quite specific direction and, furthermore, that this light is green. Perhaps you are at a loss to account for this inclination; you feel it very strongly, but you don't know why. Or perhaps this sort of thing happens to you so often, and turns out so reliable, that you don't give it a second thought. Either way, you will have acquired a propensity to believe. And let's suppose further that experimental tests reveal that this results from your eyes being open, turned in the right direction, etc. Yet it seems that this need not involve any conscious experience at all; it could continue throughout to *look* pitch dark, for example. Perhaps this case initially sounds very odd indeed: yet in fact some people who have suffered brain damage can apparently arrive at some beliefs about their environment by using their eyes while all the time protesting that they have no conscious visual experiences (the phenomenon is called 'blind-sight', see Weiskrantz 1980).

However, to concede the possibility of this odd sort of case isn't decisively to undermine the belief-acquisition theory. For we might argue that there will still remain many relevant differences between the propensities to believe which you would have in this abnormal case, and those you would have if you were in a normal perceptual situation (which, at least for human perceivers, involves not only seeing but awareness that one is seeing). To begin with, in the abnormal situation, you would presumably not believe that you were seeing the light, nor that the light appeared to be green; and you would continue to believe that everything looked pitch dark. It would be quite different in a normal perceptual situation. In other words, the difference between the imagined case of acquiring beliefs about the world non-experientially and a standard case of perception will show up as an *overall* difference in the totality of beliefs acquired. And it does seem very difficult to imagine a case where (i) one acquires *all* the beliefs or propensities to believe associated with ordinary human perception, including beliefs about one's own state of mind, and yet (ii) there is nothing which it is like, experientially speaking, to acquire these beliefs. With a bit of care, therefore, we might still hope to be able to characterise perception in terms of the sort of beliefs acquired therein.

In summary, we can agree that there need be nothing which it is distinctively like, experientially speaking, to *have* certain beliefs or propensities to believe, and also that beliefs *can* be acquired without conscious experience even via a sense organ. But these concessions do not force us to accept that we could acquire just the sort of complex patterns of belief characteristic of human perception and yet there still be nothing experiential which it is like to do so.

9   Finally, what is the relation of all this to physiology? We have been arguing that perception involves, at the end of the causal process, some state which normally results in the acquisition of appropriate beliefs. But the neuro-physiologists tell us that seeing, for example, involves goings-on in the visual cortex. What is the relation between these two accounts? Well, why not say that *these are just two ways of describing the same thing*? The inner object theorist has dire difficulties in reconciling his dualistic account with a scientific view of perception: but our talk of propensities seems as if it should cohere nicely. Propensities to believe – the suggestion runs – are brain states, differently described. Here we get the first glimpse of the possible shape for a general non-dualist theory of the mind: mental happenings, in this case the experiences which are acquisitions of propensities to believe, are events in the brain under a different description. This bold thesis will have to be explored at length in Chapters XI to XIII, so we will say no more about it here. For the moment, we merely note this potential compatibility between our theory and physiology as another mark in its favour.

There is much more to be said about the belief-acquisition theory of perception. We have suggested (§2 and VII.1) that beliefs have to be caused in 'the right kind of way' for there to be a case of perception: but there are tangled problems lurking here. And more needs to be said in order to quiet the worry that the theory leaves out the experiential or phenomenological character of perception (for a discussion of related matters see Chapter XV). However, we have already said enough at least for introductory purposes. The key idea that perception is to be understood as a mode of acquiring information about one's environment has turned out to be attractive and problem-solving, and it can be defended at least against some initial objections. At the moment, therefore, it looks as though work on this sort of theory is a promising strategy (it is, if you like, a progressive research programme in the sense of V.2). And on this optimistic note we pass on from the topic of perception.

IX

ACTION AND VOLITION

1   As outlined in VI.7, our strategy is to approach the mind from the outside inwards. In other words, we want first to discuss the fundamental capacities for perception and action which form (so to speak) the input and output interfaces between the mind and the world, before we go on to deal with the more purely internal workings of the mind, such as beliefs and desires, sensations and thoughts. Having discussed perception at length in the last two chapters, we now turn to consider the topic of action.

Not everything you do is an action in the sense we are going to be interested in. You move your eyeballs when asleep, you perspire and digest your food, you occasionally lose some hair, you grow older and eventually die: and while these are all things you can be said to do, they will not count as actions in the full-blown sense that is our concern here. An action in our stricter sense is something which is – so to speak – up to you; within limits you have some choice about whether to do it or to refrain. For example, it is up to you whether or not you move your arm or start running, open the door or saw the logs, wake the baby or commit adultery. It is not in the same sense up to you whether you move your eyeballs while asleep; you just have no choice in the matter – your eyeballs move whether you want them to or not. Likewise, chasing sheep or fetching balls are things the dog does on purpose, and it has considerable control over these performances: but it is not up to the dog whether or not it breathes.

A genuine action, we might perhaps say, is something you could sensibly be asked to do or to refrain from doing. Sitting down, fetching balls, washing dishes, voting Conservative are all actions of varying degrees of sophistication; these are things we could ask you to do or not to do. But it would be pointless to say to you 'Stop perspiring this minute!' or 'Stop digesting the food in your stomach!' You can, of course, be asked to do something that will bring

119

it about that the perspiring stops (you can take a rest) or that the digesting of food in the stomach stops (you can make yourself sick); but that is another matter. While we can imagine creatures for whom digestion *is* a matter of choice, who have voluntary control over the later stages of their digestive processes just as we have voluntary control over (say) chewing and swallowing, that is evidently not how things are with humans. For us, digesting is not an action.

This notion of action is related to the idea of responsibility: humans, at least, may sensibly be held answerable for their genuine actions in a way that they can't always be held answerable for their other doings. Or, at least, so it certainly seems. However, the whole question of free action is an extremely thorny one, and we will set it aside until Chapter XVIII.

To repeat, actions – in the sense that interests us – are doings which are up to you. You have some choice in the matter whether you raise your arm or start running; you can't in the same way choose whether or not to digest the food in your stomach. Could we sum up these introductory remarks by saying that actions are things done intentionally?

This generalisation obviously won't do as it stands because there can be unintentional actions. For example, Jack can unintentionally hit the ball into the net, Jill can unintentionally wake the baby, and yet these are still doings in which Jack and Jill are active. However, the notion of something's being done intentionally or on purpose does seem quite central to the concept of action in the following way. Jack counts as having actively done something in hitting the ball into the net because that involved his intentionally playing a backhand drive. Likewise, Jill counts as having actively done something in waking the baby because that involved her intentionally sawing logs. Suppose, by contrast, that what woke the baby was Jill's crashing onto the glass table in a dead faint, so in this case Jill did nothing intentional at all: then while we can say Jill's *fall* woke the baby, it would surely be rather misleading to say *Jill* did so – and even if we did say that, we would evidently not be imputing to Jill an action in the stricter sense we are interested in. Putting it crudely, unintentional, inadvertent or accidental doings will count as actions just in so far as they involve some core of intentional action. So despite the fact that actions need not be intentional, the central concept we need to get clear about is still the notion of intentional action, the notion of doing something on purpose.

These initial remarks, we hasten to note, certainly don't add up to a precise, hard-edged characterisation of the category of action. We have in particular left it open what it is for some unintentional doing to 'involve' an intentional action. And what are we to say about such marginal cases as those unremarked hand-wavings, scratchings, finger-tappings and so on which accompany our more considered performances? These usually do not involve anything intentional – yet they are like actions in being doings we can reasonably be asked to desist from. Still, our rough remarks will do as an introduction.

2   As good a place as any to begin our enquiry into the nature of action is with the question raised by Wittgenstein: 'What is left over if I subtract the fact that my arm went up from the fact that I raised my arm?' (1953: §622). Evidently, your arm can go up without you intentionally raising it; perhaps your elbow is jogged, or someone is pulling at strings tied to your wrist, or is giving electric shocks to your arm muscles. Not all occasions when your arm goes up are occasions when you act: so what makes the difference between the arm-risings which are genuine actions and the ones which are not?

As an initial response, we might say something like this: 'In order for my arm to rise without my actively raising it, there will have to be some external cause for the movement – a gust of wind dragging at the umbrella that I am holding, someone jogging my elbow, or such like. If I raise my arm myself, however, there is no need for such an external cause for the movement of my arm: the cause will be internal to me. The movement will be due to the contraction of my muscles, which in turn is due to nerve impulses, and so on. In short, the difference between mere bodily movement and genuine action is the difference between external and internal causation.' But clearly, this account will not do as it stands; twitches, spasms, nervous tics and reflex jerks have internal causes yet are not at all the sort of things which we want to count as actions. Indeed, if there was no more to intentional action than internal causation, then there would be no reason why the internally caused movements of plants, or even the movements of a watch, should not count as fully-fledged actions. Still, it seems easy enough to amend our first account of action to avoid such absurdities: intentional actions are in some sense things you put your mind to – so surely what we need to say is that actions must ultimately have internal *mental* causes. A reflex muscular spasm, like the movement of a plant or a watch, has (in a broad sense) an internal cause: but a genuine action has mental antecedents – your mind has some part to play in the performance of the action.

Note that, while we can say that actions have mental causes, we cannot reverse this claim and say that all movements with mental causes are actions. After all, anxiety may make your hand shake, or embarrassment make you twitch, and these shakes and twitches are not actions despite their mental antecedents. So the presence of mental causes is only a necessary condition of genuine action, and not a sufficient condition.

There already emerges from these sketchy remarks a certain parallel with our treatment of perception. Perceiving an object, we argued, involves something mental – i.e. experiences – caused by the object. We are now suggesting that action likewise involves a causal process: you only count as raising your arm if the arm goes up as a causal result of something mental. In respect of each theory, we need to ask about the mental end of the causal processes: what are experiences? what are the initiating mental causes of action? And just as we began our earlier investigations into perception by looking at the historically important sense-datum theory of experience, so the present enquiry will begin by looking at versions of the historically influential volitional theory of action.

3   What are the mental antecedents of action? What sort of mental happenings or states are the initiating causes of an intentional action?

Our first thought might be that action always proceeds from *desire*. In other words, actions are things which you do either because you specifically want to do them, or because you believe that they are the means to other things you want. When you actively raise your arm, your arm goes up because you simply want it to go up (perhaps you are testing to see if you can still move it after an accident), or because its going up is required for something else you want (perhaps you want to vote and think that you need to raise your arm to vote, or you want to signal the start of the race and think that raising your hand is the way to do it, or you want to point to the Pole Star ...). By contrast, non-actions like spasms or twitches happen independently of your wants, i.e. they occur whether you want them to or not.

But there is an apparent difficulty with this plausible first thought, which can be brought out by the following argument:

(D) Our desires – or at least the more basic ones – are not themselves states we have much control over; it is not usually up to us whether we feel thirsty and want a drink, or whether we want to be warmer, or whether we feel sexual desires. Our beliefs likewise are not normally under voluntary control; for example, many are acquired perceptually, and perception involves a causal process whose workings are not up to us. So, if we characterise actions as doings caused by desires (in company with appropriate beliefs), this suggests that states which aren't up to us automatically produce actions without further intervention on our part; and this in turn would imply that our actions too are not up to us. This conclusion makes a nonsense of the whole concept of action as we have introduced it.

As we will see later (§7), the argument just sketched is resistible: but if you are impressed by it, then the suggestion that something intervenes between desire and action will seem very attractive. Between the desire to kiss Jill and the action comes the choice to act on that desire rather than to more wisely resist: the desire inclines our will towards kissing Jill, but to produce an action there must be an independent act of will. Or, as Reid put it:

> Desire, therefore, even when its object is some action of our own, is only an incitement of will, but it is not volition. (*Active Powers*: II.i)

A volition, he explains, is an act of will: and he observes that 'when we will to do a thing immediately, the volition is accompanied with an effort to execute that which we willed'. Thus we are invited to view the situation in terms of a three-stage model. First we have desires, and no doubt beliefs too, which influence the will but do not causally determine its activities; secondly, the will acts (or in other words, there is a volition); and finally, there is the effort to produce the action – i.e. the muscles get going.

If you accept this model, then your answer to the question we posed at the beginning of this section will take the form of a *volitional theory of action*. In other words, you will say that the immediate mental antecedents of actions are volitions or acts of will; it is volitions which initiate the causal process of acting.

This sort of volitional theory has been immensely popular in the history of philosophy. It is there in the work of Hobbes, who wrote:

> In *deliberation*, the last appetite, or aversion, immediately adhering to action, or to the omission thereof, is that we call the WILL; the act, not the faculty, of *willing*.   (*Leviathan*: I.vi)

When all relevant desires and beliefs have had their say, as it were, something else has to intervene in order to produce the action, namely the willing. Locke similarly asserts

> we must remember, that *volition* or *willing* is an act of the mind directing its thought to the production of any action, and thereby exerting its power to produce it.   (*Essay*: II.xxi.28)

And he adds that 'the *will* is perfectly distinguished from *desire*' (II.xxi.30). Locke makes it clear that he thinks of actions as caused by volitions: indeed on his view it is precisely in virtue of being produced by a volition that a bodily happening counts as an action. Berkeley too spoke of volitions, e.g. in the second of his *Dialogues*:

> I never use an instrument to move my finger, because it is done by a volition.   (*Works*: 173)

And Berkeley again happily uses the phrase 'act of will' as an equivalent to 'volition'. Hume likewise thought that action requires a causal connection between 'an act of volition, and a motion of the body', and asserts that

> When a person is possessed of any power, there is no more required to convert it into action, but the exertion of the will.   (*Treatise*: I.i.4)

In other words, if you have the power to raise your arm, for example, then what is needed to get the arm into motion is an act of will. Finally, we may note that this key idea that a volition or willing is crucial for action retains its popularity right into the present century. To take just one example, H.A. Prichard thought that the right answer to the question 'what was the activity by performing which I caused my hand to move?' was 'willing the existence of the movement' (1949: 32). Admittedly, there are differences in the way the volitional theory has been developed by different philosophers, but there is an impressive degree of agreement on the centrality of the notion of an act of will or volition, however exactly that notion is to be defined.

In sum: the volitional theory of action which sees actions as causally initiated by acts of will has a prestigious pedigree. It is also, as we shall now see, a disaster.

4 Just what is a 'volition' or 'act of will'? Locke breezily asserts that

> it being a very simple act, whosoever desires to understand what it is will ... find it by reflecting on his own mind and observing what it does when it wills. (*Essay*: II.xxi.30)

With equal confidence, Prichard asserts that willing is

> a *mental* activity of a certain kind, an activity of whose nature we are dimly aware in doing the action and of which we can become more clearly aware by reflecting on it. (1949: 189)

Suppose, however, that you are at the bank; the cashier passes over a familiar slip of paper, saying 'sign here, please' and you oblige. Now your signing is certainly an action. But is it, in the typical case, preceded by any conscious mental event of which you are even dimly aware? Does introspection or reflection really reveal an internal 'act of will'. Surely you will normally sign 'straight off' without deliberation, without consciously setting yourself to perform the task, without mental or physical effort. Contrary to Locke's confident claim, echoed by Prichard, introspection does not seem to reveal the volitions which supposedly prompt any action. And we are left quite in the dark about how to answer questions such as those raised by Ryle:

> Can [volitions] be sudden or gradual, strong or weak, difficult or easy, enjoyable or disagreeable? Can they be accelerated, decelerated, interrupted or suspended? Can people be efficient or inefficient at them? Can we take lessons in executing them? Are they fatiguing or distracting? Can I do two or seven of them synchronously? ... Can I forget how to do them? Can I mistakenly believe that I have executed one, when I have not, or that I have not executed one, when I have? At which moment was the boy going through a volition to take the high dive? When he set foot on the ladder? When he took his first deep breath? When he

counted off 'One, two, three – Go', but did not go? Very, very shortly
before he sprang?   (1949: 63-4)

The defender of the volitional theory owes us answers to such
questions, yet it is, to put it mildly, very unclear indeed how he is to
proceed. Still, let's waive these preliminary points, important
though they are: for there is an even more telling difficulty for the
theory. The volitional theory is intended to be a universal account
of the nature of *any* action: we will now show that it cannot
possibly provide such an account.

You will doubtless have already noticed that the cast-list of
supporters of a volitional theory of action includes many who were
also devotees of an inner object theory of perceptual experience.
This is no coincidence: there are many parallels between the two
sorts of theory. For the present, we can bring out their crucial point
of similarity as follows. Any sane theory of seeing, for example, will
allow that visual perception in the end leads to the acquisition of
information about our environment. But according to the inner
object theory, there is a crucial intermediary element in the overall
process that leads from the world to our visual beliefs, namely the
awareness of sense-data before the mind's eye. Likewise, any sane
theory of action will allow that action springs ultimately from our
desires and the beliefs which shape and channel our desires. But
according to the volitional theory there is a crucial intermediary
element in the overall process that leads from our desires to our
doings in the world, namely a volition or act of will. Now, we
objected to the inner object theory on the grounds that, in
purporting to explain what it is to perceive ordinary outer objects,
it smuggled in the scarcely disguised notion of perceiving inner
objects. And we argued that, if there is a puzzle about the nature of
the ordinary visual sense, then there is equally a puzzle about the
nature of this mysterious inner seeing of inner objects. In an exactly
parallel way we can now object to the volitional theory on the
grounds that, in purporting to explain what it is to perform an
ordinary action such as raising one's arm, it helps itself quite
explicitly to the notion of an *act* of will. And again, *if there is a
puzzle about the nature of ordinary outer acts then there is equally
a puzzle about the nature of inner acts of the mind.*

We are trying to get a clear view of the distinction between
bodily happenings which are actions and those we passively
undergo. But we must remember that there is equally a distinction

to be made among *mental* events between our actions and things which merely happen to us. For example, we suffer a stab of pain, are suddenly reminded by a particular smell of a long-forgotten childhood event, cannot help hearing the clap of thunder, start to feel hungry. These are all things which happen to us, which are not matters of choice. By contrast, we may try to turn our attention from the pain by thinking about philosophy, we may compose in our heads a sonnet about childhood, calculate how far away the storm is, and decide on the menu for dinner. These are mental *actions*, doings which are in some important sense up to us. Now, if the distinction between bodily actions and passive bodily happenings needs clarifying, then the parallel distinction between mental actions and passive mental happenings needs clarifying no less. So if we are to get clear about the difference between raising one's arm and the arm merely going up, it's no good saying that the action is distinguished by being caused by an antecedent mental act of will, for *that* reduplicates the problem on the mental stage.

If our ambition is to provide a general account of the nature of action, we cannot presuppose the notion of a mental action - for that simply raises the question 'what's the difference between performing an *act* of will and merely finding that one's will has undergone a certain change?' Plainly, we can't say that acts of will are distinguished by being caused by yet further mental acts, for that would be to set off an entirely vicious infinite regress: if performing any act requires us already to have performed a prior act, how could we ever get started? In short, then, appealing to inner acts in the theory of action is no more explanatory than appealing to inner perceptions in the theory of perception.

5   The volitional theory of action is badly misguided. So where do we look next for an account of the antecedents of action? Well, in rejecting the volitional theory we certainly have not demolished *every* version of the idea that something intervenes in action between our desires and our movements: we have only shown that we get into embarrassing difficulties if what intervenes is itself thought of as a kind of action. So there might still be room for a new, non-circular, account which shares with the volitional theory its key idea that some further mental phenomena intervene in action after the initial setting of one's desires and relevant beliefs.

What about saying, for example, that actions always involve a prior act of choice? But putting the question like that immediately gives the game away: if choices are mental *acts* then we will again need to know what the difference is between actively fixing one's will and merely finding that one's will has changed. Mental choices are no more explanatory than volitions.

What about the recently popular idea that an action always involves a *trying* which mediates between our desires and our eventual movements? Unlike the notion of a volition, this is at least something which we are all familiar with; no one doubts that there is such a thing as trying to do something and perhaps succeeding or perhaps failing. So, can we say that what distinguishes actions is that they always involve tryings in this familiar sense?

Well, first let's note that trying to attract Jill's attention, for example, is ordinarily a matter of waving your arms about in the hope she will see you, trying to start the car involves pulling out the choke and turning the ignition, while trying to win the match is a whole complex of actions. Even in the case where a trying leads to no physical activity (e.g. because you are suddenly paralysed) there is perhaps the inner mental act of setting oneself to do something, of putting in some mental effort. We can argue, therefore, that tryings – far from being the inner mental causes of action – are themselves typically actions in their own right. So the attempt to explain the notion of action in terms of the idea of trying is, like the volitional theory, doomed to circularity again.

Second, the claim that a trying always intervenes between one's desires and one's actions is implausible for the simple reason that there seem to be many things we do without trying – for example, we don't usually have to *try* in order to raise our arms. In fact, we normally use the word 'try' only when there is some difficulty in the performance or doubt about the outcome. To say that action *always* involves a trying presupposes the possibility of dissociating the meaning of the word 'try' from these thoughts of difficulty or doubt that are usually in our minds when we use the word. And can we be sure that we know what the word means when these apparently crucial associations are removed? Isn't the notion of trying, thus purified, beginning to look as thin as the notion of volition upon which it was supposed to be an improvement? (We should note, however, that our rather brusque dismissal of the notion of trying is controversial: see Hornsby 1980.)

What about the idea that the intervening factor between our

desires and our actions is simply an *intention*? After all, we are discussing the nature of intentional action, so what more natural than to say that the essential element in the causal generation of action is an intention to perform it. However, if what is meant here is a *considered* intention formed in advance of the action (perhaps as the result of deliberation), then it is plainly false to claim that all actions spring from intentions in this sense. Jack suddenly kisses Jill: afterwards he says, quite truly, 'I'm sorry, I don't know what came over me! I didn't have any intention of kissing you tonight ...' Yet, although Jack had no settled intention to kiss Jill, his act was done on purpose – it wasn't like some reflex movement or nervous tic. Jack simply acted, as we say, on the spur of the moment, without prior intention. Equally on the spur of the moment, you find yourself bidding much more at the auction than you had intended: yet as you raise your arm you are certainly acting intentionally, with the purpose of bidding. Your action was unplanned but not unpurposed. And these are merely somewhat dramatic examples of what happens all the time: remember the occasion at the bank when without hesitation you signed that slip of paper passed over by the cashier. Writing your signature is certainly an action, yet it would seem to be mere dogma to insist that it must therefore have sprung from a speedily deliberated prior intention. In short, there are very many things which we do, and do on purpose, yet without having had any settled prior intention to do them.

Still, it is of course true that when we act intentionally we are in some crucial sense acting with an intention – even if not necessarily with some previously settled or articulated intention. But acting with an intention in this sense is not a matter of acting as a result of some intervening mental happening which occurs, so to speak, between one's desires and one's movements. On the contrary, as we shall see shortly, to act with an intention is to act as a direct result of certain background desires and beliefs. We don't need to bring intervening factors into the story at all.

6   Let's ask again: what is it for something to be done on purpose, with an intention? Elizabeth Anscombe makes exactly the right initial move when she says that doings which are intentional are to be distinguished from the rest in virtue of being those

to which a certain sense of the question 'Why?' is given application; the sense is of course that in which the answer, if positive, gives a reason for action.   (1963: 9)

In other words, an action is intentional if there is an answer to the question 'why did the agent do that?' which explains the action by giving the agent's *reasons* for so acting.

And what is it for an agent to have reasons for acting? Suppose Jack raised his arm: why did he do that? Because he wanted to vote for the motion, and believed that, on the present occasion, raising his arm would be voting for the motion. And why did Jill flick the switch? Because she wanted to turn off the light, and took it that by flicking the switch she would get the light to go off. And to turn to a case of animal agency, why did Fido rattle the cupboard door? Because he wanted to get at the bone inside, and took it that shaking the door would get it open so he could reach the bone. In each case, the agent has reasons for acting in virtue of having relevant desires and beliefs. Note, by the way, that these relevant desires and beliefs need not be consciously entertained or thought about: Jack perhaps consciously reached his desire to vote for the motion, but Jill's simpler desire was very probably as unreflective as Fido's. As we remarked before, not all intentional actions flow from prior deliberations.

In our three examples, specifying the agent's reasons for acting is a question of mentioning a desire together with a belief to the effect that the action in question was the appropriate way of satisfying the desire: we render the behaviour comprehensible by seeing the agent as pursuing his or her aims in an intelligible way. Generalising, then, let's say that reasons for acting are appropriate combinations of desires and beliefs. Of course, the relevant desire is sometimes too obvious to need explicit mention, and then we only bother to describe the agent's beliefs: 'Why is Jack wearing jeans at the formal reception?' – 'Because he thought that the invitation was to an informal party, and he supposed that everyone else would be wearing jeans.' Here we probably don't need to add 'and he wanted to wear the same sort of clothes as everyone else'; for that, we might suppose, can be taken for granted. Equally, we can often explain an action adequately enough for ordinary purposes simply by mentioning the appropriate desire, because we can take the relevant belief for granted: 'Why is Jill walking to her car carefully carrying a saucer of mud?' – 'Because she wants a laboratory sample of soil from the boggy land at the bottom of the field for bacteriological analysis.' Here we need hardly add 'and she thought that by carrying the mud back to her car etc.'; the rest of the story here will be easy to fill in once we know the relevant desire. But note that if Jack *didn't* want to dress like everyone else, for example, then the belief we explicitly attributed to him would not adequately explain his action. Likewise, if Jill *didn't* think that she could get the mud to the laboratory by carrying it in a saucer to her car, then the attributed desire wouldn't explain her action. So, in these cases where we only bother to mention one or other part of the agent's reason for action, the unmentioned component is still required for a fully-fledged explanation of the action.

To give someone's reason for acting, therefore, we must typically mention a desire which he has and a corresponding belief to the effect that the action done is a means of securing the desired end. (The exception will be when the agent's desire is just that a certain action be performed, i.e. when he does *A* for no reason other than he wants to do *A*; in this case there is no need for a belief to link what is desired to the action performed.)

However, isn't this formulation open to a rather obvious objection? For surely people sometimes intentionally do things which it would be odd to describe them as *desiring* to do. Cowardly Jack reluctantly goes to the dentist: he might well object to the description that he *desired* to go to the dentist and claim that he went on purpose but despite his desires! Again, Jill succumbs on the spur of the moment to a second helping of cheesecake: she might afterwards say to herself 'I shouldn't have done that, I didn't really want it.'

Well, let's agree that not all actions flow from desires properly so-called. So what we really need here is not the everyday notion of desire so much as the generalised semi-technical notion of a 'pro-attitude' which will, to quote Donald Davidson, cover

> desires, wantings, urges, promptings, and a great variety of moral views, aesthetic principles, ... and public and private goals and values in so far as these can be interpreted as attitudes of an agent directed towards actions of a certain kind. The word 'attitude' does yeoman service here, for it must cover not only permanent character traits that show themselves in a lifetime of behaviour, like love of children or a taste for loud company, but also the most passing fancy that prompts a unique action, like a sudden desire to touch a woman's elbow.   (1963: 4)

In the ordinary sense, Jack may not want to visit the dentist, but if he thinks that he really should then he has to that extent an attitude which inclines him towards doing so – i.e. he has a 'pro-attitude' towards visiting the dentist. Likewise, Jill succumbs to a passing pro-attitude towards a second helping and takes it against her more settled desires. Henceforth, then, when we loosely talk of actions as springing from 'desires', we intend the term to be understood in an attenuated, technical sense equivalent to 'pro-attitude'. Note that we have here yet another parallel with our discussion of perception. In presenting the belief-acquisition theory we were forced to acknowledge that we probably need to work, not with the notion of belief, but with some more generalised notion of information-registering states (see VIII.5); the present move from the ordinary notion of desire to a generalised notion of desire or pro-attitude is similar.

Following Anscombe, our fundamental suggestion is that an action is intentional only if it is done with reasons in the light of which the agent's behaviour can be seen to be comprehensible. To specify reasons which make the behaviour comprehensible is to specify a relevant desire or pro-attitude, and a belief to the effect that the action done will lead to the end desired. We now need, however, to bring out a quite crucial point that has so far been left implicit. In order to explain someone's action, it is not enough to specify a desire and belief which the agent has and which make the action comprehensible; if we are to have a correct explanation, the action must have been done *because* of that desire and belief. Suppose for example that Jack opened the window while wanting some fresh air and believing that he would get fresh air by opening the window. That belief and desire evidently make opening the window a sensible thing to do in the circumstances – but for all that, they may not actually have operated as Jack's reasons for opening the window on this occasion. He may instead have opened the window because he wanted to talk to Jill who is standing outside, and believed that opening the window would facilitate conversation. More generally, one might on a particular occasion have a number of different packages of beliefs and desires such that each package would make reasonable one and the same course of action: in explaining the action we must therefore pick out one (or more) of the packages as actually operative in producing the action. To repeat: to explain an action we must do more than simply specify beliefs and desires that would make the action comprehensible; we must say that the agent acted *because* of those desires and beliefs.

7   But what about the volitionist's argument (D) – sketched in §3 above – which was supposed to show that something must intervene between a desire and its upshot? Well, the point we have just made about the need to use a generalised notion of desire in the theory of action is perhaps already enough to take much of the sting out of this argument.

The essential thought in (D) was that, if we try to define actions as doings to be explained by reference to desires, then since desires are not 'up to us' the same will hold even of our supposedly intentional actions. Well, let's grant that our most basic urges are indeed not under our control – we can't help it when we feel thirsty, for example. But many, or perhaps even most, of the desires or pro-attitudes involved in the explanation of human action are in some measure 'up to us' (at least in the casual everyday sense of that phrase which matters at the moment). To revert to our earlier examples: it surely is to some extent up to Jack whether he wants to look like everyone else at the party – we can sensibly ask whether he ought to feel like that, we may perhaps hold him accountable for still succumbing to the temptation to feel that way, and so on. And Jill's desire for a laboratory sample, which is likely to be the result of some deliberative process, is even more clearly something for which it could make sense to hold her accountable (for example, we can ask whether she has deliberated carelessly or well). Even in the case where Jill succumbs to the fancy for a second helping of cheesecake, there is the question whether her contrary desires should not have been more firmly held. In all these cases, then, the complex of desires which lie behind an action is itself, by and large, something for which the agent has some degree of responsibility: so the consequent action will also be to some extent something for which the agent can be held to account. Hence there is, after all, no quick inference from the claim that intentional actions are doings which spring from our desires (in the broad sense) to the paradoxical general conclusion that our actions are never really up to us after all.

Of course, we are here touching on some difficult and extremely complex issues, to which we will have to return in our concluding chapter on free will. But our present point is a very modest one – we simply want to note that the simple-minded argument (D) doesn't cause insurmountable difficulties for the idea that a doing is 'up to us' even if it is brought about by an appropriate desire. That sweeping argument for the necessity of postulating an intervening factor between our desires and our actions can be resisted.

8   Putting together the strands of our discussion, we can sum things up by saying that a doing is an action only if it involves something done intentionally, i.e. something done *because* of an appropriate pro-attitude and corresponding belief. It seems, therefore, that we have at last arrived (after a detour via the volitional theory) at the correct formulation of the core of a causal theory of action – *the mental causes of those behavioural episodes which count as intentional actions are simply beliefs and desires*. To answer Wittgenstein's question: the difference between your arm going up and your raising your arm is a matter of appropriate causation by beliefs and desires.

We started off these discussions (in §2) by specifying a necessary condition for action: actions have mental causes. But in the course of refining this condition, we seem to have ended up with something which is plausibly also a *sufficient* condition for action. In other words, it seems not only that actions must be appropriately caused by beliefs and desires, but also conversely – any behaviour caused by appropriate beliefs and desires will be an action, at least so long as this happens in the normal kind of way. We do need the qualification about 'the normal kind of way' in order to bar some bizarre cases where things go haywire, and there are interesting problems lurking in this area analogous to those which prompted us to talk of the normal causal routes when discussing perception in VII.1 and VIII.2. But we cannot explore these issues here.

Obviously, there remains more to be said. However, we will have to delay taking up any further issues about action until Chapter XVII, for we now have an even more pressing need – namely to discuss the notions of belief and desire that have come to play such an important role in our investigations.

X

TWO THEORIES OF BELIEF

1   We have some tendency to reserve the term 'belief' for special use in speaking of states of mind subject to conscious deliberation – as when we speak of a man's religious or political beliefs. But in this chapter and the next, we will be using the word in a more general way which also covers less reflective states that register information, where no conscious thought processes are involved (see VIII.5). If you flicked the switch because you unthinkingly took it for granted that it would put on the light, we will still say that you believed that flicking the switch would put on the light.

Likewise, we normally reserve the term 'desire' to cover a fairly limited class of wants and inclinations: by ordinary standards, for example, it would sound odd to describe your reluctant feeling that you should visit your cantankerous aunt as involving a desire to do so. But we will continue to follow our practice in the last chapter (IX.6) and use the term as a generously wide catch-all for pro-attitudes.

We speak not only of believing *that* something is the case, but also of believing *in* something (e.g. one can believe in homeopathic medicine, in the virtue of chastity, in God). Beliefs of the second kind normally encompass beliefs of the first kind, perhaps together with additional attitudes of trust or reverence. For example, believing in homeopathic medicine involves a number of beliefs to the effect that particular homeopathic remedies actually work, and perhaps also a general attitude of trust towards homeopathic techniques. We can take beliefs of the first kind as basic, and they will be our concern here. So, what is it to believe that p, where 'p' holds the place of a suitable sentence?

With only a little artificiality we can also ascribe desires by using 'that'-clauses. If Jack wants to go to the cinema, then he desires-it-to-be-true that he goes to the cinema; if he wants to kiss Jill, then he desires-it-to-be-true that he kisses Jill. If Jill wants an apple, then she desires-it-to-be-true that she eats an apple (or that she possesses an apple, or that she φ's an apple for some other suitable φ). And so on. We can therefore take our question about desires to be: what is involved in desiring-it-to-be-true that *p*, where '*p*' again holds the place of a suitable sentence?

The restriction to 'suitable' sentences here is essential, for interrogative or imperative sentences obviously cannot be used to complete a 'that'-clause. It would simply be ungrammatical to say 'Jack believes that *paint the door red!*' or 'Jill desires-it-to-be-true that *is the door red?*' What we need in 'that'-clauses are declarative sentences which express propositions that can be true or false. Using a bit of standard jargon, we might therefore say that both beliefs and desires are *propositional attitudes*: to have a belief is to hold some proposition to be true, to have a desire is to want some proposition to be true. And these are just two from an extended family of propositional attitudes – for we may also hope a certain proposition is true, expect it to be true, regret its truth, etc.

We will be discussing what are arguably the most basic propositional attitudes, i.e. beliefs and desires; and we will be concentrating very largely on the first of these. In this chapter our particular concern is with two classic theories of belief, inspired respectively by David Hume and Gilbert Ryle. There is perhaps room for scholarly debate in each case as to how far these two philosophers are really committed to the theories which are conventionally attributed to them: but we will not delay over this point.

2   First, let's gather up a loose end from our discussion of perception in Chapter VIII. There we argued that perception is, very roughly, a matter of the acquisition of beliefs. But this account would be embarrassingly circular if beliefs themselves were states to be analysed in broadly perceptual terms (see VIII.4). For example, if having a belief essentially involved *images* perceived in the mind, then the belief-acquisition theory would be no more acceptable than the sense-datum theory: in both cases we would only be explaining outer perceptions in terms of inner perceptions in a quite unhelpful way. In this section and the next, therefore, we will argue that what we might call 'imagist' theories of belief are unacceptable. And we will take as our target Hume's account of belief,

which seems on the face of it to have been more or less straightforwardly imagist.

Having a belief, according to Hume, requires having in mind certain ideas – or, as he puts it, 'conceiving the ideas according to the proposition'. Thus believing that your cat is black involves having in mind an idea of a cat and an idea of black (plus some sort of association between the two ideas). But what, in Hume's sense, are ideas? He tells us in the opening paragraph of his *Treatise*:

> All the perceptions of the human mind resolve themselves into two distinct kinds, which I shall call IMPRESSIONS and IDEAS. The difference betwixt these consists in the degrees of force and liveliness, with which they strike upon the mind, and make their way into our thought or consciousness. Those perceptions, which enter with the most force and violence, we may name *impressions*; and under this name I comprehend all our sensations, passions and emotions, as they make their first appearance in the soul. By *ideas* I mean the faint images of these in thinking and reasoning. (I.i.1)

Hume adds in a footnote to this passage that

> By the term of impression I would not be understood to express the manner, in which our lively perceptions are produced in the soul, but merely the perceptions themselves.

So, for Hume, an impression is the end product of the perceptual process, a fleeting inner mental object (see VII.4); and an idea is 'a faint image' of an impression. But the faint image of, say, a visual impression is presumably itself something seen in the mind's eye (and similarly for the other senses); it seems, therefore, that Hume's ideas are supposed to be image-like. Hence, his theory of belief – according to which having a belief requires us to have ideas in mind – can be said to be an imagist theory.

As Hume notes, however, there must be more to having a belief than just 'conceiving the ideas according to the proposition' – for there is evidently a difference between merely conceiving a proposition and assenting to it.

> Suppose a person present with me, who advances propositions, to which I do not assent, ...; 'tis evident, that notwithstanding my incredulity, I clearly understand his meaning, and form all the same ideas, which he forms. My imagination is endow'd with the same powers as his; nor is it possible for him to conceive any idea, which I cannot conceive; or conjoin any, which I cannot conjoin. I therefore

ask, Wherein consists the difference betwixt believing and disbelieving any proposition?   (I.iii.7)

The question is a good one, but Hume's initial answer is thoroughly unconvincing:

> this difference lies not in the parts or composition of the idea, which we conceive; it follows, that it must lie in the *manner*, in which we conceive it. ... [As] belief does nothing but vary the manner, in which we conceive any object, it can only bestow on our ideas an additional force and vivacity.   (I.iii.7)

And elsewhere he writes that

> belief is nothing but a more vivid, lively, forcible, firm, steady conception of an object, than what the imagination alone is able to attain.
> (*Enquiry*: V.2)

Now, Hume himself noticed one immediate consequence of the claim that the difference between belief and unbelief is just the distinction between having lively and feeble ideas. He cheerily asserts that two people reading the same book, one as a romance, the other as a true history, will receive the same ideas, but the second reader (who believes what he reads) will have 'a more lively conception of all the incidents' (*Treatise*: I.iii.7). But this claim has only to be stated to be seen to be false. Suppose you first read a book as an historical novel, and are then told that it is in fact largely true; surely the resulting change in your beliefs need involve no change at all in the force or vivacity of the ideas which the story produces in you! Again, both Tolstoy and Herzen describe happenings during the burning of Moscow by Napoleon's troops, one in his novel *War and Peace*, the other in his autobiographical masterpiece *My Past and Thoughts*: to suggest that the difference between reading the two accounts, one as a fiction and the other as reportage, is a difference in the vivacity of the ideas produced seems simply preposterous.

3   Interestingly, Hume was uncomfortable with his equation of belief with a lively conception – in the Appendix to the *Treatise* he writes that belief

> makes [ideas] appear of greater importance; infixes them in the mind; and renders them the governing principles of all our actions.

The last point is surely an absolutely crucial one: a thought is held as a belief rather than entertained as a fancy only if it guides behaviour (including, of course, our linguistic behaviour in answering questions, etc.). If you imagine that there is a tiger in front of you, that is merely a pleasing conceit; if you really believe that a tiger is there, then you take to your heels.

Let's overlook Hume's disastrous first thought about the difference between belief and mere fancy, and grant that his second thought is better. Beliefs, then, are to be distinguished not by their supposed 'vivacity' but by their being states which guide action. However, Hume remains committed to holding that both believing that p and also merely entertaining the thought that p involve having a conception that p – where this is in turn a matter of having in mind certain ideas. This crucial commitment is still open to objection, on at least three counts.

First, there is the very general point that Hume's theory is naturally read as being dualist 'in the broad sense' (see VII.7), and is objectionable for that reason alone. Ideas are presumably non-physical objects, and that immediately introduces problems about how they can be causally related to the world. We won't say anything more about this point.

Second, having ideas before the mind is, for Hume, more or less a matter of having faint images in mind. But particular images can be before the mind at one moment but not the next; and certainly the same image will not consciously be there for weeks on end, whether we are awake or asleep, and whatever we are doing or thinking about. The presence of a particular idea in the mind will therefore be, in a word, *episodic*. And if having a belief involves having certain ideas in mind, then beliefs too must be episodic. In general, however, beliefs are *not* episodic; nor are they always consciously in mind while they are being held. For example, it remains true that Jack believes that snow is white even while he is entirely absorbed in a cricket match, or while he is fast asleep for the night. He does not stop believing that snow is white whenever his attention is wholly taken up with some more weighty matter, nor does he stop believing for the night only to revive the belief each morning. If someone asks you whether Jack believes that snow is white, it would be absurd to reply 'I don't know, I'll check whether he's playing cricket' or 'I'll see if he is awake'. The vast majority of our beliefs are not consciously in mind at any particular time. It was, most likely, true of you as you began reading this paragraph that you believed, as you still believe, that zebras are striped while giraffes are not; but it most certainly does not follow that you were then consciously thinking of zebras, giraffes and their stripes or lack of them, nor that you were picturing them by means of 'faint images' or 'ideas' (in fact, you may never have consciously formulated the thought that giraffes lack stripes before). Of course, coming to believe something (e.g. in perception) is often a conscious episode, occupying our attention for a time; but – to repeat – the attitude of belief thereby acquired is not typically episodic.

The Humean could at this point mount a strategic retreat and agree that it is a mistake to suppose that having a belief is always a conscious episode involving images in the mind. What Hume should have said, perhaps, was this: 'There need only be ideas before the mind when one is actively entertaining a conception; and to have a certain belief one need not at the time be entertaining any relevant conception – it is enough that one has a disposition to entertain the relevant conception on appropriate occasions. In other words, to have a belief involves, not the continuous conscious awareness of ideas in the mind, but rather a certain tendency to bring ideas to mind when the occasion arises.' However, while this revised Humean account avoids our second objection, it still faces a damning third difficulty.

The simple un-Humean truth is that we have very many beliefs which are associated with no characteristic imagery at all. It might be said, falsely but with a modicum of plausibility, that when we are actively thinking about some simple perceptual matter like the colour of post-boxes then we must have in mind 'faint images' of post-boxes. But it is not at all plausible to say that there is imagery essentially associated with the beliefs that the U.S. budget deficit is too high, or that seven eights are fifty-six, or that Chekhov is a much greater playwright than Shaw, or that neutrinos have zero mass, or ... Of course, when you think on a particular occasion about the U.S. budget deficit (for example), this may be *accompanied* by imagery – perhaps you imagine the President, or a dollar note, or a page from the *Wall Street Journal*. But this imagery is pretty arbitrary and quite certainly inessential. The fact that yesterday your belief about the budget deficit was associated with one play of images, and today it is associated with a quite different set of images obviously does *not* entail that your belief itself has changed at all. To repeat: imagery is inessential to belief.

A supplementary difficulty for Hume is this. We ordinarily make judgements about what another person believes without speculating even for a moment about the images which might be in his mind. If you decide that the *Guardian*'s economics editor believes that the U.S. budget deficit is too high, then this does *not* require a prior investigation to see what, if anything, he has by way of 'faint images' in the mind when he thinks about the matter! Or to take a more mundane case: you no doubt would agree that your mother believes that milk keeps better in the refrigerator. On the Humean account, your mother's belief essentially requires at least a disposition to have appropriate 'ideas' in her mind. But you have almost certainly never attempted to investigate whether she has any appropriate imagery associated with this belief. So, on the Humean account, it seems that you are not really entitled to the assumption that she believes that milk keeps better when cold. And this is surely a conclusion to be avoided if at all possible.

4   The Humean imagist theory of belief is a mistake. But, as we noted before, Hume did come to see one very important point – namely that beliefs are 'the governing principles' of our actions. Can we put this point about the intimate relation of belief and action to work as the basis of a better theory?

Suppose you believe that it is about to rain, and go outside to get the washing off the line. Here you act because of your belief, and wouldn't have so acted if you hadn't had that belief: the belief and the behaviour go together. But obviously, although the belief and the behaviour may well go together, we cannot say that they are one and the same thing. It is plainly possible to believe that it is about to rain *without* proceeding to get the washing in. What if you were detained by a phone call, heard a child scream out upstairs or had just got in the bath? We can imagine a wide variety of circumstances in which you believe it is about to rain but do not get the washing in: so we cannot simple-mindedly identify the belief with that particular bit of behaviour (or, for analogous reasons, with any other behaviour). Indeed you may have the belief when engaged in no relevant behaviour at all.

Still, it might reasonably be said, when you have a certain belief there is at least a *disposition* to behave in an appropriate way. Although you did not get the washing in when you believed that it was about to rain, it is probably true that you *would* have got it in if the phone hadn't rung just then, if the child hadn't screamed or if you hadn't just got into the bath. This points towards a more sophisticated account of the relation of beliefs to behaviour: beliefs are to be identified, not with bits of behaviour, but with dispositions or tendencies to behave in certain appropriate ways depending on the circumstances. For example, your belief that it is about to rain is nothing other than a disposition on your part to bring in the washing (in appropriate circumstances, with no distractions), to take your umbrella if you are going into town, not to bother watering the garden, and so on. On this view, beliefs will be the 'guiding principles' of your actions in the sense that they are dispositions to certain complex patterns of behaviour.

The classic presentation of this view is to be found in Gilbert Ryle's enormously influential book *The Concept of Mind*. Ryle asserts that

> Dispositional words like ... 'believe' ... signify abilities, tendencies or pronenesses to do, not things of one unique kind, but things of lots of different kinds.   (1949: 118)

This suggestion is very attractive: however, it is only as clear as the pivotal concept of a disposition or tendency which it employs. So, what is a disposition?

A number of rival views about dispositions have been canvassed, but the obvious place to start is with Ryle's own position. Let's consider his brief discussion of two very simple examples of dispositional properties, namely brittleness and solubility:

> The brittleness of glass does not consist of the fact that it is at a given moment actually being shivered. It may be brittle without ever being shivered. To say it is brittle is to say that if it ever is, or ever had been struck or strained, it would fly, or have flown, into fragments. To say that sugar is soluble is to say that it would dissolve, or would have dissolved, if immersed in water.   (1949: 43)

According to Ryle, then, for X to have a dispositional property is simply a matter of an appropriate 'iffy' statement about X being true – 'X is soluble' means (roughly) *if X were put in water, it would dissolve*, 'X is brittle' means (roughly) *if X were firmly struck it would shatter*, and so on. Dispositional properties therefore contrast with properties such as being cracked or cubic which do not readily invite definition in 'iffy' terms. To say that the glass is cracked or that the sugar lump is cubic is not, at least on the face of it, to say something which needs to be unpacked into subjunctive conditionals.

Let's grant that there is some distinction to be made between dispositional properties and the rest: what is more controversial is the precise way in which Ryle wants to elucidate this distinction. As we have just seen, he claims that having a disposition consists in nothing more than the truth of some 'iffy' statements. An alternative view might be that dispositions are underlying states which *make* 'iffy' statements true. But Ryle rejects this alternative. He maintains that, if the glass has the (non-dispositional) property of being cracked or the sugar lump is cubic, then they are respectively in certain states; but to be brittle or soluble is strictly speaking not to be in any particular state at all:

> To possess a dispositional property is not to be in a particular state, or to undergo a particular change; it is to be bound or liable to be in a particular state, or to undergo a particular change, when a particular condition is realised.   (1949: 43)

So, if a dispositional property is what Ryle says it is (i.e. not a state), and having a belief is having a complex dispositional property, then strictly speaking a belief is not a state which underlies behaviour. To say that someone has a given belief is not, as one might suppose, to describe his internal state but just to say that certain 'iffy' statements are true of his behaviour. Applying this to the particular case of Jack's belief that it is about to rain, we get something on the following lines:

(1)   Jack's believing that it is about to rain is simply a matter of its being true that: if circumstances *A* were to obtain, Jack would get in the washing; if circumstances *B* were to obtain, he would take his umbrella; if circumstances *C* were to obtain, he wouldn't start watering his garden; and so on.

On Ryle's view, then, talk about beliefs can be cashed out into 'iffy' talk about overt behaviour patterns without reference to internal states; and when we see this, the temptation to think of beliefs as mysterious states of mind (or worse, as states of our Cartesian Minds) disappears.

As we said, a dispositional theory of belief has considerable attractions. But Ryle's particular version of the theory is a mistake: in §6 to §8 we will offer three arguments against it, which might be labelled the Explanation Argument, the Asymmetry Argument and the Regress Argument respectively. We should stress, however, that our complaint will be against Ryle's way of developing the idea that beliefs are dispositions, and not against that general thesis itself. In the next chapter it will be shown how we can avoid the difficulties which beset the Rylean position by taking a different view of the dispositions which are beliefs. Still, in order to appreciate the virtues of the Mark II theory, you first need to see the failings of the Mark I model. And since getting clear about the notion of belief is absolutely crucial for our general account of the mind, it is worth expending some effort over the point. Before turning to criticism, though, a brief aside (which can be omitted on a first reading).

5   Ryle's theory of belief is often said to be a *behaviourist* one. We should pause to say a little more about this bit of jargon.

Behaviourism – in the sense of the term we are interested in here – aims to translate away talk of beliefs, desires and the like into complex 'iffy' talk about behaviour. The general idea is that we can thereby give a gloss of respectability to discourse about the mind: talk of beliefs does not after all refer to puzzling internal states, but only to patterns of behaviour. We can, however, distinguish sub-varieties of this view, which differ in the ways in which they are prepared to describe those behaviour patterns. At one extreme is the hard-nosed suggestion that, in defining beliefs, we should restrict ourselves to using specifications of bodily movements couched entirely in scientific terms (so we may only talk, for example, of the agent's left hand moving with such-and-such velocity in such-and-such a trajectory). At the other extreme there is a much more relaxed position which allows itself to specify relevant behaviour patterns in the everyday vocabulary we use for describing human activities (so we may talk, for example, of the agent reaching for a cup). Let's call these extremes *hard* and *soft* behaviourism respectively. There are some interesting intervening possibilities on the hard/soft scale, but we needn't go into details here.

Now, it is plain that Ryle's position, at least as we have described it, is a kind of behaviourism (in the sense explained): however, it is a very soft behaviourism. In the specimen account (I) we gave of what it is for Jack to believe that it is about to rain, we allowed ourselves to describe his relevant behavioural tendencies in the everyday vocabulary of action – in appropriate circumstances, Jack *gets in the washing,* he *takes an umbrella,* he doesn't *water his garden.* For a behaviourist, this 'softness' has both disadvantages and advantages.

On the debit side, a soft behaviourism which analyses talk of beliefs in terms of everyday talk about *actions* still leaves us inside the circle of broadly mentalistic concepts. A harder behaviourism at least offers the prospect of taking us right outside the family of mentalistic concepts, by boiling down talk of beliefs to 'iffy' talk about physical behaviour described in scientific terms. Indeed, some philosophers would say that the ambition to cash out mentalistic descriptions in terms of crisply physicalistic descriptions is of the very essence of *real* behaviourism, and that Ryle's softer and more relaxed position shouldn't really be called behaviourism at all, since it doesn't do enough to make beliefs 'scientifically respectable'. There is something to be said for this terminological stipulation. But the fact remains that the majority of philosophers would casually refer to the position we have attributed to Ryle as a kind of behaviourism – so we had better stick to this common wider usage, and distinguish real behaviourism (as some would have it) by its distinctive 'hardness'.

To repeat, soft behaviourism offers us no prospect of analysing talk of beliefs in entirely non-mentalistic terms. On the other hand, it has the advantage over hard behaviourism on the score of intrinsic plausibility. To see this, note first that there is no one set of movements, described in purely physical terms, which constitutes (say) gathering in the washing. Everything depends on where the washing is relative to the agent and how it is all hung up. In different cases, quite different sets of physical movements, with different orientations and velocities, will be needed to get in the washing: the set of physical movements which in one case counts as getting in the washing would in another case leave the agent's hands clutching at thin air. In short, types of movement picked out in purely *scientific* terms don't neatly match up with types of action picked out in *everyday* terms. Having noted this point, let's return to the behaviourist's suggestion that we analyse beliefs in terms of patterns of behaviour, and ask which is the more plausible – to analyse the belief that it is about to rain in terms of patterns of *action* such as gathering in washing, or to analyse the belief in terms of patterns of skeletal orientation and velocity of movement? Surely the former! In fact it is difficult to see even how to make a start at developing the latter, hard behaviourist, alternative.

There is more to be said about the hard/soft distinction: but, having noted the distinction, we need not pursue the issue any further here because the three arguments we will be offering in the rest of this chapter sink behaviourism anyway, hard or soft. For economy of exposition, we will direct the arguments against behaviourism in its Rylean form as exemplified by (I) above. But it will easily be checked that the arguments carry equally against harder forms of behaviourism, since nothing will hang on precisely how the behaviour in any proposed 'iffy' analysis of beliefs is to be described.

6　　The first worry about Ryle's theory is simply this. Having a certain belief is often the cause of some consequent behaviour; but according to Ryle having a belief is a matter of there being lots of 'iffy' facts concerning one's behaviour; and surely packages of 'iffy' facts about behaviour can't themselves be the *causes* of behaviour.

This argument is undoubtedly on the right lines. But there can be disputes about the role of mental causality in our behaviour (as will emerge in Chapter XVII): so to avoid unnecessary complications it is worth shifting ground a little, and talking not of causes but of *explanations*. Thus reconstructed, the argument runs as follows. It is surely incontrovertible that we appeal to people's beliefs in explaining their behaviour patterns. But if having a particular belief just *is* a matter of there being certain patterns in one's behaviour, then how can citing a belief explain the behaviour? On Ryle's theory, this would seem to collapse into a vacuous attempt to explain something by reference to itself.

Ryle's behaviourism is thus, so to speak, an inverted image of Descartes's dualism. Descartes regards mental states like belief as being entirely distinct from anything physical, so it is very difficult to see how on this theory mental states can possibly explain behaviour (see IV.5). Ryle, by contrast, collapses facts about mental states into complex facts about behaviour patterns, so this time there isn't *enough* difference between the two for the one to explain the other.

This point comes out especially clearly if we return to our Rylean attempt (I) to spell out what is involved in Jack's believing that it is about to rain, and consider the first conditional in the analysis. This reports a particular 'iffy' behavioural fact about Jack, namely that in a situation of the kind *A*, he would get in the washing. It is very natural, and surely true, to say that this behaviour pattern obtains *because* of Jack's belief. In other words, we surely have

(E) It is true that, if circumstances *A* were to obtain, Jack would get in the washing, *because* Jack believes that it is about to rain.

But now let's plug into (E) the Rylean account of the meaning of 'Jack believes it is about to rain', as given in (I). Then we get

(E*) It is true that, if circumstances *A* were to obtain, Jack would get in the washing, *because* if circumstances *A* were to obtain, Jack would get in the washing; if circumstances *B* were to obtain, he would take his umbrella; if circumstances *C* were to obtain, he wouldn't start watering the garden; and so on.

If you look at (E*) carefully, you will see that it reports an entirely uninformative logical inference of the form 'it is true that *p because* we have *p* and *q* and *r* and so on'. And that is no more explanatory of the fact about Jack's behavioural tendency than it would be explanatory of Jill's wealth to say 'she's rich because she's rich and famous and forty'! So (E*) is devoid of serious explanatory content: by contrast, whatever the exact status of (E), it seems to have *some* real explanatory content. Hence (E*) and (E) cannot be equivalent after all.

In short, to summarise the Explanation Argument: On the sketched Rylean account of the meaning of 'Jack believes that it is about to rain', (E) and (E*) come out as equivalent. But these are patently not equivalent. So the Rylean view must be wrong.

7   Consider next the question of how you get to know about your own beliefs. Even if we concede that it is possible for you to make the occasional mistake about what you believe, it surely has to be granted that you are generally in a position of reliable authority so far as knowing your own beliefs is concerned. Further, you do not acquire this generally reliable knowledge of your own beliefs by carefully watching your own behaviour as a spectator might. To tell whether you yourself believe that the U.S. budget deficit is too high, for example, you don't have to wait to catch yourself in revealing behaviour! Again, you know whether you believe that Jill is pretty without having to watch out for tell-tale external clues about your behavioural tendencies (in the way that

you have to rely on behavioural clues to determine whether someone else thinks that Jill is pretty). Generalising the point, there is evidently a difference between the typical way we get to know about our own beliefs and the way we get to know about other people's. In other words, there is an asymmetry between the first-person and third-person routes to knowledge about someone's beliefs. But this seems to be inexplicable on the Rylean dispositional theory.

The Humean, to return to him briefly, at least had an account of the difference between the way you gather knowledge of your own beliefs and the way you know about someone else's beliefs – i.e. he had an account of what we will call 'The Asymmetry'. On his view, you get to know about your own beliefs by introspecting the 'ideas' you have before your own mind, while you get to know about other people's beliefs by examining their behaviour for external signs of their internal ideas. This account no doubt exaggerates and misdescribes The Asymmetry: but a Rylean, on the other hand, seems to have difficulty in allowing that there is any asymmetry between first-person and third-person cases at all. On his view, there is no internal state which one needs to be in if one is to count as having a belief – all that is required is that certain 'iffy' claims about your behaviour are true. So there is no internal state of belief which the possessor could get to know about in some special way; there are only the complex, 'iffy', behavioural facts which are in principle equally accessible to everyone. The behavioural facts about you which constitute your beliefs will be as available to Jack or Jill as they are to yourself. Other people will get to know about your beliefs by observing your behaviour patterns – and on Ryle's theory it seems that you will have to get to know about your beliefs in exactly the same way.

In short, to summarise the Asymmetry Argument: For Ryle, beliefs have (as it were) no 'inside' – which entails that we cannot have 'inside knowledge' of our own beliefs. But we do have such knowledge. Hence Ryle's theory is wrong.

8   Our first two arguments against Ryle are damaging; but – in case anyone is tempted to side-step these arguments by denying the Asymmetry and heroically insisting that we *can't* explain behaviour by mentioning an agent's beliefs – it is worth offering a further,

double-barrelled, argument which gets to the heart of what's wrong with Ryle's version of the dispositional theory. We can call this the Regress Argument.

Consider again our gesture towards giving an account of what it is to believe that it is about to rain. We said, in a Rylean spirit, that Jack has this belief if, in circumstances *A* he would get in the washing, in circumstances *B* he would take his umbrella, etc. Now let us press for more details here: how are we to fill out the place-holder '*A*', for example? In what sort of circumstances will Jack's belief that it is about to rain result in his getting in the washing? Well, presumably Jack must have certain other beliefs – such as the belief that the washing is out on the line (if he has forgotten that it is there, then he obviously won't get the washing in when he thinks that it is about to rain). And he must also have certain desires – such as the desire that the washing doesn't get wet (if, for some reason, he actually wants the washing to get wet, then obviously he will not bring it in). Generalising the point, we can say that the circumstances in which the belief that it is about to rain produces a particular given upshot will be circumstances in which the agent has appropriate background beliefs and desires. So, if we are going to try to analyse what it is to have a certain belief in terms of a package of 'iffy' statements, then *these conditionals must themselves mention the agent's background beliefs and desires*.

This leads to two related difficulties for Ryle. First, the Rylean theory was supposed to get rid of the temptation of thinking about beliefs as ghostly mental states by the simple device of cashing out talk about beliefs in terms of complex talk about behaviour. We can now see that this is impossible. We can only specify the behavioural facts which might plausibly constitute having one particular belief in terms of propositions which mention other beliefs: we can take things on another step by cashing out talk of these further beliefs by mentioning more 'iffy' behavioural facts which involve yet further beliefs. But however far we press the Rylean line, we can't escape mentioning more beliefs, i.e. we can't end up with a purely behavioural analysis. So the idea that facts about beliefs are just 'iffy' facts about behaviour must be rejected.

Second, consider the point that in analysing a belief we must mention desires. What are desires? The very same motivation which presses a Rylean to say that beliefs are not inner mental states of a Humean kind – and indeed are not inner states at all – would seem to apply again to the case of desires. In other words, if Ryle's account of belief is at all attractive, then it should be equally attractive to say that desires are likewise not inner states; rather, to have a desire is just for a package of 'iffy' statements to be true of your behaviour. What is it, for example, for Jack to want the washing to dry? On a Rylean account, it is for Jack to have suitable behavioural tendencies – for instance the tendency to hang the washing outside in circumstances A^*, and also to put it in the dryer in circumstances B^*, and so on. But suppose we ask: how are we to fill in the place-holder A^*? In what sort of circumstances will Jack's desire to get the washing dry result in his hanging it out? The answer will refer to his beliefs and desires. If Jack's desire to stay indoors to watch the match on television is greater than his desire to get the washing dry, then he will not hang it out. If he believes that it is about to rain, then his desire to dry the washing will again not lead him to hang it outside. So, if we are trying to analyse what it is to have a certain desire in terms of a package of 'iffy' statements, then these conditionals must in particular mention the agent's beliefs.

The thorough-going Rylean therefore is committed to holding that beliefs are to be analysed in terms of 'iffy' propositions which mention desires, and desires are to be analysed in terms of 'iffy' propositions which mention beliefs. For example, Jack's believing that it is about to rain consists in such facts as that he gets the washing in if he doesn't want to get it wet. And his desire that the washing doesn't get wet consists in such facts as that he gets the washing in if he believes it is about to rain. Here we seem to be going around in a very small circle. To put the point more generally, an agent's belief that it is about to rain (according to the Rylean account) consists in 'iffy' facts about his behaviour, which involve his desires. And these desires in turn consist in 'iffy' facts about his behaviour, which mention his beliefs including the belief we started off with! The idea that facts about beliefs are just 'iffy' facts about behaviour thus ends up in a futile regress.

9   So far we have examined two theories of belief, Hume's and Ryle's, and found both to be unacceptable. Their faults are in a way mirror images of each other. Hume's theory tries to answer the question 'what is a belief?' by taking an inner look to discover what is inside the mind when one believes, and – at least in its initial

version – the theory radically underplays the role of belief in the production of action. We might say that Hume's theory is too concerned with the inward character of beliefs. Ryle by contrast is not concerned enough, for he denies that beliefs are internal states at all, and that gets him into the three problems we have outlined. We need a better theory which avoids both excesses.

XI

THE FUNCTION OF BELIEFS

1   After our negative attacks on Hume and Ryle, we must now turn to develop a positive theory of belief. Since we have already argued that perception is essentially a matter of the acquisition of beliefs, and that action is behaviour caused by appropriate beliefs and desires, the account we give of belief must be central to our whole conception of the mind, and will need to be explored and defended at some length. Our exploration starts in the present chapter, which outlines a skeleton account of the nature of belief-states. The discussion continues in the following chapter which aims to put some more flesh on the bare bones, and incidentally sketches a companion theory of desire.

We begin by returning to Ryle's version of the idea that beliefs are behavioural dispositions. In the previous chapter, we offered three objections to this theory of belief: but it turns out that all three objections can be met by making what seems on the surface to be a simple alteration to the theory. Consider again the Rylean analysis, which runs along the following lines:

(I)   Jack's believing that it is about to rain (for example) is simply a matter of its being true that: if circumstances *A* were to obtain, Jack would get in the washing; if circumstances *B* were to obtain, he would take his umbrella; and so on.

As Armstrong (among many others) has commented,

> it goes profoundly against the grain to think of the mind as [mere patterns of] behaviour. The mind is rather what stands behind and brings about our complex behaviour.   (1965: 74-5)

In particular, it goes against the grain to think of *beliefs* as mere patternings of behaviour: for surely they are what cause such patternings. Armstrong suggests, however, that we can acknowledge this point while still continuing to speak of beliefs as dispositions, if we are prepared to abandon the mistaken Rylean view that dispositions are not states. Contrary to Ryle, we should recognise that

> dispositions, properly conceived, are really states that underlie behaviour and, under suitable circumstances, bring about behaviour. ... a mental state [is] *a state of a person apt for producing certain ranges of behaviour.* (1965: 75)

Armstrong's suggestion, therefore, is that we should reconstruct the dispositional theory of belief within the framework of a view which treats dispositions as causally effective states which underlie behaviour. This gives us something on the following lines:

(II)   Jack's believing that it is about to rain (for example) is a matter of his *being in some state which is causally responsible for its being true that*: if circumstances A were to obtain, Jack would get in the washing; if circumstances B were to obtain, he would take his umbrella; and so on.

But what is the significance of this apparently simple revision? What is the difference between saying with Ryle that beliefs are not states and claiming with Armstrong that they are?

The best way of exploring this issue is to re-examine the objections we raised against the Rylean Mark I theory and show how the Armstrong-style Mark II theory can cope with them. And we will take first the Regress Argument. Before doing this, however, we should briefly pause to note the similarity between the Armstrong view of dispositions and the explicit definition of the notion of a propensity which we gave in VIII.6. 'Someone has a propensity to be φ', we said, 'if he is *in a state such that* he will be φ, unless some special blocking factors intervene.' Now, the use of the two different terms 'disposition' and 'propensity' is not intended to signify a particularly deep distinction. When we talked of a propensity before, we simply had in mind an (Armstrongian) disposition or tendency of a very simple kind – i.e. a state that typically results in a fairly uniform kind of upshot, unless special countervailing factors happen to come into play. But beliefs are much more complex states than that, for a belief can be manifested in a vast variety of ways, depending on the context. Beliefs are not simple propensities but (if they are dispositional at all) they are, to use a suggestive term of Ryle's, *multi-track* dispositions.

2   The Regress Argument against Ryle turned on the point that, when we try to spell out in detail the Mark I account of what it is to have a certain belief, we are forced to mention other beliefs and desires. The 'iffy' facts about behaviour which supposedly constitute a particular belief are not *purely* about behaviour, but must also concern further mental states.

But doesn't the same go for the Mark II story about Jack's belief that it is going to rain? This still gestures towards the desired account by airily using phrases like 'in circumstances *A*, Jack would get in the washing'. As with the original Rylean account, we can again press for details here. And as before, when we spell out the circumstances in which Jack would indeed get in the washing, we must necessarily mention his other beliefs and his desires. Hence, if this is an objection to the Mark I theory, shouldn't the same point also sink the revised Mark II theory? Well, not so – because there is a quite crucial difference between the ambitions of the two styles of theory. This point is very important, so let's try to make it clear.

The Mark I Rylean theory asserts that Jack's having a certain belief is a complex 'iffy' fact about how he would behave in various circumstances. The theory is thus a *reductionist* one: in other words, its intention is to reduce or cash out talk about beliefs in terms of talk about something else, namely behaviour patterns. This intention is thwarted by the point just mentioned, namely that beliefs cannot be analysed in purely behavioural terms, however far we push the analysis.

The revised Armstrong-style theory, by contrast, asserts that Jack's having a belief is a matter of his being in a particular state which is responsible for certain behaviour patterns. This time there is no ambition to reduce talk about beliefs to talk about behaviour. Beliefs remain what we always took them to be, i.e. states of the person who has them – states which, to repeat Armstrong's words, 'stand behind and bring about behaviour'. All the theory aims to do is to tell us more about a particular belief-state by telling us how it can interact with other states to produce various kinds of behaviour: in other words, it tells us about the place of one belief-state in a pattern of possible states. For example, the belief that it is about to rain is (roughly speaking) the state which combines with the desire to dry the washing and the belief that washing left out in the rain will get wetter, so as to produce the action of getting in the washing; and so on. The fact that this specifies the belief-state by reference to other mental states is no objection to the Mark II theory, because *this* theory has no reductive ambitions: the theory does not want to translate away talk of beliefs into talk about behaviour. As we saw in X.8, the most which we can hope for is an account of how one mental state relates both to behaviour and to other mental states, and this is what (II) gives us.

3   The two other objections to the Rylean Mark I theory were the Asymmetry Argument and the Explanation Argument.

We argued that Ryle's view that beliefs are not internal states makes it very difficult to account for The Asymmetry which exists between the first-person and third-person routes to knowledge about one's beliefs. If beliefs have, as it were, no 'inside', then how could one have any 'inside knowledge' of one's own beliefs? This difficulty simply doesn't arise for Armstrong's version of the dispositional theory. For the Mark II theory insists that beliefs are states, and hence is quite consistent with the stronger claim that beliefs are internal states knowledge of which is acquired in one way by the person whose state it is, and in another way by other people.

By way of an aside, it is well worth saying a little more about The Asymmetry. The natural way to explain it is via an 'inner sense' theory, which postulates a faculty of introspection. According to this sort of account, we can get to know what we believe by 'looking inside' our own minds: other people can't look inside our minds in the same way, and this accounts for The Asymmetry.

This general approach is arguably correct: but we should be very chary of taking the idea of introspection – of 'looking inside' – too literally. If we suppose that we know our own minds by means of a quasi-visual inner sense, then this naturally prompts the suggestion that what we find when we take an internal look must be quasi-visual inner objects, perhaps 'faint images' or 'ideas'. In short, pressing the visual metaphor here may tempt us into taking a Humean view of the contents of the mind (see X.2). But fortunately we can dispense with the metaphor.

Let us consider more carefully what is needed if The Asymmetry is to exist. There are two essential requirements:

(a) there must be a reliable connection between your judging that you believe that *p* and your actually believing that *p* (for many different propositions *p*),

and

    (b) the reliable connection mentioned in (a) must not involve observations of your own external behaviour.

If (a) holds, then your thinking *I believe that p* will generally be a reliable sign that you actually do believe that *p*: that is, your judgement that you believe that *p* will reliably be true. But a source of reliably true judgements is, by ordinary standards, a source of knowledge. So your judging that you believe that *p* will regularly count as your *knowing* that you believe that *p*. And if (b) holds, this knowledge of your own mind will not be based on the sort of observations of behaviour that other people have to rely on when judging what you think – in short, there will be a first-person/third-person asymmetry.

The obvious way to secure the truth of (a) and (b) is to suppose that there are some internal causal linkages which enable the reliable acquisition of beliefs about one's own belief-states. And given our earlier view of perception as a matter of the causally based acquisition of beliefs, such a set-up can perhaps be regarded as constituting an 'inner sense'. However, there is no need to regard this as involving anything much like vision: the situation could be a lot simpler. Maybe there is just a pretty direct causal link between the state of believing that *p* and the state of believing *I believe that p*, a link that doesn't go via any complex information-processing mechanism akin to the visual system. In this simple case, (a) and (b) will be true – i.e. there will be a reliable connection between your belief that *p* and your belief that you believe that *p*, which is not based on observations of your own external behaviour. Hence The Asymmetry can still be accounted for, even though (in the imagined situation) there is no process of introspection in anything much like the literal sense of 'looking inside'.

A computer analogy may help here, so long as it isn't taken too seriously. Suppose your microcomputer is so programmed that it can reply to the query 'what are you doing?' with a suitable report about where it has got to in running its program. Then the following could happen. We hear its disk drives whirr away, and think 'it has got to the point where it has to consult its file store': we type in 'what are you doing?' and the machine displays the message 'I am consulting my file store!' Hearing the whirr of the disk drives, we know that this is an appropriate display on the basis of our external observation of the machine's 'behaviour'. The computer itself, on the other hand, doesn't have to go through any routine of 'inspecting' its own behaviour; it certainly doesn't listen out for the whirr of its disk drives. Nor does it engage in the problematic perceptual task of taking a look at its own innards. Indeed, there need be no serious information-processing task involved for the computer at all: the programmer has merely set up a simple and direct correlation between being at a certain point in its program which involves consulting its file store, and a disposition to display an appropriate message in response to queries. Stretching a point, we might say that there has been set up a direct connection between being in a certain internal state and the machine 'believing' that it is in that state; and this results in an asymmetry between how we get to know what's going on and how the computer itself 'knows' what's happening.

Now, as we suggested before, it could be similar with you. There could be a simple direct connection between being in a certain internal state (believing that p) and your thinking that you are in that state – and this is enough to result in The Asymmetry between how others get to know what's going on and how you yourself know it. In summary, then: so long as we allow that beliefs *are* internal states (as does the Mark II, Armstrong-style theory), it is possible to accommodate the existence of The Asymmetry, and to do so without having recourse to any visually loaded notion of introspection.

4   We turn now to the remaining objection we raised against the Rylean theory in the previous chapter. The Explanation Argument turned on the point that if (as Ryle insists) facts about beliefs are just 'iffy' facts about behaviour, then it is vacuous to explain these 'iffy' facts by citing the belief. The Mark II theory simply side-steps this objection: on the new theory, beliefs are states genuinely distinct from the behaviour patterns they cause, and so citing the state is potentially explanatory of the behaviour.

It might be protested that this response is too quick: for consider again, as we did in X.6, the explanatory claim:

(E)   It is true that, if circumstances A were to obtain, Jack would get in the washing, *because* he believes that it is about to rain.

On the Mark II theory, it might be argued, this comes out equivalent to something like:

(E**) It is true that, if circumstances *A* were to obtain, Jack would get in the washing, *because* Jack is in some state which is causally responsible for it being true that: if circumstances *A* were to obtain, Jack would get in the washing; if circumstances *B* were to obtain, he would take his umbrella; if circumstances *C* were to obtain, he wouldn't start watering the garden; and so on.

And this, the objector might insist, is again simply vacuous (cf. the argument of X.6). However, this protest is misplaced. For a start, (E**) isn't vacuous at all. On the contrary, it tells us that Jack's tendency to gather in the washing is the causal result of something which is also responsible for some other 'iffy' facts about his behaviour. This requires there to be a real connection between the particular behaviour pattern to be explained and some other behavioural facts about Jack – and claiming that there *is* such a connection could obviously be informative and illuminating.

5   To summarise the discussion so far: the Armstrong-style Mark II theory, properly understood as lacking reductive ambitions, avoids all three of the difficulties which sank the original Mark I theory.

Now Ryle's dispositional theory claims that facts about beliefs are (suitably complex, 'iffy') facts about behaviour. So, the theory in this version is obviously incompatible with the dualist view that facts about mental states are facts about what goes on in our immaterial Minds. And it is equally incompatible with the more specific Humean suggestion that facts about beliefs are facts about a special sort of thing called an 'idea'. The Mark II theory is, on the face of it, very different in this respect. It holds that facts about beliefs are facts about states which are causally responsible for behaviour patterns, and (the persistent dualist might insist) it would be quite consistent to go on and say that these states are states of our immaterial Minds, or states which consist of having Humean ideas in mind. In other words, our revised theory, far from being a reductionist or behaviourist theory, actually seems compatible with a broadly Humean theory of belief – more generally, it is compatible with a range of dualist theories!

Still, the revised theory is none the worse for that, and we can certainly recommend it without being guilty of backsliding into some kind of dualism. For even if it is consistent to add to the Mark II theory the rider '... and the states in question are immaterial states of our Cartesian Minds', it is of course equally consistent to add '... and the states in question are physical states'. The theory may itself be neutral between dualism and (say) an Aristotelian naturalism; but this means that it can consistently be developed in either direction. Of course, we think (like Armstrong himself) that it should be developed in the second, naturalistic direction: for given our general arguments against dualism — which we need not rehearse again — there is every reason to hold that the states which causally underpin our behavioural tendencies are in fact physical states.

Let's move, therefore, from the non-committal version (II) to a more explicit third version of the dispositional theory:

(III) Jack's believing that it is about to rain is a matter of his being in some *physical* state which is causally responsible for its being true that: if circumstances *A* were to obtain, Jack would get in the washing; if circumstances *B* were to obtain, he would take his umbrella; and so on.

And similarly, of course, for other beliefs. On the basis of our everyday biological knowledge, it is reasonable to hold the relevant physical states are neuro-physiological ones.

6   According to this third version of the dispositional theory, belief is an inner physical state — more narrowly, a neuro-physiological state. But there is a sense in which the theory only identifies the state *indirectly* by specifying its role or function in producing behavioural upshots: it certainly doesn't give us a direct description of that state in neuro-physiological terms. However, this is no criticism of the theory: indeed, as we shall now argue, it is a positive strength.

Consider for a moment the concept of having measles; it is plausible to say that to have measles is, by definition, to be in a physical state which is causally responsible for a certain set of typical symptoms. So here again we are identifying an underlying state indirectly, via its observable upshots. Still, if we enquire further about the state in question, we can arrive at a general physiological account which associates measles with infection by a particular type of virus. Anyone who has measles will be infected with this same type of virus. Now, is the case of having a particular belief similar? Can we expect there to be a single physiological description which applies to anyone who believes that it is about to rain?

It seems not. Even if we restrict ourselves to the case of human believers, it does not seem at all likely that each and every one of us who believes that it is about to rain shares a common neuro-physiological state. To make one simple point: the brain is a remarkably adaptable organ – our mental life can survive even quite extensive brain damage because functions previously performed by the damaged part can often be relocated. Given this plasticity of brain function, it seems entirely possible that the neural state which is causally responsible for the tendency to bring in the washing in circumstances *A* (and so on) may substantially differ from person to person. In other words, the particular state which is the state of believing that it is about to rain may be physically different in different people. And if we now cast the net wider to include animal believers, Martians and the like, then the supposition that all those who believe that it is about to rain share a common physical state would seem to be entirely gratuitous.

Another computer analogy may well help (though it should again be accompanied by a warning against taking such analogies too seriously). Suppose you have a chess-playing computer whose hardware has become somewhat ramshackle. In particular, its memory has been expanded using a variety of add-on or plug-in components. As a result, some of its memory store is located on floppy disks, some on magnetic tape, some on various sorts of silicon chips and some perhaps on fancy bubble-memory devices. Now, consider the machine's 'belief' that it should develop its knights early when playing the Sicilian Defence: this 'belief' is that physical state which is causally responsible for its playing thus-and-so in various circumstances. The very complex state in question will presumably be located somewhere in the computer's memory store, to be recalled when needed. But there is no reason at all why it should always be held in the same place, or even in the same physical device. In other words, the relevant memory state may sometimes be a state of a floppy disk, sometimes a state of some magnetic tape or whatever. The computer can continue to be in the same 'mental' state while the physical state in virtue of which it satisfies a constant 'mental' description changes. And what is true of a single computer is even more obviously true when we compare different computers. Your machine and ours may be running the same program, and may therefore both 'believe' in developing knights early when playing the Sicilian Defence: but the respective machines have different hardware, so their states when described in physical terms are quite different. In a phrase, *shared software does not require identical hardware*.

What goes for computers goes too for human chess players: there is not much reason to suppose that for all the time during which you believe in getting your knights developed early there is a single brain-state which is responsible for your behavioural disposition. And when we compare, say, human chess players with Martian players, then there is even less reason to think that a single physiological description will apply to all believers in developing one's knights early.

We might put this absolutely central point about the Mark III theory as follows. To identify a state as a belief-state is to identify it by the way it causally functions in co-operation with other states to produce behaviour. Physical states which are, neurophysiologically speaking, of different kinds can still play the same functional role at different times or in different people. So we can't identify believing that it is about to rain (for example) with a particular type of physical state picked out in neuro-physiological terms. That is, we can't assume that everyone who believes that it is about to rain must always satisfy one and the same neuro-physiological description. But this does not mean that belief-states are not physical states: it only means that different particular instances of believing that it is about to rain can be constituted by instances of different kinds of physical state.

The example of the chess-playing computer should show that there is no mystery about this point. In fact it is merely an application of a very general truth about broadly functional concepts. Consider, to take an even simpler example, the notion of a *piston*. To identify something as a piston is to identify it functionally, in terms of its role within certain mechanisms, rather than in terms of its physical constitution. Different sorts of piston can be built in different ways, of different sorts of stuff, so there is certainly no general law of the kind 'any piston has such-and-such a physical constitution'. But this of course does not mean that pistons are non-physical objects – it simply means that different particular pistons are physically constituted in different ways. This humdrum example shows that there should be nothing puzzling about the fact that classifications of physical objects in terms of their *function* can cut across classifications in terms of *physical make-up*. Things can be of the same functional type (i.e. perform the same function) while having different constitutions. Likewise, the classification of physical states in terms of their function can cut across classifications by reference to their physical make-up. Different brain-states can be of the same functional type while having different neuro-physiological constitutions.

7   According to our current theory, then, beliefs are states essentially identified by means of their causal function in interacting with other states to produce behaviour. So our theory might very well be called a *functionalist* theory (but see XII.5 for some cautionary remarks about this labelling). Note, though, that a belief is still to be identified by means of the way it disposes you to act in various circumstances, so we could equally well continue to call our descendant of the Rylean account a *dispositional* theory. This theory is naturally construed as taking belief-states to be physical states (as in the Mark III version), for these are surely what do causally underpin behaviour: more particularly, belief-states are neuro-physiological states. But, to repeat the absolutely crucial point, in picking out something as a belief-state we are not concerned with its intrinsic physical properties but with its function; and the same function could on different occasions or in different people be played by physically different states.

This theory can be elegantly summarised if we allow ourselves to stretch the Aristotelian terminology of matter and form which we introduced in Chapter VI so that it applies to states of Substances as well as to the Substances themselves. Then we can say that the *matter* of a belief-state is physical, but its *form* (the 'what it is to be what it is') of a belief-state is its function.

So much, then, for our initial outline sketch of a dispositional/functionalist theory of belief. The theory is evidently a naturalistic one in the sense that it invokes no entities unrecognised by the natural sciences (the relevant matter here is physical). But the theory is only as good as its pivotal notion of the 'function' or 'role' of a belief-state. We will continue to explore this notion in the next chapter.

XII

FUNCTIONALISM AND FOLK PSYCHOLOGY

1   In the previous chapter, we sketched the bare bones of a theory of belief which has its origin in the work of Ryle and Armstrong. We need next to put some flesh on the skeleton, for our account of the role played by a particular belief in producing behaviour has so far been doubly schematic. Consider again the given instance of the Mark III theory:

(III)   Jack's believing that it is about to rain is a matter of his being in some physical state which is causally responsible for its being true that: if circumstances *A* were to obtain, Jack would get in the washing; if circumstances *B* were to obtain, he would take his umbrella; and so on.

One respect in which (III) is merely schematic is in its use of the open-ended formula 'and so on'. Now, it is easy enough to begin filling out that final clause: we all know the sorts of behaviour which would in various circumstances manifest the belief that it is raining. But what is the basis of this knowledge? How do we know what other 'iffy' claims are covered by the use of 'and so on'?

We will tackle this problem indirectly, by noting that a similar problem is raised by the other respect in which (III) is schematic. For how are we to fill out those phrases 'circumstances *A*', 'circumstances *B*'? When we first touched on this issue (in X.8) we pointed out that, if we are to specify the circumstances *A* in which Jack's belief that it is about to rain will lead him to get in the washing, then we will have to mention some of his other beliefs and desires. We might mention, for example, his belief that the washing is outside, and his desire that it gets dry. We will also have to mention his lack of more pressing desires (such as the desire to see the end of the match on television, which would stop him going outside for the washing, though it wouldn't be enough to stop him going outside to rescue his child). These points seem absolutely obvious: we all know that they are the sort of thing that must be taken into account if we are to specify circumstances where Jack's belief will indeed lead him to fetch in the washing. But *how* do we know this?

The first thing to note is that, while filling out that schematic reference to 'circumstances *A*', we are quite certainly not exercising some special knowledge which concerns only the belief that it is about to rain. We have never had to learn a separate lesson about the motivational properties of this particular belief: rather, we are drawing on knowledge which concerns beliefs more generally – we are bringing to bear some common-sensical general principles about how beliefs and desires interact to produce actions.

Let's briefly discuss a couple of these principles. Consider first the *Fundamental Principle*, as we might call it, which is very roughly this: if someone desires that *p*, and believes that *p* will come about only if he does *X*, then, in the absence of countervailing desires, he will as a result usually do *X*. Applied to Jack's case, the Fundamental Principle implies – among many other things – that if he desires that the washing gets dry, and he believes that the washing will only get dry if he fetches it in, then (in the absence of countervailing desires) Jack will typically fetch in the washing. Now, this does not yet relate Jack's action to his belief that it is about to rain; but suppose that we also accept a *Consequence Principle*, to the effect that people normally believe the most obvious and immediate logical consequences of their other beliefs. Then, applying this to our present example, we can take it that if Jack believes that it is about to rain (and also thinks that washing left in the rain gets wet, thinks that there is no one else to fetch it in, etc.), then he will tend to believe that his fetching in the washing is required to bring it about that the washing gets dry. So, given these assumptions about Jack's background beliefs and desires, the Fundamental Principle and the Consequence Principle taken together will link his belief that it is about to rain to his action of fetching in the washing. In this way our grasp of principles like the two just mentioned helps us to specify the background circumstances *A* in which Jack's belief does normally lead to that particular behavioural upshot.

Similarly, these same two general principles, combined with other assumptions about his background beliefs and desires, will link Jack's belief that it is about to rain to the action of taking his umbrella (suppose, for instance, that Jack wants to stay dry and believes that, if he doesn't take his umbrella when it is about to rain, then he will get wet). On other assumptions still, the principles will link the same belief to the action of putting on a hat. And so on. As we spin the possible background beliefs and desires, the fixed principles will imply different possible resulting actions. Or to put it all another way, our principles imply that if Jack believes that it is about to rain, then there will be *many* true 'iffy' claims of the kind 'if Jack also has such-and-such beliefs and desires then he will normally do so-and-so'. In one fell swoop, therefore, our principles enable us to tackle both respects in which (III) is schematic – they help us to fill in those references to circumstances *A*, etc., and at the same time they also deal with the open-ended character of (III).

2   To repeat, we can fill out the details in (III) in virtue of our grasp of principles such as the Fundamental Principle and the Consequence Principle. But of course, the role of such principles is not simply to help us with the philosophical thesis (III): on the contrary, they play an immensely important role in our everyday, common-sense explanations of each other's behaviour. Suppose you want to understand someone else's behaviour: what you need to do is to come up with an appropriate psychological story about her, a description of her beliefs and desires such that you could reasonably expect someone who had *those* mental states to behave in the way observed. The Fundamental Principle is obviously crucial here: a standard first move in rendering a stretch of behaviour comprehensible is to try and see the agent as acting on the basis of a belief/desire pair which (according to the principle) would lead to the observed action. Here is Jill walking towards her car carefully carrying a saucer of mud. You initially find the sight extremely puzzling – what on earth is going on? You then remember that she wants a sample of soil for bacteriological analysis, and things fall into place: for you know how this desire can combine with an appropriate belief to yield mud-gathering behaviour. And this is, of course, not a *special* bit of knowledge about the desire for a sample of soil for bacteriological analysis: on the contrary, you are obviously bringing to bear the Fundamental Principle about how people act in the light of their beliefs and desires.

The Fundamental Principle encapsulates a bit of common-sense folk wisdom which belongs to what might happily be called *folk psychology.* The Consequence Principle also belongs here; and so do many other, more or less rough, generalisations about beliefs and desires. Thus we have various important Perceptual Principles, which relate people's (or animals') beliefs to their perceptual environment: for instance, someone looking at a medium-size object, in good light etc., typically comes as a result to believe that there is an object of roughly that kind in front of him. And to take just one slightly more complex example: consider what happens when different desires, as we say, pull us in different directions. A key fact here is that, when faced with two alternative goods to aim at, both of which are desirable, people do not automatically try for the alternative they would prefer to get. Rather, they take into account the relative likelihood of successfully getting what they want. We standardly prefer £120 to £100: but we would normally pass up an outside chance of getting £120 in favour of the dead certainty of getting £100. We discount the greater attractiveness of the £120 roughly in proportion to the probability of failing to get the money; and, since the heavily discounted value of this chancy option is much less than £100, we go for the second option. This illustrates what we can call the Utility Principle. Roughly speaking, people assess the relative merits of two courses of action not simply by the value of the alternative goods that might be secured, but by reference to the *expected utility* of the two options (where the expected utility of an option is the value that might be secured, discounted by the likelihood of failure).

As we said, such principles obviously play a very important role in our everyday psychological understanding of each other: they provide the framework within which we ordinarily explain behaviour. So we must now say a little more about their structure and status.

3   Note firstly that the principles we have so far stated are rather imprecise: people *tend* to do what they think is required to satisfy their desires, people *normally* believe the most obvious consequences of their other beliefs. Could we firm up these common-sense principles to make them absolutely precise? Apparently not. After all, whatever beliefs and desires Jack has, he could suddenly suffer one of those strange lapses of attention, or one of those puzzling failures of logic to which we are all prone.

Perhaps, as we say, his mind suddenly goes blank. In such cases the expected action does not ensue. And so long as we are considering principles couched in everyday psychological talk, it seems that these principles must leave loop-holes to allow for lapses of this kind. Our principles will also be subject to unpredictable failures – unpredictable, that is, from the point of view of folk psychology – which result from various kinds of neuro-physiological malfunction (induced by knocks on the head or drugs for instance). In short, therefore, our principles must remain rather soft-edged and continue to speak of what normally tends to happen in certain circumstances: the search for absolute precision here looks misguided.

This first point about the imprecise nature of everyday pyschology incidentally shows that the schematic (III) isn't quite right as it stands. For it implies that, given Jack believes that it is about to rain, then in circumstances *A* he *will* get in the washing. But an appeal to the Fundamental Principle and the Consequence Principle will only support something of the form 'if circumstances *A* obtain then he will *normally* get in the washing'. In other words, (III) implies that Jack's belief will in a given context definitely lead to a particular upshot; but our fuzzy principles only imply that they will normally produce that upshot. So we really ought to soften up (III) as well. Instead of relating Jack's belief to what he would (definitely) do in various circumstances, it should instead relate the belief to what Jack would typically do in those circumstances – i.e. what he would normally do, barring lapses, neuro-physiological malfunction etc.

So much, then, for the imprecision of the principles of folk psychology: we must next consider their status.

We all acquire a grasp of the broad principles of folk psychology as we learn to operate with the concepts of belief and desire (and their extended family of related concepts). Of course – and this is a very important point – this isn't to say that we learn the principles *explicitly*. On the contrary, you have probably never encountered a statement of the Fundamental Principle or the Utility Principle before. Just as you learn to speak grammatically without explicitly learning the rules of English grammar, so you learn ways to structure acceptable psychological stories about people without explicitly learning that these structures can be described by the principles of folk psychology.

It is a nice question how far these principles actually help to define the notions of belief and desire, and how far they record general truths about beliefs and desires which could have been otherwise. We might well suppose, for example, that beliefs and desires *must* be related to action via the Fundamental Principle: in other words, states which don't dispose you to act in appropriate ways just wouldn't count as beliefs and desires. So this first principle is a plausible candidate for being 'true by definition'. On the other hand, it would seem to be an empirical question how good believers are at drawing new consequences from their current beliefs: animals and children are less good at this than adults. So any moderately specific version of the Consequence Principle will perhaps record a generalisation which *could* have been false. But, all in all, the question of the exact status of the principles of common-sense or folk psychology is a decidedly murky one, which we will here have to leave unresolved. And it is another nice question how far we can press the intuitive distinction we have just been using between what is 'true by definition' and what is merely an empirical fact. Perhaps we should simply be content to say that the principles of folk psychology – and derived principles in the style of (II) and (III) – are important general truths, and leave it at that.

Our third and final point about the principles of folk psychology arises from the fact that those we have mentioned so far have all been very simple and very general. But of course the surface structure of our common-sense psychological theory is immensely complex and finely detailed. We have an extensive range of finely differentiated mental concepts, and we can cope with a multitude of interrelations between them. Note, in particular, that there are differences of nuance between (say) 'Jack believes that it is about to rain', 'Jack takes it that ...', 'Jack thinks that ...' and 'Jack assumes that...'. For example, talk of belief proper is perhaps most appropriate where there has been an element of deliberation or public affirmation. It is for this reason that we tend to prefer saying something like 'Fido thinks that his Doggiebix are in the cupboard' when we see the dog scrabbling at the cupboard door; it seems rather less felicitous to say that Fido *believes* the biscuits are there. Again, note that there are differences of nuance between (say) 'Jack desires that the washing gets dry', 'Jack wants the washing to get dry', 'Jack prefers ...' and 'Jack longs for ...'. Generalisations like the Fundamental Principle are obviously intended to abstract from fine differentiations of this kind. Although our principles refer to 'beliefs' and 'desires', they are not supposed to be about beliefs *as contrasted with* other belief-like states which register (correct or incorrect) information; nor are they about desires *as contrasted with* other pro-attitudes. Rather, our principles are intended to state how belief-like states as a class interact with pro-attitudes as a class.

Now, it seems that if we are to command a perspicuous overview of folk psychology, then we must indeed first try to describe the structure of a basic pattern of psychological explanations, which we can then proceed to overlay with a variety of finer discrimina-tions, explanatory epicycles and so forth. If we tried from the start to illuminate the structure of common-sense psychology while respecting all the fine differentiations of our everyday psychological concepts, then the task would be quite impossible. If we are to shed any light in this area, it seems that we must begin by abstracting from the surface details and operate with generalised notions of belief and desire (or better, 'belief-like, information-registering state' and 'pro-attitude'). We have already noted the pressure to employ generalised notions, stripped of nuance, in VIII.5 and IX.6: we are now insisting that this move towards generalised notions is a precondition of any useful theorising in this area.

4   Let's summarise the position we have reached. To believe that it is about to rain is, according to the 'softened up' Mark III version of our broadly dispositional theory, to be in a state which is responsible for our normally acting thus-and-so in various cir-cumstances. On general grounds, it is reasonable to suppose that the states which are responsible for these behavioural patterns must be brain-states – in a sense, therefore, beliefs are brain-states. But what makes a given brain-state a case of believing that it is about to rain is not its intrinsic physical constitution, but rather the role or function that it normally plays (in interaction with other states) in producing behaviour. And what is the distinctive role of (say) the belief that it is about to rain? We answer this question by appealing to some general principles of folk psychology – these tell us how beliefs in general interact with each other and with desires to produce behaviour, and we can infer how the belief that it is about to rain in particular will interact with other states.

We have not explicitly said much about the associated notion of desire, except to insist repeatedly that beliefs and desires work *together* to produce behaviour. But this is enough to suggest the general shape that our matching account of desire must take. Since beliefs are physical states which work together with desires, desires had better be physical states too (at this late stage in the game, we certainly don't want to reintroduce any puzzling interactions between the physical and the non-physical). And surely what makes a physical state a desire is going to be a matter of the *role* of the state in producing behaviour, and not a question of its physiological constitution. A functionalist account of desire beckons.

To spell that out: The desire to eat an apple (for example) is a state which is responsible for your having tendencies to act thus-and-so in various circumstances. It is again reasonable to suppose that the state which is responsible for these behavioural tendencies must be a physical one – in a sense, desires too are brain-states. But what makes a given physical state a case of desiring to eat an apple is not its intrinsic physical constitution, but rather the role or function that it plays (in interaction with other states) in producing behaviour. So what is the distinctive role of this desire? We answer this question by appealing once more to some general principles of folk psychology – these tell us how desires interact with each other and with beliefs to produce behaviour, and so we can infer in particular how the desire to eat an apple will interact with other states. In this way, we can construct a (III)-like account of particular desires.

But aren't our stories about beliefs and desires now *too* symmetrical? – we have said that beliefs are states located by the way they interact with other beliefs and desires to produce action, and that desires are also states located by the way they interact with other desires and beliefs to produce action. Surely we must be able to say something about what *distinguishes* belief-states as a class from states of desire.

Of course: but we can again turn to folk psychology for help. We have already mentioned (§2) the existence of various Perceptual Principles which relate people's beliefs to their environment. Our desires are not related to our current environment in the same direct way: however there are a number of everyday principles which relate some desires, at least, to states of bodily deprivation such as lack of food or sleep. So we can perhaps say this, by way of distinguishing beliefs and desires: beliefs are states of a class many members of which can be picked up by perception, whereas desires are states of a class some members of which can be engendered by deprivation. Putting it crudely, beliefs are the sort of thing you get when you look at the world, desires are what you get when you go without things you need, like food or sleep. Hence a full story about beliefs and desires must not only mention their specific effects – as in (III) – but also say something more general about their typical causes. We need not go into further details here, however, for this addition merely enriches the functionalist story, and doesn't introduce any radically new issues.

5   To round off our extended discussion of the dispositional/ functionalist theory of belief and desire, we should consider two final issues. In the present section we will consider the important distinction between 'hard' and 'soft' functionalism. And in the next section, we will say a little about the implications of our theory for the problem of our knowledge of other minds.

In X.5 we contrasted two kinds of behaviourism which differ in the ways in which they are prepared to describe the behaviour patterns which allegedly constitute beliefs and desires. The hard behaviourist holds that in defining beliefs we must describe the relevant behaviour patterns in purely physical terms: the soft behaviourist like Ryle allows himself the more relaxed vocabulary of the everyday description of actions. Now, the same choice of options also faces the functionalist. His basic idea is that beliefs are states identified by their role in producing behaviour – but does this mean behaviour as picked out in purely scientific terms (skeletal movements with certain velocities and trajectories), or does it mean behaviour as ordinarily described in the vocabulary of human action?

Armstrong, for example, takes the first option, and argues that it is indeed compulsory if his position isn't to collapse into circularity.

> We may distinguish between 'physical behaviour', which refers to any merely physical action ... of the body, and 'behaviour proper' which implies a relationship to the mind. ... Now if in our formula [namely that a belief, for example, is a state of the person apt for bringing about a certain sort of behaviour] 'behaviour' were to mean 'behaviour proper', then we would be giving an account of mental concepts in terms of a concept that already presupposes mentality, which would be

circular. So it is clear that in our formula, 'behaviour' must mean 'physical behaviour'. (1968: 84)

In short, then, Armstrong commits himself firmly to what we can call *hard* functionalism, which aims to characterise mental states in terms of outputs described in the language of physiology.

By contrast, the functionalism which we have been expounding in this chapter has been of a decidedly *soft* variety. For we have suggested that in order to specify the sort of behaviour which will manifest a given belief in various circumstances we need to follow some principles of folk psychology, and these principles obviously do not categorise behaviour into classes of skeletal movements, but rather deal in everyday actions like gathering in the washing, collecting umbrellas or drinking a cup of tea. In Armstrong's terminology, therefore, we have been outlining an account of mental concepts in terms of 'behaviour proper'. But then how can we avoid the accusation of circularity?

We could perhaps put Armstrong's worry like this. In Chapter IX we analysed the notion of 'behaviour proper' – i.e. action – in terms of the fundamental pair of concepts, belief and desire: we said that 'behaviour proper' involves intentional action, which is physical behaviour appropriately caused by beliefs and desires. We have now outlined, in Chapter XI and the present chapter, a soft functionalist theory, which identifies beliefs and desires by their role in producing actions. At bottom, then, we have said that actions flow from beliefs and desires, while beliefs and desires are dispositions to action – and *that* looks viciously circular.

But this response would involve a misunderstanding. We haven't been trying to *do away with* talk of action in favour of supposedly independent talk of beliefs and desires, or vice versa. That is indeed impossible – the notions of belief, desire and action are too tightly interrelated for that. So our ambitions have been more modest: we have just been trying to explore the interconnections between this close-knit family of concepts, without any reductionist intent. Folk psychology involves interpreting someone as a perceiver with beliefs and desires which lead him to act in the world – and there are not two or three or four separate stages in this enterprise. Rather we have to develop all the pieces of our interpretative picture about Jack at once: the pieces of the jigsaw have to fit together according to common-sense principles such as the Fundamental Principle and the Consequence Principle, and the emerging picture has to match up with Jack's physical circumstances. In particular, the interpretation must fit Jack's physical behaviour, rendering it a comprehensible pattern of 'behaviour proper'. There is no circularity in all this because, to repeat, there is no aim of analysing away any of the concepts of action, belief or desire.

In short, then, soft functionalism – properly understood – is not viciously circular. The problematic option, despite Armstrong's defence, is hard functionalism. For a theorist who says that a belief is a state apt to produce certain kinds of behaviour surely faces the question *what kind of behaviour?* At the very least, he owes us some means of filling out the now familiar schema (III). But, as we saw, the natural way of filling out that schema is by appeal to principles of folk psychology; and this is the very move that takes us inevitably towards a soft variety of functionalism. Hence the defender of hard functionalism must eschew this attractive move and fill out (III) in some quite different way. And, to put it mildly, it is very difficult to see what plausible alternative move is open to the functionalist here. The hard functionalist seems to inherit here some of the difficulties which, as we hinted in X.5, also face the hard behaviourist.

So, our money is on soft functionalism. We should note, by the way, that there are some writers who would not apply the term 'functionalism' to this position at all, and who would insist on restricting the label to what is, in our terms, hard functionalism (just as some writers reserve the term 'behaviourism' for hard behaviourism – see X.5). On the other hand, other writers with positions like the one presented here do describe their views as functionalist. It has to be frankly acknowledged that there is a terminological mess in this area, and we offer the hard/soft distinction as a small contribution towards retrieving a degree of clarity.

6   Finally, we turn to the issue of our knowledge of other minds: can we ever really know what someone else believes or wants, thinks or feels? We first raised this question at the very beginning of Chapter I, only to set it aside again for much later discussion. As we noted then, we are tempted to regard other people's mental states as hidden away inside their minds; and this idea readily gives rise to nagging doubts about whether we can ever

get to know about these hidden internal states. Is Jill's external behaviour really an adequate guide to her private mental life? This sort of sceptical worry is, as we shall see in Chapter XIV, exceptionally tempting in the case of our knowledge of other people's sensations. But for the moment let's concentrate on the case of belief: is another person's outward behaviour really a safe guide to her inner beliefs?

The Asymmetry between the grounds for first- and third-person ascriptions of belief seems to encourage scepticism here. It is so very tempting to say that we know about our own beliefs in a peculiarly intimate way, and that by contrast our judgements about other people's beliefs can be little better that wild stabs in the dark. A Humean account of belief, in particular, would lead to exactly this sort of view. According to Hume's first thoughts at any rate, having a belief is simply a matter of having suitably 'lively' ideas tucked away in the mind. And this liveliness is naturally thought of as having no necessary link with any outward behaviour pattern; rather, it is an intrinsic quality of the idea, which only the person who has the idea can be directly aware of. So, on Hume's first theory, what makes a mental state a belief is its intrinsic inner quality. But in that case how could you ever know that another person like Jill has beliefs – i.e. inner states with the right intrinsic character – underlying her external behaviour?

The Rylean theory, if it worked, would squash all such doubts. For according to Ryle, beliefs are not hidden internal states, because they are not internal states at all: facts about beliefs are just general 'iffy' facts about behaviour, and these facts are, so to speak, out on the surface. However, as we have seen, this theory of belief is unacceptable; we have offered in its place a theory more in the style of Armstrong. But the Mark III theory, it might be argued, reinstates beliefs as states of which we can have especially direct first-person knowledge, so doesn't this also reinstate the possibility of a radical scepticism? Won't we be left with the original worry about how we can ever know about anyone else's state of belief?

Well, note that our theory inherits from Ryle the crucial insight that what makes a state a belief or desire is precisely the way in which it is manifested in behaviour. In other words, beliefs are not identified by an intrinsic character like 'liveliness' but by their function in producing behaviour. If Jack is exhibiting the right behaviour patterns, and these flow from some underlying states, then by our theory he has the corresponding beliefs and desires:

beliefs and desires just are what show up thus-and-so in behaviour. On this view, therefore, there is no room for a wild scepticism about what other people think and want. If we can observe enough behaviour and find the right sort of patterns, then this necessarily gives us good evidence of their beliefs and desires.

This point is worth labouring. Suppose you are trying to understand and explain Jack's behaviour. To this end, you construct a hypothesis about his beliefs and desires which is in accordance with the general principles of folk psychology, and which fits Jack's behaviour well. As with any explanatory hypothesis, the fact that it apparently *works* is some real reason to suppose that it is true. Of course, for all that, your story about Jack's beliefs and desires could be wrong. One extreme possibility is that Jack's behaviour is not properly caused by his internal states at all: he may, perhaps, be a remotely controlled Martian robot, and folk psychology doesn't really apply to him after all. Another, much more reasonable, possibility is that Jack's behaviour is indeed being brought about by beliefs and desires, but you are wrong about what these are. There is a rival second hypothesis, which is still structured in accordance with the principles of folk psychology, and which actually fits his behaviour better.

In short, then, your story about Jack's beliefs and desires is more or less risky. But that's how it is with explanatory stories generally, and your psychological story is none the worse for that. For example, a physiological explanation of Jill's current illness is open to similar risks. Maybe – though this is a wild thought – Jill doesn't physically function like the rest of us, and so standard theory doesn't apply at all in her case. Or much more plausibly, the given explanation of her ailment can be challenged by a rival explanation in the standard style that better fits all the facts. But the potential fallibility of particular medical explanations is no reason for wholesale scepticism: there are well-established ways of minimising the risks of error, and doctors often know perfectly well (by any sane criteria of knowledge) what is wrong with us. Similarly, the fallibility of particular psychological stories is no reason for wild scepticism. We can consistently recognise the fallibility while still wanting to insist that we have familiar ways of checking our stories and reducing the risks of error, and that we often know perfectly well (by any reasonable standard) what our friends or relations believe. After all, just try doubting, in a real-life case, that your mother believes that grass is green or that butter keeps better in the refrigerator or that the moon isn't made of green cheese.

On our dispositional/functionalist theory, then, the ascription of beliefs to other people is in much the same boat as any other explanatory move which goes beyond what can be observed. Things can go wrong: but this in itself is no reason for thinking that talk of other people's beliefs is peculiarly risky, or for leaping instantly to a sweeping scepticism about our knowledge of other minds. So, at least as far as states like beliefs and desires are concerned, our general approach shows how we can avoid an extreme scepticism about other minds. But this perhaps does not take us very far: for as we remarked before, the deep roots of the worry that we can't really know another person's mind lie in reflections, not about their propositional attitudes, but about their sensations. These roots will have to be explored in Chapter XIV.

XIII

ASSESSING THE FUNCTIONALIST THEORY

1   It is time to take stock. Over the last few chapters, the beginnings of a theory of the mind have emerged. We first elucidated the notions of perception and action in terms of the fundamental pair of concepts, belief and desire. We then offered what we called a dispositional/functionalist account of this fundamental pair. Three classes of question now arise. First, how does the view we have arrived at relate to other views in the philosophy of mind? If our position now is (broadly speaking) a kind of functionalism, then how does it relate to all the other 'isms' which contemporary philosophers have discussed? Second, can the sort of account which we have offered of the propositional attitudes of belief and desire be extended to cover other sorts of mental state or process? Can we, for example, give an account of sensation or conscious thought which is in the same general spirit? Or does our account need to be augmented by something radically different if it is to cover the whole of our mental life? Third, we must ask about the wider implications of our view: can it accommodate, for example, our ordinary conception of ourselves as free agents?

In short, we must ask about the rivals to our theory, about its coverage and about its implications. In this chapter we will be concerned very largely with the first of these topics. The other topics belong to Part III.

2   Let's begin, though, with some remarks about the Aristotelian roots of functionalism.

In Chapter VI, we set an agenda for discussion which owed everything to Aristotle's insight that the mind is to be regarded as a set of capacities. From this anti-Cartesian perspective, a discussion of the nature of the mind best proceeds by examining the exercise of

177

our various capacities for perception and action, belief and desire, and so on. As we followed through this agenda, however, the arguments have been shaped by considerations drawn from other philosophers, and Aristotle's own views on these topics haven't been explicitly discussed. Still, the positions we have developed all have Aristotelian echoes, to say the least. And in particular, the broadly functionalist framework we have been recommending has clear Aristotelian antecedents.

To illustrate the last point, let's very briefly consider a couple of examples, starting with the discussion of anger in Book I of *De Anima*. Aristotle notes the dependence of 'affections of the soul' (i.e. states of mind) on bodily conditions; and he suggests that anger, for example, is a particular happening in a body 'as a result of this cause, and for the sake of that end'. Since it involves bodily happenings, anger falls within the province of the physiologist. However, Aristotle continues,

> the student of nature and the dialectician would define what anger is differently. For the latter would define it as a reaching out for retaliation or something of the sort, the former as the boiling of the blood round the heart. Of these definitions, the first gives the form or defining essence, the other the matter.   (403a29-b3)

There is an immediate parallel here with our treatment of belief and desire (see XI.7). The student of nature tells us about the physiology of anger or belief or whatever: but that still leaves us with the question of what makes some physical happening count as having a particular mental character. For instance, what makes the happening which is materially a 'boiling of the blood' (or whatever) a case of anger? The answer, Aristotle supposes, is something to do with its connections with retaliation and such-like behaviour. The natural way of developing this thought is in the direction which associates form with function.

As a second example, we might consider what Aristotle himself says about desire, where he again puts the matter/form to work. Aristotle's material description of desire is to be found in *De Motu Animalium* ('On the Movement of Animals'). The physiology is decidedly antiquated: Aristotle talks of heating which results in the expansion of a gaseous stuff called 'connate spirit', which is in turn what moves our limbs. But the quaintness of this is beside the point. What matters is that Aristotle clearly distinguishes the question of the physiology of desire from the issue of what makes something count as a desire. And on the second issue – the formal description of desire – Aristotle's view is recognisably close to ours. Desire as such is necessarily connected to action: as Aristotle puts it in the *Metaphysics*.

> Everything which has a rational capacity, when it desires that for which it has the capacity, and in the circumstances in which it has the capacity, must do this. (1048a13-15)

For example, when a reader desires to read a certain book, in circumstances where the book is to hand (and there are no countervailing considerations), then he will read it: the desire necessarily produces appropriate action. And it is clear that Aristotle treats this relation between desire and appropriate action as being of the essence of desire: what makes something a desire is precisely its role in producing behaviour.

Functionalism, in our broad sense, thus has distinguished antecedents. But it also has important rivals. So we turn now to the main business of this chapter, a review of the relations between various rival positions and the one we have been defending.

3   'Logical behaviourism', 'physicalism', 'the contingent identity theory', 'anomalous monism', 'eliminative materialism', 'the token identity theory' ... That's just a handful of labels for some of the various 'isms' or general theories you can encounter in the recent philosophy of mind. Yet so far – you might well protest – we have only looked at *two* such theories, Cartesian dualism and functionalism. So haven't we given an extremely biased and partial picture of the scene? A responsible and honest introduction to the philosophy of mind must surely examine more than two possible views out of so many!

This protest would be mistaken. We have in fact, in the course of our discussions, touched on many of the issues at stake in the various 'isms' listed: we have already given implicit evaluations of many of their central claims. It is just that, up to now, we have tried to keep the lines of argument tidy by not cluttering the discussion with too many asides explicitly comparing our position with neighbouring positions on the philosophical map. But let's now take bearings.

Consider first the term *physicalism*. This has been used in a variety of ways in the literature: but the overall tendency is to use it in a broad sense, to label the essential core of any naturalistic view of the mind. The physicalist's claim, then, is that thinking, feeling animals such as ourselves are constituted of nothing more than the ordinary physical stuff recognised by the natural sciences. The key claim, in other words, is that there is no more stuff in our make-up than complex organic molecules. We should perhaps explicitly add the further claim that these molecules obey the same physical laws when they occur as parts of human or animal bodies as when they occur in other things.

Thus defined, physicalism stands flatly opposed to Cartesian dualism, and is an essential part of any naturalistic view of man which tries to accord with the results of the natural sciences. Given the strength of our anti-dualist arguments in Part I, we have since been seeking a viable form of physicalism. We have wanted to show that beliefs and desires, and thus perception and action, are possible for creatures who have nothing more in their heads than physical brain-stuff: a proper understanding of the fundamental mental accomplishments does not require us to suppose the existence of anything immaterial. The issue for us, as for the great majority of contemporary philosophers, is no longer whether physicalism in our very general sense is true but rather what more specific brand or sub-variety of physicalism is defensible. The difficulties do not come over the question of the matter of the mind, but over its form: more precisely, the areas of real dispute don't concern the stuff we are made of but rather the precise account we give of our mental capacities. What sort of physicalist theory of beliefs, desires and so on is defensible?

4   Some philosophers have, by our lights, been either unduly pessimistic or rashly over-optimistic about the theoretical task. We will take the pessimists first. These come in two varieties. Some, perhaps influenced by Wittgenstein, have held that it is misguided even to attempt to give the type of general treatment of the nature of belief or desire which we have sketched. Attention to the details of our everyday psychological talk reveals a very complex pattern of nuanced distinctions between (say) thinking, presupposing, hypothesising, trusting that and taking it that. Likewise, we make an equally complex pattern of discriminations between (say) want-

ing, preferring, desiring that and lusting after. To flatten out all these distinctions and only discuss two catch-all notions of belief and pro-attitude is (so the argument goes) to chase illusions and seek for a kind of quasi-scientific generality where none is to be had.

Now, such scepticism about the very possibility of the sort of theorising which we have been doing has some interesting roots which we cannot explore here. However, we have already implicitly sketched an overall response to this style of pessimism at the end of XII.3. Let's cheerfully acknowledge that our discussions of belief and desire do indeed proceed at a certain level of abstraction from the surface detail of everyday folk psychology. They are none the worse for that. For we claim to be outlining the bare bones of folk psychology, not to be depicting its surface richness; and we hold that this is an essential move if we are eventually to command a perspicuous overview of the details of our folk theory. The surface play of detailed nuances and shadings is held together by an underlying skeletal structure. And to the suggestion that there is really no such skeletal structure to be found, perhaps an adequate reply is to come up with an outline general story about beliefs and desires that *is* illuminating, puzzle-solving and intellectually satisfying. We claim to have done exactly that in Chapters XI and XII.

5   The first sort of pessimist about the task of giving a theoretical analysis of our mental concepts thinks that the project is doomed from the outset. The second sort of pessimist holds that an analysis *can* be given, but maintains that it reveals our concepts to be, in one way or another, radically flawed. Perhaps analysis shows our concepts to have irremovable dualist implications; or perhaps it shows that we are committed to false empirical assumptions about the structure of human mentality. Either way,

> *our common-sense psychological framework is a false and radically misleading conception of the causes of human behaviour and the nature of cognitive activity.* ... Folk psychology is not just an incomplete representation of our inner natures; it is an outright *mis*representation of our internal states and activities.   (Churchland 1984: 43)

The everyday framework should simply be got rid of.

The situation, according to this sort of pessimist, is a bit like the situation with the concept of being possessed by a devil. We can give an explanation of what this means, and the presumptions involved in describing someone as possessed. The trouble is that these presumptions are ones that hardly anyone these days is prepared to buy (for a start, we do not believe in devils). As a consequence, we have eliminated talk of possession from our serious descriptions of each other: we no longer explain people's behaviour in such terms but deploy instead such concepts as those of clinical hysteria or epilepsy. We are left, at most, with cagy talk of 'what people used to *call* possession'.

According to this kind of pessimist, then, our everyday mentalistic talk should – at least eventually – go the same way as talk about demonic possession. In other words, we should *eliminate* the supposedly flawed talk of beliefs and desires, pains and the rest, in favour of some more respectable and well-behaved mode of talk. One recommended option is to eliminate mentalistic concepts in favour of concepts belonging to neuro-physiological science: instead of saying 'Jill is in pain' perhaps we should really say that her C-fibres are firing. And if we do continue to speak of 'pains', then this should only be done very cagily, in the heaviest scare-quotes, just as we now only talk about 'so-called possession by a devil'. Taking this option would make us, to use a standard label, *eliminative materialists*. Alternatively, we might seek instead to replace common-sense concepts with the refined constructs of a future cognitive psychology which employs notions of information-processing borrowed from computer science: this would make us – to coin a new phrase – *eliminative cognitivists*.

The suggestion that, at the end of the day, the concepts of folk psychology will prove to be in some sort of a mess cannot be dismissed out of hand. But a great deal of hard work will be needed to establish that any alleged mess is real and not apparent, for the price of accepting eliminative materialism or eliminative cognitivism is obviously so very high. It means that we are as mistaken in describing ourselves as having beliefs and desires as our forefathers were in occasionally describing themselves as possessed: and *that* is very hard to credit. (Note, by the way, the difference between this extreme position and sceptical worries of the kind we tried to block in XII.6: the traditional sceptic presupposes that we know very well in our own case that we have beliefs and desires, and he raises doubts about whether we can know this about anyone else. The eliminative materialist, by contrast, must reject even first-person ascriptions of belief.)

Now, whenever philosophical radicals offer an account of our everyday mental concepts which seems to show that these concepts are confused or embody unacceptable assumptions, philosophical conservatives will protest that the fault lies not in the concepts but in the mistaken analysis presented by the radicals. Suppose, to take a very crude example, someone argued that ordinary talk about perception commits us to accepting the existence of immaterial mental objects like 'sense-data'; and because such objects cannot be accepted by a physicalist, everyday talk about perception must be abandoned. This would hardly be very persuasive! The proper reply would be that our imagined radical philosopher has surely gone wrong in his account of what ordinary talk commits us to.

In our earlier chapters, we have offered accounts of perception and action, belief and desire, which seem at first sight to confirm that these concepts are in reasonably good order, i.e. are coherent and involve no dubious or indefensible assumptions. And even if these analyses have actually been mistaken, no reason has as yet emerged for jumping to the radical view that the concepts are not coherent and acceptable to physicalists. At this stage in the proceedings, then, pessimism of the second kind would be decidedly premature. We can't be certain that such pessimists won't in the end turn out to be right: but so far, at any rate, a more hopeful view seems the better bet.

6   It would be over-hasty to say that we can give no theoretical analysis of mental concepts: we also have no reason yet to say that, while we can give analyses, these show the concepts to be faulty. So we will here resist both brands of pessimism about our theoretical project. But of course this does not mean that we should leap to accept over-optimistically simple accounts of our mental concepts.

One over-simple way of accommodating our mental concepts to a general physicalist outlook is to claim that statements about mental states can be *reduced* to, or *translated* into, equivalent statements which are clearly about bodies. Now, claims about beliefs (for example) can hardly be translated into neuro-physiological talk about brains. Pretend that, whenever someone believes that it is about to rain, his brain will be in a special neuro-physiological state S picked out in scientific terms: it still will not follow that the two assertions 'Jack believes that it is about to rain' and 'Jack's brain is in state S' actually mean the same. It is quite implausible to suppose that your talk about Jack's belief is actually synonymous with talk about some neural state which is no doubt entirely unknown to you (as if you have been talking neuro-physiology all the time, without realising it). If we are to translate away mental discourse it must be into terms which are accessible to the ordinary speaker. And the only plausible way of doing this would be to try to translate mental talk into talk about overt, observable behaviour. Thus we arrive at a form of *behaviourism* (sometimes called 'philosophical' or 'logical behaviourism'). But we have examined this Rylean view already, in X.4 onwards, and found it open to conclusive objections.

Here is another over-simple way of reconciling our use of mental concepts with our basic physicalism. Consider for a moment the relation of talk about water to talk of H_2O, or talk about lightning to talk of discharges of electricity. In each case we have an everyday term and a corresponding scientific term: the two terms pick out the same sort of thing, but are not straightforwardly synonymous. Just as the designators 'Jack's niece' and 'Jill's cousin' may refer to one and the same person, but pick her out in different ways, so 'water' and 'H_2O' refer to the same stuff but pick it out in different ways (roughly, by its superficial properties, and by its chemical composition respectively). We might say that the terms have the same reference, but have a different sense or descriptive content. Likewise, the terms 'lightning' and 'electrical discharge' may both refer to the same sort of thing, but they pick it out in different ways (by its appearance, and by its constitution). Now, why not treat the relation of folk psychology to neuro-physiology in the same way? Why not say that the folk concepts are used to pick out in *one* way the same sort of state that some scientific descriptions may pick out in *another* way?

The suggestion, in short, is that just as water and H_2O is the same type of stuff differently described, so the belief that it is about to rain and some brain-state S may be the same type of state, differently described. And this suggestion invites generalisation: in a similar vein, we might say that sensations too are brain processes. Now, as J.J.C. Smart noted in a hugely influential paper, this

is not the thesis that, for example, 'after-image' or 'ache' means the same as 'brain process of sort X' (where 'X' is replaced by a description of a certain sort of brain process). It is that in so far as 'after-image' or 'ache' is a report of a process, it is a report of a process that *happens to be* a brain process. It follows that the thesis does not claim that sensation statements can be *translated* into statements about brain processes. ... All it claims is that in so far as a sensation statement is a report of something, that something is in fact a brain process. Sensations are nothing over and above brain processes.   (1959: 55-6)

So the claim is that a given type of mental state is identical with a type of brain-state: call this the *type identity theory*. But again, this view is one we have already discussed, at least in its application to beliefs (in XI.6: we will return to its application to sensations in XV.7). We noted before that it does not seem at all likely that each and every one of us who believes that it is about to rain (for example) shares a common neuro-physiological state. The brain is a remarkably adaptable organ, and it seems entirely reasonable to suppose that the neural state which is causally responsible for the same behavioural patterns may substantially differ from person to person. In other words, particular *instances* of the belief that it is about to rain are no doubt constituted by particular neural states, but these may very well be different sorts of neural states on different occasions or in different people. At least in the case of states like belief or desire, the over-optimistic type identity theory has to be rejected.

Our Mark III dispositional theory, however, still encourages the identifying of beliefs with brain-states: but the identity holds between particular instances of belief and particular instances of brain-states, rather than between types of beliefs and types of brain-states. See again XI.6 for a more detailed explanation of this point. We might call this sort of position the instance identity theory — or, to use its official but much less perspicuous name, the *token identity theory*.

7   Early versions of the idea that mental states are brain-states, differently described, tend not to be very clear as to whether this was a claim about types of states or about particular tokens or instances. In other words, early versions do not distinguish clearly between the type identity theory and the rival token identity theory, though (on the whole) proponents wrote as if favouring a type theory. The undifferentiated versions went under a number of

labels: 'central state materialism', 'Australian materialism', 'the contingent identity theory'. The first label signals the contrast between identity theories and behaviourism. The behaviourist claims that mental discourse is really disguised chat about external behaviour, i.e. about what is going on at the periphery of the body: the identity theorist has it that what is being referred to are internal states underlying the behaviour, i.e. what is going on centrally. The second label reminds us of the distinguished part played by a number of philosophers working in Australia (such as J.J.C. Smart and David Armstrong) in developing identity theories. The third label, however, raises a troublesome issue worth pausing over (although the following discussion can be omitted on a first reading).

Are statements identifying mental states with brain-states necessarily true? Or are the identities contingent – in other words, could they possibly have been false, could the world actually have been such that mental states were *not* brain-states? Is Smart right, for example, when he says that aches *happen to be* brain processes?

This question is rather tangled, not so much because of issues belonging specifically to the philosophy of mind, but because of the puzzling nature of the general notions of necessity and possibility which are involved here. However, without getting too embroiled in controversial issues of philosophical logic, we can safely make two points.

First, let's consider again the core claim of Chapter XI, namely that Jack's believing that it is about to rain is a matter of his being in some state which is causally responsible for certain 'iffy' behavioural facts. When we first presented this claim in XI.5, we noted that it seems compatible with dualism – for couldn't the dualist still insist that the state in question is an immaterial one? But maybe this appearance of compatibility is misleading. For we argued in Chapter IV that there are serious difficulties in the way of making sense of the notion of non-material things causally affecting the physical world. And if these arguments, or others to the same effect, can be made to stand up, then it is not after all a coherent option to suppose that the state causally responsible for Jack's behaviour pattern is a non-material state. In that case, it is *necessarily* the case that Jack's belief is some physical state.

In short, then, there may well be a priori arguments which establish that belief-states must be physical states of some kind or other. On the other hand (and this is our second point) there are certainly no experience-independent arguments to establish that our belief-states are specifically states of the brain as opposed to states of the heart, liver or whatever – at least so long as we identify the brain independently of its function, as the greyish mass of tissue in our heads. The states ultimately responsible for certain of our behavioural tendencies have turned out to be something to do with our brains; but, before the empirical investigations that established this, we would have had no a priori reason to suppose that mentality was linked to this grey stuff rather than that pink stuff. Aristotle, for example, famously thought that the brain was a cooling device (rather like a car radiator), and he located the seat of our mental functions at the heart.

To echo Smart, then, we can surely say that it has *turned out* that our mental processes are brain processes and not heart processes. But of course, this isn't exactly what Smart claims: for he says that aches, for example, *happen to be* brain processes – and it is open to argument whether this comes to quite the same. It is one thing to say that a certain fact can only be established empirically; it is another thing to say that it only happens to be the case and could possibly have been otherwise. There may perhaps be necessary features of the world, things that don't just happen to be so, which still can only be established empirically: this thesis has been argued with great rhetorical verve by Kripke (1980) – but obviously it would take us much far too far afield to explore the point any further here.

In summary: (A) the fact that mental states are identical to physical states (i.e. some physical states or other) is arguably not contingent – i.e. it perhaps could not have been otherwise. (B) We can agree with the Australian materialists' observation that it has turned out that our beliefs (for example) are brain-states rather than heart-states. But (C) this is arguably not equivalent to their official claim that our beliefs just contingently happen to be brain-states.

8   There is one other currently popular 'ism' to which we should very briefly refer, namely *anomalous monism*. This view, which is particularly associated with Donald Davidson, is a 'monism' in the sense that it maintains that there is only one fundamental kind of thing, namely physical objects. So it is again a brand of physicalism.

It is 'anomalous' (from the Greek *anomos*, meaning 'lawless') in the sense that it denies that there are law-like connections between mental and physical characteristics. Davidson's own arguments for this position are difficult, but it gets support from our broadly functionalist approach.

Consider again a type identity theory of the kind we have already rejected, which identifies mental states of type *M* with physical states of type *P*. Presumably, the defender of this identity would not want to say that the fact that certain states are both *M* and *P* is merely an *accident*. Rather, the connection between the mental and physical characteristics of the states will be, in a word, law-like. The anomalous monist, on the other hand, maintains that there can't be laws relating mental characteristics to physical ones (or at least, he must hold such laws to be the exception rather than the rule). Take once more the example of believing that it is about to rain. As we have already noted, it is highly unlikely that there is actually any general truth of the kind 'whenever someone believes that it is about to rain, he will be in the characteristic neural state *P*'. And even if some such general truth did happen to obtain, it would not be a hard-and-fast *law* – for (given the plasticity of the brain) you *could* believe that it is about to rain, you could be in a state with the right functional role, without being in that neural state *P*. So, as we said, our sort of functionalist account of belief would give support to the anomalous monist's rejection of laws relating the mental to the physical.

9   That completes our review of neighbouring positions in the philosophy of mind. It has been brisk but, we hope, enough to show how our earlier discussions relate to a wide spectrum of different theories in the philosophy of mind. We must now turn to ask what problems our current, broadly functionalist, position faces.

The first problem is simply this: can our theory concerning beliefs and desires be generalised to cope with mental states that are not propositional attitudes? Consider, for example, the state of having a pain. Whereas belief is typically belief that something is the case, and desire can be treated as desire that something become the case, obviously having a pain is never having a pain that something be the case! Pains do not have any propositional content; so can our functionalist theory cope with them? That must be the topic of Chapters XIV and XV.

A related thought is that functionalism can't deal with the phenomenon of *consciousness*. After all, you might be tempted to say, machines can have internal states with functional properties, but can't really be conscious. Now, the notion of consciousness is an exceedingly slippery one: however, two main things it covers are the having of experiences and the having of thoughts. The first of these topics we have promised to discuss in our next two chapters: the topic of thought (and particularly of intelligent, self-conscious, discursive thought) we will discuss in Chapter XVI. This will take us firmly into those mental realms which are distinctively human.

The topics just mentioned need to be dealt with because they may seem to resist the broadly functionalist approach so far adopted. In other words, they threaten to show that the coverage of our approach is radically incomplete. The last topic for discussion arises in a different way. Abstracting from the details of our discussions, we have been defending a kind of physicalism. You are made of physical stuff which is, one may reasonably suppose, subject to the same causal laws as everything else. But if your behaviour is, in the end, a result of physical processes which are subject to the laws of physics, then surely your actions are causally determined to be as they are. Which seems evidently to imply that you do not have free will. And that is, to say the least, a deeply alarming conclusion. So our final topic, after the preparatory Chapter XVII, will be the broad issue of freedom and causality.

Part III

SENSATION, THOUGHT AND FREEDOM

XIV

SENSATIONS:
THE PHENOMENOLOGICAL THEORY

1   In Chapters XI and XII, we defended a broadly functionalist theory of beliefs and desires. According to this theory, the belief that it is about to rain (for example) is a physical state, identified not by its intrinsic physiological properties but by its role in producing behaviour. As we put it before, the 'what it is to be what it is' of a belief is its function. Now, can we generalise this approach to cover other types of mental state? What about sensations – such as feeling pain, for example? Can we give a functionalist analysis of these, or must we look for a quite different kind of account?

There are conspicuous differences between sensations and states like belief and desire. Take the case of feeling a painful tingling. This experience is not *about* something in the way that beliefs or desires, hopes or fears are about something: we have no locution of the form 'Jack tingles that *p*' or 'Jill has a pain that *p*'. Generalising, we cannot ascribe simple bodily sensations by using a 'that'-clause – i.e. sensations are not propositional attitudes in the sense explained in X.1. Because of this rather fundamental difference, we perhaps shouldn't expect a theory of sensations like pain to run exactly parallel to our account of attitudes like belief. Still, let's begin by briefly considering the prospects for a functionalist theory of pain.

What is the function or causal role of pain? At bottom, it seems plausible to say, the business of pain is at least typically to alert us to bodily damage or malfunction, and to spur us into protective or avoidance behaviour. For instance, a painful 'burning' sensation (as we call it) is normally produced by a skin-damaging contact with a hot surface and eventuates in a speedy attempt to withdraw from that surface. Generalising the point, let's say as a first shot at an account of pain roughly in the functionalist style of Chapter XI that

Jack is in pain if he is in a state standardly produced by bodily damage or malfunction, and which in turn produces reactions like tears and moans, and prompts avoidance responses.

This is, of course, far too simple. Note that the sort of responses actually produced by pain will depend a lot on the associated beliefs and desires of the sufferer. The wounded fugitive may manage to suppress his moans in order to avoid discovery by his pursuers. And the long-term victim of a painful condition perhaps doesn't even have to make an effort any more to suppress the signs of his pain. Again, in some situations pains are welcomed rather than avoided (pain is, for example, the antidote to morphine poisoning). The situation is evidently complex. Still, as a second shot, we can try this: pain is a state normally due to bodily damage or malfunction and which results in a propensity (which may get suppressed) to tears and moans, and also a propensity to alleviate or bring about the cessation of the state (which may be over-ridden by other desires).

This is still too simple. But we won't pursue the fine details of a possible functionalist account of pain, because in this chapter and the next we are going to be exploring a series of related objections which – if valid – would sink *any* broadly functionalist account, whatever the exact details. There is no point in developing the sketched theory any further until these tempting blocking arguments have been cleared out of the way.

2   The functionalist's idea is that pains are states defined by their role in the causal processes typically leading to tears and groans and avoidance reactions – and these states, he will add, are physical ones. But there is an immensely strong temptation to say that this must be completely misguided, for the following reason.

A sensation, we are inclined to say, is a state with an intrinsic nature which can only be experienced by the person who has the state. When you have a pain, for example, only you yourself can be directly aware of its painfulness: you can know for certain whether or not you are feeling a pain by being aware of this inner felt quality of your experience. This intrinsic quality of painfulness (the argument continues) surely cannot be identified with anything recognised by the functionalist theory – for you can establish that you are in pain without establishing anything about the causal powers of your state. And even if there is some general correlation between your feeling a pain and your going in for characteristic 'pain behaviour' (complaining, groaning, rubbing the affected spot), this correlation isn't what makes your sensation a pain. To put it bluntly, what makes a pain a pain isn't its relation to anything else but is its intrinsic painfulness as recognised by introspection. The functionalist story, which tries to define what a pain is by its causal relations to behaviour, is therefore quite wrong.

This line of objection to a functionalist account (*any* functionalist account) of pain is very attractive. Another way of bringing out its undoubted appeal is as follows. Imagine a community of Martians who, like us, occasionally damage themselves: and when they do, they seem distressed, groan or weep, attend to the affected spot, avoid repeating the damage, and so on. In short, let's suppose that the Martians often exhibit behaviour exactly as if they are in pain. Now, given that this behaviour flows from an internal state of the Martians (and they are not merely pretending, etc.), this is enough – on a functionalist theory – to show that the Martians are often genuinely in pain: for the theory holds that pain just is an internal state apt for bringing about that sort of behaviour. But surely, the anti-functionalist will want to protest, this cannot be right. The internal state which produces pain behaviour in Martians might not feel anything like what pain feels to us: and if the state hasn't got the right phenomenology - the intrinsic painful feel – then it cannot be a genuine pain-state after all.

In summary, this attack on functionalism rests on the rival view that what makes something a pain is essentially its recognisable inner quality of painfulness, a quality which can in no way be identified with its causal function. In Saul Kripke's words, pain is simply 'picked out by the property of being pain itself, by its immediate phenomenological property' (1980: 152). The account of pain here naturally generalises to other sensations: they too are defined by their immediate phenomenological properties – i.e. by their 'feels' as recognised in conscious awareness. This general anti-functionalist view invites the label *the (pure) phenomenological theory* of sensation, or 'the PP-theory' for short. It will be our topic for the rest of this chapter.

3   The PP-theory is evidently enticing; indeed, it is so intuitively persuasive that to deny it can seem tantamount to saying that we

never really feel pain. But all the same, we will be arguing that the theory faces overwhelming difficulties. So we should immediately stress that we are dealing with a disputable *theory* here: to repeat, what is at stake is the philosophical claim that pain (for example) is to be defined, without any reference to its behavioural function, in terms of an inner quality we are consciously aware of. And challenging this definition of pain no more implies that we don't really have pains than (say) rejecting the dualist theory involves denying that we have minds in the ordinary sense.

Let's first pause to show that the argument for the PP-theory sketched in the previous section actually carries very little weight. A key thought was as follows: we can establish that we are in pain without thereby coming to know anything about the physical state we are in — hence pains cannot be (functionally defined) physical states. But this bit of reasoning, once frankly brought out into the open, has an embarrassing similarity to Descartes's Argument for dualism which we showed to be invalid in Chapter III. Descartes, it will be recalled, tried to prove that we are distinct from our bodies by appealing to the fact that we can establish that we exist (by arguing 'I think therefore I am'), while leaving the existence of our bodies open to philosophical doubt. Likewise, the present reasoning aims to show that our pains are distinct from any functional state by appealing to the fact that we can establish the existence of our pains (by introspection), without thereby settling the existence of any functional state. The new argument is evidently no better than the old one. To put it crudely, it doesn't follow from the premise that *a* and *b* can be held apart in our thought that they are really distinct in the world (see III.7) — and this point holds good not only for pairs like George Orwell and Eric Blair, or a person and her body, but also for pain and a certain functional state.

In addition to this Cartesian element in the case for the PP-theory, the other crucial element was the idea that when we introspect we are aware of a special intrinsic quality of painfulness. But that idea is also open to fundamental criticism.

Of course, any theory must acknowledge that when we judge ourselves to be in pain, we do not do so on the basis of an inspection of our own behaviour. Jill can say whether she is in pain or not without having to wait for tell-tale signs; she doesn't have to listen out for moans and groans, nor does she have to watch in the mirror to catch herself grimacing or rubbing the affected spot. In short, Jill's claim to be in pain is not based on the sort of publicly available evidence which other people have to rely on to support their claims about her. Now, given that (a) first-person claims about one's own pains are not based on an inspection of the publicly available evidence, it seems only a very small move to infer that (b) first-person claims must be based instead on an examination of the private evidence as revealed to our internal mental gaze. What is more natural?

It is then but a short step to the PP-theory. For once we are working with the idea of a kind of inner vision which surveys the contents of our own minds, it seems compelling to say that a self-ascription of pain is grounded in the inward observation of some special sort of quality – we recognise some 'immediate phenomenological property', to use Kripke's words again. And this quality would presumably be what makes a pain a pain: surely, so long as the right inner 'feel' occurs, the sensation in question is a pain no matter what else is happening. In other words, any correlation between this introspected inner quality and outward behaviour patterns would seem to be inessential to the sensation's status as a genuine pain. Which takes us back to the PP-theory.

In short, one move that sustains the PP-theory is the slide from (a) to (b). But this slide, though so tempting, is certainly not compulsory, and we have already shown how to resist a parallel slide in our discussion of belief. There we noted that we can account for what we called The Asymmetry between first-person and third-person routes to knowledge about beliefs without resorting to any quasi-visual notion of introspection. What we need to say is that there is typically a direct causal link between the state of having a certain belief and a readiness to judge that one has that belief (see XI.3). Similarly here: we can again accommodate the evidential asymmetry between first-person and third-person judgements that one is in pain without resorting to some dubious notion of the internal recognition of 'immediate phenomenological properties'. Why not just say, analogously to our treatment of the belief case, that the asymmetry is due to there being a direct causal link between a pain-state and the readiness to judge that one is in pain? Then Jill's judgement that she is in pain is not based on some putative inner observation of special 'phenomenological properties', any more than her judgements about her own beliefs are based on any process of looking at the internal scene. In both cases she can say straight off, without any prior process of quasi-visual introspection, what she believes or feels. On this sort of account, assent to the truism (a) need not lead us on to make claim (b) and so at least one route to the PP-theory can be blocked.

4　　We have tried to diminish the immediate appeal of the PP-theory by undermining some of the considerations initially offered in its favour. However, this is not yet to show that the theory is actually false: so we now turn to the main line of attack. Later, in §6, we will give reasons for saying that the PP-theorist can't even make sense of the idea that someone else is in pain. But let's not pre-judge that argument. We will allow, for the moment, that our theorist can at least understand the claim that someone else is in pain, and we will ask instead: can he ever have good reasons for supposing that such a claim (as understood by him) is true?

On reflection, the PP-theory seems to have the embarrassing consequence that you can never have strong grounds for believing of anyone else that she is in pain. The basic argument is as follows:

(S)　Suppose that the PP-theory is correct: suppose, in other words, that a state may have all the behavioural associations of pain and yet not be a pain, because what is required for a genuine pain sensation is the right phenomenological 'feel'. How then could you ever be sure in the case of another person that she is in pain? All you have to go on is her behaviour, including verbal behaviour, and perhaps some observable bodily damage. And how do you know that the sensation (if any) which accompanies her behaviour and the seen bodily damage is genuinely a *painful* sensation, with the right feel to it? Perhaps in her case an intrinsically different sensation is associated with the same behaviour pattern. After all, you can't get inside her mind to find out how it really feels to her. All you have to go on is the fact that in your own particular case there is an association between pain and certain outward physical phenomena — but that is hardly very impressive. Maybe other cases are not analogous to your own. You certainly can't argue 'there is a correlation in my case, so the same *must* hold for her too'. That would involve a wildly over-optimistic extrapolation from the one case you know. On the PP-theory, therefore, you have no very good reasons for supposing that, in the case of anyone else, 'pain behaviour' is really a sign of genuine pain. But since 'pain behaviour' is the only evidence there is, it follows that you can never have strong grounds for holding that someone else is in pain. This last conclusion is naturally taken as entailing that we can never *know* that someone else is in pain; and so the the PP-theory drives us into a radical scepticism.

We can put the argument another way. Consider again the Martians mentioned in §2: they are just like us in respect of their functional states, but the PP-theorist wants to press the intuition that they might all the same not really feel pain – and hence that pain must be distinct from any functionally defined state. We now want to turn this line of thought back against the PP-theorist. For suppose it is said that what makes some state a case of pain is something quite other than its functional role. Then how can we have any reason for confidence that our next-door neighbours are not like the Martians, and share our functional states without experiencing genuine pains?

Faced with argument (S), the defender of the PP-theory has only two options. Either he must seek to rebut (S) by showing that the alleged embarrassing consequence does not really follow, and that we can – even on the PP-theory – have strong grounds for believing that another person is in pain. Or he must allow that the conclusion follows but insist that it is not absurd. We will argue that neither of these options is tenable, though readers already convinced of the strength of argument (S) can skip to §6.

5   First, then, we will reinforce argument (S) by considering a very suggestive model which we have taken over, with only slight modifications, from James Hopkins (1975). Imagine that we are living in a world that is nearly all black and white and shades of grey (like on an old-fashioned television). However, everyone has his own set of special cards. These cards have a grey back, visible to everyone. But the cards' inner faces are visible only to their holder, and each has a different vivid coloured patch. Indeed, these faces are so vivid that they produce in us strong emotional reactions, so one card, say, makes us want to cry when we see it, another makes us smile and so forth. Naturally enough, we want to talk about these peculiarly intense colours – the most vivid things in all our experience – and we unreflectively fall into the habit of talking

about 'the crying colour' to refer to the colour on the card which happens to make us cry, 'the smiling colour' for the colour which makes us smile, and so on.

In this imagined world, however, it would make good sense for someone – Jack, let's suppose – to wonder whether the colour which *he* calls 'the crying colour' really is the same as that which someone else calls by the same label. Of course, the colours are alike in inducing tears in their respective beholders, but that isn't what is in question: what is being asked is whether the colours are intrinsically alike, in respect of the way they *look*. Jack might guess that everyone's crying cards are all alike in intrinsic colour. But, now that he has raised the issue, he would no doubt take it to be quite possible that other people's crying cards should be different in colour, remembering that he has only one case (his own) to go on: and if the cards are different, this means that the colour he calls 'the crying colour' would indeed be different from what other people call by the same label.

Finally, suppose that – overcome with curiosity – Jack starts to peek at other people's cards. He could of course find that everyone's crying cards looked the same. But he could find that different people's crying cards were typically quite different. At this, Jack might say 'How surprising': but he could equally say 'Well, I always knew the evidence for any guess about the look of other people's cards was pretty thin'. Both reactions would seem appropriate. The evidence clearly *was* very weak: all Jack had to go on in forming expectations about what counted as 'the crying colour' for other people was the inner colour of his own crying card. But on the other hand, as Hopkins puts it, 'since that was all the evidence, what was [Jack] to do but go on it, and leave [himself] in for a surprise' when at last he peeked?

Now, the point of Hopkins's illuminating tale is this: *on the PP-theory, talk about other people's pains is in the same boat as talk in the story about other people's crying colours*. For the PP-theory says that what makes a sensation a pain is essentially its feel (independently of what other effects it has), just as what makes a card a particular colour is its look (independently of what other effects it has). Now, in the story – before Jack started peeking – we unreflectively talked about 'the crying colour', but were left with a real issue about whether the colours that make other people cry are actually the same as what *we* call 'the crying colour'. Similarly on the PP-theory; we all talk about pain, but face a real issue about whether the sensations that make other people cry and moan actually feel the same as what *we* call pain. The evidence, in the story, that the colour which makes someone else cry is the same as the colour which makes us cry is pretty weak: all Jack can do is extrapolate from his own case and hope for the best. And – still on the PP-theory – the evidence that the sensation associated with 'pain behaviour' is the same for other people as it is for ourselves is equally weak: we can only note what happens in our own case and hope that the same happens in other cases too. But maybe Jack's crying colour is red, and Jill's green (they react similarly to these different colours); likewise, in Jack's case, the sensation correlated with certain behavioural signs could have one 'feel' while Jill's sensation associated with the same behaviour has quite a different 'feel' (they react similarly to these different sensations).

Of course, there is one cardinal difference between the case of pain and the card story. In the story, Jack could peek and see how things really stand with other people's cards. But we cannot peek inside other people's minds to see what their sensations are like. However, that can hardly *improve* the evidential situation in the pain case! The bold extrapolation from our own case is not strengthened by our being told '... and what is more, it's actually impossible to check out the results'. Hence the privacy of sensations provides no escape from the conclusion that – on the PP-theory – it is a risky and thinly supported assumption that other people feel genuinely painful sensations when they damage themselves.

To sum up. The PP-theorist, it seems, must rely for his attributions of pains to other people on an Argument from Analogy (as it is standardly called). He must extrapolate from his own case and hope that other people's situations will be analogous. Such arguments are necessarily weak.

Now, could the defender of the theory bite the bullet and claim that our assumption that other people feel pain really is only a weakly supported conjecture? Well, you might *say* that – and the PP-theory runs so very deep in our everyday thinking that its sceptical implications about our lack of knowledge of other people's sensations can seem intuitively compelling (much more compelling than sceptical worries about other people's beliefs – cf. XII.6). However, on serious reflection it is difficult genuinely to *believe* that sort of sceptical claim. Faced with the child who comes crying for comfort having just badly grazed her knee, could you really think: it's only a weakly supported guess that she is in pain?

Again, consider the provision of anaesthetics for patients under-going surgery; can you really suppose that it is only a risky bet that these people actually need the stuff? (Maybe their sensations are not really painful, so why not just temporarily paralyse them with curare to keep them still under the surgeon's knife? Do we really only give anaesthetics *just to be on the safe side*, because they *might* feel pain?) A little honest reflection shows that the sceptical conclusion of argument (S) cannot be seriously entertained. But in that case, the PP-theory, which starts the whole argument off, had better be rejected.

6   The situation for the PP-theorist is arguably even worse: not only has he difficulty in justifying the attribution of pains to other people but, antecendently to that, he has difficulty in even *making sense* of the claim that other people have pains. For on the PP-theorist's view what is the meaning of the term 'pain'?

The PP-theory rests on the idea that a sort of inner vision reveals to us what pains really are. This conception almost inevitably gives rise to the further idea that by paying attention to what we feel when we are in pain we can provide ourselves with a private definition of the word 'pain'. We can pinch ourselves and say: *that* is what I mean by 'pain' - and someone else is in pain if she too has one of *those* sensations. The idea, in other words, is that the meaning of the word 'pain' can be entirely fixed from the first-person perspective by reference to the putative introspected quality of painfulness; other people count as being in pain simply if they too have the same thing, irrespective of the behavioural accompaniments. All this, of course, underpins the PP-theory again.

But is this story about sensation words like 'pain' really coherent? This question raises a large family of troublesome issues, some of which we have already touched on; here we will point to just one more difficulty. Let's grant for the sake of argument (and many would say that this is already to concede far too much) that we can make sense of the suggestion that you could introduce a term 'S' to label your own experiences by saying 'this is S' while pointing inside yourself to some suitable mental occurrence. Well, this at best latches 'S' onto something in *your* mental world. And so how, on this story, are you to give any content to the idea that *another* person might also have S? How can you give the term S, supposedly learnt in its first-person applications, a third-person use?

The reply may go: 'Someone else has S if she has the *same* as what you have when you have S – and where's the problem in understanding that?' But by hypothesis, what the other person has is something in her mind, whereas sensation S is something in your mind; and what greater difference could there be between the cases? How, then, can what she has be 'the same' as what you have? 'That's an entirely perverse objection! She can surely have a sensation which has the *same character* as S – except for the obvious fact that it is hers rather than yours!' But how can this talk of the other person having a sensation of the same character be explained from the perspective of a PP-style account of sensation words? Are you supposed to point at suitable pairs of your own sensations, and say 'this is what I mean by sensations having the same character'? That manoeuvre would merely raise the same difficulties as the original attempt to apply 'S' to another person – how can noting similarities among your own experiences give any content to the notion of similarities between different people's experiences? So how does the PP-theorist explain 'same character' here? (Obviously he can't say that different people's sensations have the same character if they are, for instance, both in pain, or both tingling or whatever. That would just take us round in a circle.)

To put the main worry here in a slightly different way: the notion of 'having the same kind of sensation' is just as problematic, and raises the same philosophical questions, as the more specific notion of 'having a pain'. Yet the PP-theory helps itself to interpersonal uses of the former notion in its attempt to explain the interpersonal applications of the latter. And that begs the question. So it seems that the PP-theorist has no acceptable route from his supposed grasp of 'pain' as applied to his own case to an understanding of what the term means as applied to other people.

7   To conclude this chapter, we should briefly note that the attack on the PP-theory over the last four sections ultimately owes everything to the profound discussion of sensation concepts in Wittgenstein's *Philosophical Investigations*. A detailed treatment of Wittgenstein's work would, however, require two or three chapters

to itself; we must content ourselves with quoting a few illustrative passages which relate to some of the points we have been making.

Wittgenstein battles long and hard against the temptation we noted in the previous section – i.e. the temptation to say that we each fix which sensation we mean by 'pain' by (so to speak) pinching ourselves hard, introspectively noting how it feels and saying 'something like *that* is a pain'. He argues at length that this private baptismal ceremony can't in fact confer the required sense on a word like 'pain'. Some strands of this discussion have become known as the Private Language Argument (which is, of course, an argument *against* the very idea of a privately defined language of sensations). But the proper exegesis of this Argument is hotly disputed, and we had better avoid the interpretative morass by looking instead at another famous episode in the *Investigations* – namely the 'beetle in the box' argument, on which Hopkins's card story is modelled:

> If I say of myself that it is only from my own case that I know what the word 'pain' means – must I not say the same of other people too? And how can I generalize the *one* case so irresponsibly? Now someone tells me that *he* knows what pain is only from his own case! – Suppose everyone had a box with something in it: we call it a 'beetle'. No one can look into anyone else's box, and everyone says he knows what a beetle is only by looking at *his* beetle. – Here it would be quite possible for everyone to have something different in his box. One might even imagine such a thing constantly changing. – But suppose the word 'beetle' had a use in these people's language? – If so it would not be used as the name of a thing. The thing in the box has no place in the language-game at all; not even as a *something*: for the box might even be empty. – No, one can 'divide through' by the thing in the box; it cancels out, whatever it is.   (1953: §293)

Consider the PP-theory again: this, as we suggested before, is allied to the idea that we each use the term 'pain' to pick out the sensation defined by the introspected quality of our own experience – to pick out, as it were, the beetle found by taking a look in our own private box. But if this is how 'pain' is used, then who is to say that other people share the same sensation, have the same sort of beetle in their boxes? And so who is to say that other people mean the same thing by the word (how can we generalise so irresponsibly from just one case)? It looks as if 'pain', thus understood, could have no genuine public use: when other people use the word, we would have little reason to suppose we knew what they meant. Conversely, if the word is given the shared public sense which we certainly appear to give it, then it isn't being used as if to pick out a beetle in a private box.

Now, to repeat a point we made at the outset, rejecting the PP-theory in favour of functionalism (or some alternative) is rejecting a particular theoretical picture of what makes a sensation a pain. More precisely, it is to reject the idea that what makes something a pain is an introspectable property which is independent of its behavioural function. We are not denying that pains are painful: all we are denying is a certain bad theory about pains.

Let's try to make this last point absolutely clear. Someone could speak of the phenomenological property of painfulness just as a long-winded way of talking about the trite fact that pains hurt. But such ways of speaking are much more often bound up with a particular picture of sensations which assimilates pains to crying colours (as in Hopkins's story) or beetles in boxes (as in Wittgenstein): pains are identified by their phenomenological quality as revealed by a kind of inner vision, just as colours or beetles are identified by ordinary vision. And that picture, far from being trite or truistic, is deeply misguided. Pains are not inner somethings identified as such by an inward look at what can only be privately known to us, and about which we cannot really communicate. And their being painful, the functionalist will insist, is not their having some special property independent of their causal role in producing aversion reactions.

> 'But surely you will admit that there is a difference between pain-behaviour accompanied by pain and pain-behaviour without any pain?' – Admit it? What greater difference could there be? – 'And yet you again and again reach the conclusion that the sensation itself is a *nothing*.' – Not at all. It is not a *something* [i.e. not some thing recognised by introspection], but not a *nothing* either! The conclusion was only that a nothing would serve just as well as a something about which nothing could be said [like the beetle in a box].   (§304)

Yet such is the tenacious hold of the PP-theory on our imaginations that – despite everything we have said – Wittgenstein's conclusion here can still seem absurdly paradoxical: in denying that pains are inner things recognised by introspection he seems to be denying that we have pains at all.

> The paradox disappears only if we make a radical break with the idea that language always functions in one way, always serves the same purpose.   (§304)

We tend to suppose that a judgement like 'I have a pain in my knee' must work similarly to (say) the judgement 'I have arthritis in my knee' – as if in the one case we are identifying an inner mental something (the beetle in our box), and in the other case an inner physical condition, but in analogous ways. But we must not run the cases together. In the arthritis case, the judgement is indeed based on an act of recognition; one observes, assesses evidence, applies tests or criteria and thereby identifies the state. But in the pain case, as Wittgenstein puts it,

> what I do is not ... to identify my sensation by criteria, but to repeat an expression.   (§290)

The PP-theory would have it that we are observing and recognising an inner something with an immediate phenomenological property. But, as we suggested before, perhaps all that happens is that we can just 'repeat an expression' – i.e. say straight off, without relying on observational evidence at all, whether we are in pain or not.

There is very much more to be learnt from reflecting on Wittgenstein's discussion of sensations; our few quotations hardly hint at the depth of his investigations. But perhaps we have already said enough earlier in the chapter to achieve our central purpose – namely, to undermine the phenomenological theory of sensation. Of course, setting aside one rival theory is not in itself enough to vindicate a functionalist approach: there are plenty of problems remaining. They will be the topic of the next chapter.

XV

SENSATIONS:
FUNCTIONALISM AND CONSCIOUSNESS

1   At the beginning of the previous chapter, we sketched a rough outline of a functionalist account of pain. Pain – the suggestion went – is a physical state due to bodily damage or malfunction and which results in propensities to 'pain behaviour' (tears, moans, attempts to bring about the cessation of the state, and so forth). This theory faced a vigorous challenge from the initially attractive PP-theory. We therefore went on to argue at length that the PP-theory should be rejected. But fending off one line of attack is obviously not enough to substantiate a functionalist approach to sensations.

In particular, it might well be protested that we haven't yet dealt with the underlying worry about functionalism which makes the rival PP-theory initially attractive. For surely, the critic will say, it is the case that being in pain is a conscious experience in a sense that having a belief isn't. There is something which it is like, experientially speaking, to have a pain; but there is nothing that it is like to possess a given belief (see VIII.8). Yet this crucial difference between sensations like pain and propositional attitudes like belief is not reflected in our sketched functionalist theories so far. On the contrary, both pains and beliefs alike are simply treated as states that intervene between surface stimulations (of skin or eyes or whatever) and behavioural outputs. So isn't the functionalist theory of pain guilty of treating pains and beliefs too much alike, and ignoring the phenomena of conscious experience?

It is true, the critic might continue, that the discredited PP-theory fumbles the issue of consciousness. For that theory construes what we are conscious of as a special sort of quality – an 'immediate phenomenological property' – which floats free from the causal relations of pain. And if we allow painfulness to peel right apart from behavioural function, then how can we ever defensibly hold that someone else has a painful sensation associated with their 'pain behaviour'? An adequate theory must improve on the PP-theory by somehow dovetailing together the conscious aspect and the causal role of pain. This may prove difficult – but the trouble with a purely functionalist account, the argument concludes, is that it tries to dodge the problem by talking only about the causal role of pain and ignoring the key issue of consciousness.

2   This criticism demands a response, and in the next section we will begin to develop possible lines of reply for the functionalist. But first let's consider a cruder suggestion. It might be thought that we can very easily steer between the extremes of the PP-theory and the functionalist theory by offering a 'mixed' theory, which claims that a state counts as a pain if it has *both* the right phenomenological property *and* the right causal function. What is wrong with this simple-minded way of capturing both the experiential and the causal aspects of pain within a single theory?

Well, there are at least three problems with this procedure. (a) The mixed theory and the PP-theory share the idea of phenomenological properties – and it is recourse to this idea, with its associated introspectionist account of how we know about our own states of mind, which is arguably the fundamental mistake in this area (see XIV.3). (b) If you countenance the idea of phenomenological properties, then it is difficult to see how to prevent a mixed theory collapsing into the original pure theory. For suppose it is said that a genuine pain must both have the right phenomenological properties and also satisfy some extra condition (e.g. a functional one). This apparently means that someone could quite consistently have experiences with the right phenomenological properties – so they feel just like pains – but which aren't really pains because the extra condition for genuine pain isn't satisfied. And this implication seems very implausible: if something definitely *feels* like a pain then surely it *is* a pain! Hence, so long as a theory of sensations contains as an ingredient the idea that pains (for example) have an intrinsic quality of painfulness recognised as such by introspection, it is difficult not to take this phenomenological aspect as definitive of pain. Finally (c), a mixed theory is still going to have problems explaining how we can ever have strong grounds for saying of someone else that she is in pain – for what will warrant the claim that someone else's experiences have the right 'immediate phenomenological properties' to count as real pains?

The prospects for a mixed phenomenological theory are, in short, no brighter than those for the rejected pure version.

3   The critic of functionalism we imagined in §1 stressed two related differences between propositional attitudes like belief and sensations like pain. First, you are typically *conscious* of your pains in a way that you are not always aware of your beliefs: and second, there is *something that it is like* to be in pain but not something that it is like to have a belief. We will leave consideration of that slippery talk of what experience is like until §7, and we will begin by considering the equally slippery notion of consciousness.

The ordinary pre-theoretic concept of consciousness is a mess. A little of this mess can be tidied up by introducing a distinction between *intransitive* and *transitive* uses of the word, which we can indicate by using subscripts. Being conscious$_i$ is a matter of being awake, alert, non-comatose – thus, after she has had the operation, we may ask whether Jill has come round from the anaesthetic by enquiring 'Is she conscious$_i$ yet?' By contrast, being conscious$_t$ is being aware *of* something or aware *that* something is the case. Obviously, these notions are closely related: to be conscious$_t$ of something, you normally have to be conscious$_i$ – and conversely, you cannot normally be conscious$_i$ without being conscious$_t$ of the world. But even here things are a bit complicated. The sleep-walker who wends her way carefully downstairs and out into the garden is arguably conscious$_t$ of her surroundings in *some* sense although she is not fully conscious$_i$; and the brain in a vat (cf. III.2) is perhaps conscious$_i$ without being conscious$_t$, given that his experience is totally delusory and there is nothing suitable for him to be conscious$_t$ of.

This initial distinction, however, does not get us very far. Ordinary discourse hints at a sharp division between things having or lacking consciousness$_i$: we are tempted to suppose that the question whether something is conscious$_i$ or not admits of a simple yes/no answer. But there are problematic grey areas – consider the dreamer, the man in a trance or the sleep-walker again. And rather differently, the examples of various kinds of animals, from apes down to ants, also suggest that there are many kinds of intervening conditions between the consciousness$_i$ of a normal human adult and the brute unconsciousness of a stick or stone. Any attempt to impose a black/white distinction on the graduated facts here seems badly misguided (cf. IV.3).

The situation with our pre-theoretic notion of consciousness$_t$ is no better. Consider Jack who is driving home along a twisty country road while talking to Jill about the film which they have just seen. He swerves slightly to avoid a small rock fallen at the side of the road. His driving surely shows that he was conscious$_t$ of the presence of the rock (if he hadn't seen the rock, he wouldn't have swerved). On the other hand, Jack was absorbed in the conversation about the film, and if asked he might well say 'I wasn't conscious of anything unusual in the road' – and couldn't that remark also be understood as true? To avoid contradiction here we might try saying that 'at one level' Jack was conscious$_t$ of the rock, but 'at a higher level' he wasn't. Perhaps some such distinction between levels of consciousness belongs at the margins of our everyday folk psychology – but it is certainly not something of which we have any clear conception at all, nor do we feel much confidence in the supposed distinction.

Many philosophers have noted this unresolved messiness in our ordinary talk about consciousness. Dennett, for example, remarks that

> We *do say* that both people and animals are aware of things, that they are conscious or unconscious, that one can say what one is aware of or conscious of, and that one must be aware of something in order to recognize it. We do say these things, but we say them, even *ordinarily* (when not engaged in philosophical discussion) with misgivings. Our intuitions conflict when we are confronted with the crucial test cases. It is not merely that philosophers can generate confusions by misusing these words, but that the words in their most time-honoured uses are confused.   (1969: 130)

But if that is broadly correct, how should we proceed? Well, what is needed is evidently conceptual reconstruction rather than analysis of the inadequate concepts we already have. In other words, we need to construct some useful descriptive apparatus which will enable us to get a grip on the phenomena which are only poorly captured by our everyday talk of consciousness: and we should not expect or require our new descriptions to answer systematically to our pre-existing intuitions, because perhaps *nothing* consistently answers to those. Any way of reconstructing this area of discourse is likely to be counter-intuitive in some respect or other.

4   With that preamble, let's return to the claim that you are not continuously conscious of your beliefs in the way that you are continuously conscious of a raging toothache. There is plainly some truth in this claim; so we need to recapture this truth in a more satisfactory conceptual framework.

Let us begin, then, on the side of belief. Your belief that tigers are carnivorous, for example, is certainly not continuously forcing itself on your attention: months may go by without your being reminded of it. The belief is there, but mostly it lurks – so to speak – at the back of your mind. However, the belief can indeed be brought to your attention, you can (as we might say) become conscious of your belief. Maybe this awareness is prompted by someone asking you straight out whether you believe that tigers are carnivorous, and you can then answer 'Yes, I do believe that'.

Now, what is it to be conscious of your belief about tigers, when you *are* conscious of it? Well, consider the rather attractive idea that, just as you become conscious of something in the external world when you perceive it, so you become conscious of something in your mental world when you perceive *that* – so your conscious-ness of your belief is whatever is produced by your perception of it. This thought connects up with the now familiar idea that we have an 'inner sense' which provides us with knowledge about our own states of mind by directly producing reliably true beliefs about them (see XI.3, XIV.3). And we have already argued that, so long as we do not assimilate inner sense too closely to vision, this hypothesis should be congenial to a functionalist. Putting these ideas together gives us the following first shot at reconstructing the notion of consciousness of a belief: your consciousness of your belief that tigers are carnivorous is the state produced by perceiving that belief via inner sense, i.e. it is the state of *believing that you believe* that tigers are carnivorous.

Unfortunately, this can't be quite the whole story – for couldn't there be the following kind of case? Jack has the belief that tigers are carnivorous tucked away (as we say) at the back of his mind. He also has acquired, by a suitable causal route, the further belief that he believes that tigers are carnivorous, where this extra belief is now also lodged at the back of his mind. Even allowing for our shaky grasp on the notion of consciousness, it hardly seems very plausible to suggest in *this* case that Jack is currently conscious of his belief about tigers! How can having two beliefs stored away at the back of one's mind, passively waiting to be used, possibly constitute being actively aware of one of them? Of course, this worry is couched in metaphorical terms, yet it seems a genuine one: so we apparently need to complicate our first shot at an account of consciousness. However, on any view of belief we probably will need to develop some kind of distinction between the bulk of one's beliefs which are stored away waiting to be used, and the minority of beliefs which are actively in play at a given time, affecting one's current mental processes and guiding current behaviour. And with this distinction to hand, let's say – as a second shot – that (in one good sense) to be conscious of your belief that tigers are carnivorous involves having the *actively* deployed belief that you have that belief. More generally, to be conscious of a mental state ϕ is to have the activated belief that one has ϕ.

Now, this idea of consciousness is constructed from the notions of (a) an inner sense leading to (b) the acquisition of beliefs about one's state of mind, combined with (c) a distinction between stored beliefs and actively deployed beliefs. And the crucial point to note is that this construction only uses ingredients available to the functionalist. We have already argued that (a) and (b) involve nothing inimical to functionalism: and (c) obviously invites clarification in functionalist terms because the suggested distinction is precisely a distinction between the comparative causal roles of dormant and active states. We will therefore dub this notion of awareness which we constructed out of functionalist-approved ingredients *consciousness$_f$*.

Note, by the way, that some other uses of the notion of consciousness invite analogous treatment using the same materials. Consider Jack's driving again: he was conscious of the rock in the road in the sense that he saw it – he acquired the belief that there was a rock there, an active belief that guided his behaviour at the time. However, he did not acquire the (activated) belief that he saw the rock – which is why he says that he wasn't conscious of anything unusual. Here, Jack's lack of the 'higher level' of consciousness seems to correspond to a lack of appropriate knowledge about his own passing state of mind. As with consciousness$_f$, the crucial ingredient of the 'higher level' of awareness which is missing in Jack's case seems to be knowledge about one's own state of mind. Other cases of lack of consciousness can also be dealt with similarly. Jill's desire to hurt her mother is unconscious in the sense that she doesn't believe that she has that unpleasant desire – in fact she believes that she definitely lacks it. Again the crucial element here is the missing belief about her own state of mind.

5   We have suggested that a central strand in the pre-theoretic notion of consciousness is naturally reconstructed as consciousness$_f$, defined in terms of the idea of having (activated) beliefs about one's own state of mind. Now, turning back to the case of pain, why not say that consciousness of one's pain is also at heart a matter of consciousness$_f$? In other words, to be conscious of one's pain is also to have an (activated) belief that one is in pain. There remains the question of the distinction we noted between pains and beliefs, which we can now put this way: one is continuously conscious$_f$ of one's pains as one is not continuously conscious$_f$ of one's beliefs. But perhaps this is only to be expected for good Darwinian reasons:

> A successful type of animal, one which can look after itself, must have a sensory mechanism which will signal events likely to damage it and the signals must have priority over all others. ... It must be a sensation to which we cannot manage to remain inattentive and one which we feel compelled to bring to an end as soon as possible.   (Adrian 1947: 29)

In creatures such as ourselves, who can aspire to reflexive beliefs about our own states, beliefs about our pains will be pressed urgently upon us in a way that beliefs about our beliefs are not. It doesn't matter if the bulk of our beliefs remain unnoticed most of the time, for most of them will indeed be irrelevant to current happenings. But warnings of bodily damage or malfunction are not the sort of thing that one should readily be able to ignore; it is biologically important that we should continuously be conscious$_f$ of our pains.

A word of warning: philosophers sometimes slide from talk of 'having a pain', via talk of 'feeling a pain', into talk of 'being conscious of a pain', treating these as mere verbal variants of each other. This is thoroughly dangerous and should be avoided, as it suggests that having a pain involves a special kind of thing or quality to which we stand in a relation of inner awareness – which is just the line of thought that encourages the disastrous PP-theory. So let us make it absolutely clear that we are *not* equating consciousness of pain in that very misleading philosopher's sense with consciousness$_f$. In other words, we are not equating merely having or feeling a pain with having the activated belief that one has a pain. On the contrary, having or feeling a pain is one state and consciousness$_f$ of the pain is a second and distinct state involving a belief about the first state.

6   But isn't there a problem here? If there *are* two distinct states – the pain and the belief about the pain – then even if they normally go together don't we face the real possibility that they could come apart? In particular, aren't we committed to acknowledging the possibility that someone should *believe* that she is in pain while not *being* in pain? And doesn't this flatly contradict the traditional doctrine that we cannot possibly be in error about our own states of mind?

There is indeed a conflict here, but it is traditional doctrine which must give way. In fact, as a general thesis about the mind, the doctrine has little attraction left. Consider the case of belief again. We have noted before that our thoughts about our own beliefs are not normally based on inspection of the behavioural evidence. But the judgements we reach are still *answerable* to the behavioural evidence. We may sincerely think that we believe that *p*, but our other behaviour can speak loudly against this. Of course, we usually get things right: but people can sometimes be seriously deluded about their own beliefs – it might need a psychotherapist, for example, to reveal to Jill what she really believes about her mother. Our beliefs about such states of mind are open to correction by others – they are, in a word, corrigible. The same goes for our beliefs about our own desires and other propositional attitudes.

But even if we have to reject the general thesis that we are infallibly correct about our own states of mind, perhaps we can retain the more restricted thesis that we are infallibly correct about our own sensations. It might be argued that first-person judgements about sensations (like those about beliefs) are again not based on inspection of the publicly available evidence, but this time there is no way of overturning what we think by reference to such evidence. If someone sincerely thinks that she is in pain then, the argument goes, there can be no question of our overriding her belief and proving that she is not really in pain. (Imagine the dentist saying, in response to her complaints of agonising toothache, 'No you are not: there's nothing wrong here!') In short, then, first-person judgements about our own sensation states are incorrigible.

Even this limited argument should, however, be rejected. It is just not true that self-ascriptions of sensations are incorrigible. Consider, to use a well-worn example, the man being tortured who expects another searing pain. Suddenly, his tormentors briefly place a few ice cubes on his back. Their victim feels them and screams. He certainly *thinks* there was a stab of pain. But was there really? Knowing what actually happened, couldn't the tormentors mock their poor victim, and truly say '*that* didn't hurt'? Later, the man could perhaps become so terribly confused that it could be said of him 'he doesn't know *what* he is feeling any more'. The normally reliable linkage between the victim's sensations and his beliefs about his sensations has broken down under stress.

Here is another case. You have been suffering from recurrent toothache, which has been giving you disturbed nights. Then one night you vividly dream that you have the toothache again, and are in the dentist's chair: the dentist is approaching, about to start drilling without an anaesthetic ... You wake up with a start, rub your jaw, and say 'That damned toothache again!' But after a moment or two you realise with relief that tonight the tooth is *not* playing up, it was all just a dream. For a while when you first awoke you thought you were in pain; but you were mistaken.

Such cases are, of course, the exception rather than the norm. But they are enough to show that our beliefs about our own sensations are not infallible: here, as elsewhere, pre-existing expectations can lead our judgements astray. It remains true that first-person self-ascriptions are generally reliable in ordinary cases. But that is no problem for the functionalist: there is no reason why the causal mechanism he postulates to explain our knowledge about our own states of mind shouldn't have the required degree of less-than-perfect reliability – it is only the notion of absolutely perfect reliability that could cause trouble for him (because no physical mechanism of the kind a functionalist would countenance can be absolutely perfect). It is also true that our thoughts about our own pains are usually *more* reliable than judgements about our own beliefs or desires. But again there is no obvious reason why the functionalist shouldn't accommodate this point too, and provide a Darwinian explanation of why that should be so.

7   To summarise: We sketched at the outset an anti-functionalist argument that turned on the idea of consciousness. But we then suggested that the pre-theoretic notions of consciousness or awareness are something of a mess, needing active reconstruction rather than passive analysis. And as a first step towards an improved understanding of this area we have introduced the notion of being conscious$_f$, which involves having an activated belief about one's mental state. By construction, this notion of consciousness$_f$ is entirely respectable from a functionalist point of view. And further, we have suggested that the functionalist can also happily allow that we should normally be continuously conscious$_f$ of our pains in a way that we are not continuously conscious$_f$ about our own beliefs or desires. We might also note that the consciousness$_f$ of our pains doesn't in any sense float free from the causal aspects of pain – rather it is the same state whose presence we are conscious$_f$ of and which is defined functionally in causal terms. It seems, then, that at least some of the facts about consciousness which we imagined being invoked in an argument against functionalism can after all be accommodated by the resourceful theorist. So are there other aspects of the notion of conscious awareness which will prove more recalcitrant to a functionalist treatment?

Well, at this point let's bring into play that other troublesome idea which we imagined the anti-functionalist deploying, namely the idea that there is something which it is like to experience a particular sensation. Consider, then, the following argument which turns on this idea.

(N)   Suppose that you are given an account of the causal role of some sensation S. You are told in detail what typically brings about this sensation, and what its typical effects are. Perhaps you are also told something about the overall structure of the physiological mechanisms which are in play when sensation S is experienced. Suppose, in short, that you are given all the ingredients for a physicalist/functionalist story about sensation S. But surely, there is something else which also has to be fixed by a full account of what sensation S is, and which isn't a matter of the sensation's function, namely *what it is like to experience S*. Imagine for a moment that S is a sensation felt by Martians: then no matter how much physiological and functional information you acquire, you won't learn the absolutely crucial thing about S, which is how it consciously feels! A story about the causal role of sensation S and its associated physiology doesn't tell you what it is like, as far as experiential awareness is concerned, and so the physicalist story cannot by itself give an adequate account of its nature. Generalising the point: physicalism hasn't the resources to provide an adequate theory about sensations.

This particular line of attack against functionalism – labelled (N) in honour of Nagel 1974 – has undoubted appeal. At first sight, however, the appeal seems closely connected with the lure of the PP-theory. Indeed, if one thinks of knowing what it is like to have a pain as a matter of awareness of the 'immediate phenomenological property of painfulness', then the new line of thought coalesces with the old.

Still, proponents of the new line are wont to insist that, in using the tricky locution 'knowing what it is like to experience S', they are innocent of any flirtation with the discredited PP-theory. Their claim is that a more innocuous everyday understanding of the phrase is enough to carry argument (N). But is this so? Let's grant that there is indeed a good everyday sense of the phrase in which it is reasonable to say that the congenitally blind man doesn't know what it is like to see red. Or, to take Nagel's case, let's grant that it is correct to say that human beings don't know what it is really like ('from the inside', so to speak) to get around the world by using bat sonar. However, as we shall now show, these common-sense concessions need cause no difficulties for a broadly functionalist account of sensation.

Let us consider the history of Jill who – we will suppose – understands a fully worked-out story about the causal role of the human sensation S, and also (if you like) understands the associated neuro-physiology. However, at the outset of our tale, she has as yet not experienced the sensation herself. She can use her knowledge about the typical causes and effects of S to attribute the sensation to other people, but she has had no occasion to attribute it to herself. So at this stage, to use the phraseology of argument (N), Jill presumably doesn't know what S is like, experientially speaking: we might say too that she doesn't yet *fully* understand the term 'S'.

After a while, however, Jill does begin to have sensation *S* from time to time. But at first she fails to recognise it as such. Perhaps she doesn't consciously notice that the same experience has recurred on a number of occasions, or maybe she just thinks of it as 'that odd feeling I sometimes have'. At this intervening stage in the story, it continues to seem correct to say that (in the appropriate sense) Jill hasn't yet realised what *S* is like.

Then one day the penny drops. Jill has the sensation *S* again, and says to herself – 'Good heavens! I'd never realised it before, but I seem to have that queer feeling in just the situations mentioned in my physicalist account of sensation *S*. So *that* must be sensation *S*. I'd never paid it much attention before, but how very peculiar it feels, now I come to concentrate on it!' For a time, perhaps, Jill has to continue relying on clues from the surrounding physical context when she self-ascribes sensation *S* (so we might say 'she hasn't yet *fully* appreciated what *S* can be like'). But after the occasional false start, Jill learns to identify straight off the occasions when she is suffering *S*, without relying on the attendant circumstances. At this final stage of the story, Jill presumably does know what *S* is like, and fully understands talk of such sensations. For what more could possibly be required of her? After all, by this point she is in the same relation to her *S* sensations as we are to our pains – except that she also has a theory about them. And we, by hypothesis, do know what our pains are like.

At the beginning of this tale, we said, Jill doesn't know what sensation *S* is like. And at the end of the tale, in some quite ordinary sense, she *does* know this. What has happened in between? Two things: (a) Jill first started to have sensation *S*, and (b) Jill then learnt to identify a sensation as *S* straight off, without relying on facts about its causes and effects. In other words, she has (a) had experiences, and (b) acquired a bit of practical know-how. *But these obviously can't be captured in a theory of sensation, for they aren't bits of information.* It's no objection to an account of sensation *S* that grasping the account won't actually *give* you the sensation. And likewise, it's no objection that grasping the account – whatever it is – won't instantly enable you to say when you have the sensation. Learning to know when you have a particular sensation may take practice. For example, the blind man who has his sight restored surely won't be able to sort out the red things immediately, however great his prior theoretical knowledge about colour perception.

So the situation is this. It is true that grasping some physicalist/ functionalist theory about sensation S won't give Jill what she needs, if she is to count – in a quite ordinary sense – as fully knowing what S is like. However, this is no shortcoming in the theory, since no theory at all could give Jill what she needs. What Jill lacks at the beginning of her history is not more information that might be supplied by a non-physicalist theory of sensation S (whatever that could be). What she lacks isn't information but – as we said before – the experience and know-how which no amount of information can provide.

In summary: Argument (N), as it stands, goes wrong in presupposing that 'knowing what S is like' – in the special sense of that phrase which is in play – is a question of knowing some sort of *fact*. If you make this crucial assumption, then indeed it seems to follow that we are dealing with some special kind of 'subjective' fact which cannot be accommodated by a functionalist (or more generally, by a physicalist) theory of sensations. Thus Nagel, for example, speaks here of 'phenomenological facts' which perhaps cannot be stated in any human language – and so certainly cannot be captured in a physicalist's theory (1974: 441-2). But the crucial presumption behind all this is false. Knowing what S is like is not knowing some bit of information, and talk of what S is like should not be misconstrued as talk of a special subjective kind of fact.

Finally, it must be admitted that defenders of Nagel-style arguments will be unhappy with all this. They will want to protest that there remains an important sense of that troublesome phrase 'knowing what S is like' which *does* sustain an anti-functionalist argument. The suggestion is, in effect, that you can understand this phrase in a way that doesn't involve the PP-theory conception of 'immediate phenomenological properties', but is nevertheless stronger than the everyday notion we have just been analysing in a way compatible with functionalism. The issue is still one of hot controversy: all we can do here is record our view that a convincing case for the claim that there is a middle path has yet to be made out.

8   In this chapter, we have made two moves in response to the use of the notion of consciousness in attacks on a functionalist account of sensations. First, we suggested that one key strand in our everyday notion can be reconstructed as consciousness$_f$, which is

defined in functionalist-approved terms. Second, we have seen that the functionalist can make some good sense of talk of knowing what sensation *S* is like in a way that again preserves key pre-theoretical intuitions. Of course, fending off these attacks doesn't show that functionalism can provide a complete and philosophically adequate account of the 'conscious experience' of pain. But perhaps it is safe to say that the functionalist approach to sensations by now seems distinctly more promising than it did at the outset.

We cannot pursue the finer details of this approach any further here. But before leaving the topic, there is one last general point we should discuss, which concerns the relation between a functionalist theory of pain and a type identity theory.

In our discussion of belief (XI.6), we suggested that there is no good reason to suppose that two people who believe that it is about to rain must be in the same neuro-physiological state. In other words, there is no reason to expect a neat correlation between types of belief-state and types of neural state as picked out by scientific descriptions. Now, by contrast – it might well be argued – two people who have the same sort of pain *will* broadly share some common state of the nervous system. And can't physiologists tell us a lot about what this state is? They do important work (which is of course intended to apply to human beings quite generally) on the specific nerve-structures involved in different sorts of pain. On a more mundane level, isn't the assumption that different people's pain sensations have a common physical basis involved in the everyday practice of your local dentist? He takes it that the same physical intervention will have the same result in everybody, e.g. a local anaesthetic injected just *there* will stop the pain while he does the dental repair on a lower left molar.

If we follow this line of thought, then it is tempting to build into our functionalist account the assumption that the same physical type of state is involved in all cases of pain. This would give us roughly the following theory:

> Jack is in pain if he is in that distinctive physiological type of state (whatever it is) which is typically produced by bodily damage or malfunction, and which in turn typically produces a propensity to reactions like tears and moans, and a propensity to aversive behaviour.

The suggestion is that this state can be given a general physiological description – according to an embarrassingly popular philosopher's myth, it is the state of *having one's C-fibres firing*. We can now make an identity claim: being in pain just *is* having one's C-fibres firing (or whatever). But why not now treat this claim as the basic account of what pain is, without going round the houses via the functionalist theory? In short, why doesn't the type identity claim here supersede the functionalist theory? Maybe we need to be functionalists about beliefs, since there are no type identities to be had here: but where a simpler identity theory is available, shouldn't we prefer it?

There are three objections to this. First, there is no reason to think that there is some distinctive physical state always involved in the experience of pain. Of course, there are events in the *peripheral* nervous system which are standardly involved (including the philosopher's favourite, namely one's C-fibres firing). But these can occur without pain being experienced: for everything depends on what happens when the signals from the peripheral nervous system get to the brain. And here the situation is extraordinarily complex. It certainly isn't the case that we have a unique 'pain centre' in the brain: on the contrary 'the thalamus, hypothalamus, brainstem reticular formation, limbic system, parietal cortex, and frontal cortex are all implicated' in the experience of pain (Melzack 1973: 93). And such is the variety of types of pain, and such is the plasticity of the brain, that it is quite implausible to suppose that there is *any* general correlation of the kind 'whenever someone is in pain, he is in a physical state of the particular type *S*'. In short, the imagined type-identities are not available.

Second, even if there were some type-identities to be stated for the human case, they would be of limited interest: they couldn't tell us about pain in general. For remember that the physiology of non-human creatures that feel pain is significantly different: so – even waiving our first point – there is no likelihood of there being any interesting, cross-species, correlations between feeling pain and particular types of states identified in physical terms. Again it follows that there are no general type-identities available.

Third, and most importantly, even supposing that there were some true universal claim relating pains and types of physical state, it would be a bad mistake to interpret this claim as giving a theory of pain which might in some way supersede the functionalist theory. Rather the position is this: the identity claim would tell us about the physical constitution of pain states (tell us their 'matter', so to speak). But we could still ask what makes these states count as cases of being in pain. In other words, there would remain the philosophical task of specifying the 'what it is to be what it is' of pain. And this fundamental task of analysing what makes something count as a pain state is, in our view, accomplished by a functionalist account.

XVI

THINKING

1   The verb 'to think' – with its cognates 'thought' and 'thinking' – covers a wide variety of mental activities, states and conditions. We must begin with some distinctions.

At its simplest and least puzzling, talk about people's thoughts can be a mere stylistic variant for talk about their beliefs. Why did Jack collapse so inelegantly on the floor? – because he thought there was a chair behind him. And why did Jill open the tin marked 'sugar'? – because she thought it contained sugar. We could equally well have said 'because he believed ...' or 'because she took it that ...'. In these cases, we may suppose, the thought was not reflectively entertained. Jack didn't deliberate about the position of the chair (maybe that's what got him into trouble). Again, as we might put it, Jill *unthinkingly* thought that the tin contained sugar. The air of paradox in this description is merely superficial: there is of course no real oddity in the idea that someone's thoughts on a subject, in the sense of her relevant beliefs, may be reached and held without any reflective or deliberative processes.

We have already discussed the nature of belief at length in Chapters X to XII. Our main concern in this chapter is with the contrasting processes of discursive, deliberative thought. More precisely, we want to get a bit clearer about the sort of thing that the mathematician does as he puzzles over his problem, or the amateur carpenter does as she works out how to get her shelves to stay up, or the cook does as he plans the menu. Unlike holding a belief, thinking of this sort is indeed a process, i.e. a series of goings-on spread over time, which could perhaps be stopped in mid-course. (It makes no sense at all to say 'I was interrupted half-way through believing that I must buy some eggs'; but it does make good sense to say 'I was interrupted half-way through thinking out tonight's menu'.) This process is usually an active one: you can decide to engage in it or to desist, and you can intentionally

223

guide its course — as when you say to yourself 'I'll try out this idea and see where it gets me ...'. Again, unlike holding a belief, such thought processes are typically conscious. If you are busily thinking out tonight's menu then you are normally continuously aware that this is what you are currently doing; you are not in the same way aware of all your beliefs. You probably haven't consciously noted your belief that zebras are striped since we last reminded you of it back in Chapter X; but you have held that belief all along.

Let's fix on the term 'discursive thought' to refer to the sort of processes which we have just been describing. As we said, such processes — which are arguably distinctive of the human mind as contrasted with the minds of lower animals — will be our main concern here. We don't mean to imply, though, that there is a very sharp distinction between these cases and other kinds of thought: and it will be instructive to begin by considering another instance of thought which apparently contrasts both with plain belief and with ·discursive thought. So we turn first to what might be called 'thought as intelligent attention'.

2　　　Suppose Jack is driving along rather carelessly, not paying due attention to the road: you say, 'For heaven's sake, think what you are doing!'. Or Jill hands you the sugar bowl at tea, and you say, 'You're not thinking! I gave up sugar months ago'. Or your partner at tennis misses an easy shot he should be able to play quite well; exasperated, you say 'Come on, keep your mind on the game!' Here, what is missing from Jack's performance (and Jill's and the tennis player's) is a certain concentration on the task in hand: you want Jack and the others to keep their wits about them, to pay attention and perhaps use some intelligence.

Now, what is the difference between doing something with thought, with intelligent attention, and doing it without thinking what one is doing? This was a favourite question of Gilbert Ryle's, and he gives a most persuasive account of the type of difference involved here. Consider the tennis player, for example: what does his thinking amount to? Well, *not* in

> musing, meditating, pondering, deliberating, ruminating, reflecting or being pensive save in the unoccupied intervals between rallies, games or sets. While he is engaged in the game, with his mind on the game, he mostly is *un*reflective or *un*pensive. He is not in a brown study, nor even

in a series of fleeting brown studies: the tennis-player's thinking almost consists in his whole and at least slightly schooled attention being given to, *inter alia*, the flight of the ball over the net, the position of his opponent, the strength of the wind, and so on. His quick and appropriate responses to what occurs around him on the tennis-court show that the player is concentrating.   (1968: 211, with deletions)

The thoughtful tennis player is not doing two things at once, outwardly running and hitting the ball and inwardly cogitating: there aren't two separable performances such that one could have the thinking without the running and hitting. Rather, the player is doing one thing, i.e. playing tennis, and doing it in an intelligent and attentive manner. He is careful not to offer easy chances, he is quick to exploit chances offered to him, he intelligently positions himself on the court – and this attentiveness is obviously not separable from his playing. Ryle makes a parallel point for the case of thoughtful driving:

> Driving with care is not doing two things, as driving with a song is. I can stop driving and go on singing, or vice versa. I can do the one well and the other badly; the one obediently and the other disobediently. But I cannot stop driving and go on exercising traffic-care. In obeying your command to drive carefully, I am not conjointly obeying two commands, such that I might have disobeyed the first while obeying the second.   (1968: 213)

You can't have the attentive care without the driving, any more than you can have the grin without the Cheshire Cat. The cat counts as grinning, not in virtue of there being a mysterious associated entity ('a grin'), but in virtue of the manner in which its features are currently arranged. Similarly, the player and the driver count as thinking what they are doing, not in virtue of there being a special process of 'thought' going on behind the scenes, but in virtue of the manner and setting of their overt performances.

In this sort of case, then, to say that someone is thinking is – very broadly speaking – to characterise the manner of some activity (be it driving, playing tennis or whatever). The difference between performing an activity with thought and performing it without is a difference in overall style and setting: it *isn't* a difference in the number of things being done at once. Ryle compares talk of thinking in this sense with talk of hurrying. For again, to say someone is hurrying is to characterise the manner of his activity – walking, eating, writing, singing, driving or playing tennis. Plainly, to walk hurriedly is not to do two things at once, walking and hurrying, such that you could do the second without the first: likewise, to hurry through a meal consists in speedy eating, not in some extra activity going on simultaneously with the eating and which could be done independently. In short, hurrying is not an activity in its own right, but a manner of doing something else. Ryle claims that it is the same for many cases of thinking; to describe someone as thinking what he is doing is not to mention an autonomous activity separable from the driving or the tennis playing, but is a way of characterising the style of his performance.

Of course, much more needs to be said by way of specifying the particular styles of performance that count as thoughtful, and the mental contexts which make thoughtful activity possible. For example, the tennis player can only count as attentive towards his surroundings if his incoming perceptual beliefs are suitably rich, and are engaged in his playing. But let's not get bogged down in detail. The crucial point to grab hold of is that – in some cases at any rate – to talk of thinking is not to talk of an inner process running in parallel with some other activity, but to talk of the style and context of that activity itself. We will find that this point has a wider application.

3   Thinking, in the Rylean sense of intelligently attending to the job in hand, is not a uniquely human accomplishment. The lioness may hunt her prey with a deadly attentiveness, intelligently alert to the demands of the chase. The good sheepdog, like the shepherd, keeps her mind on the business of rounding up the sheep, the bad one is easily distracted and shows less intelligence and foresight. But there is, of course, a big distinction between *this* sort of thinking which the sheepdog and the shepherd alike can exhibit, and the sort of reflective, discursive thinking which is also available to a man, but not to his dog. So let's turn now to consider the distinctively human capacity for discursive thought processes.

Suppose that you are trying to solve a mathematical puzzle, or are working out a menu, or composing a talk on philosophy, or are otherwise engaged in deliberative, discursive thought. Even if you are doing this by yourself, without co-operating with others, you might well find it helpful to express your thoughts overtly, by jotting down notes or by talking aloud to yourself. You may in the mathematical case try various symbolic manipulations on paper to find how things turn out. In the case of preparing your talk, you may rehearse sentences aloud to see whether they run smoothly – these could roll out in neat, ready-to-type paragraphs, or much more likely it will be a gappy effort peppered with incomplete sentences and many restarts. Now, when you are shuffling symbols around on paper, we can reasonably describe you as thinking out the problem on paper. And when you compose the discourse on philosophy by talking to yourself, then we can say that you are thinking aloud. But in both cases the overt performances seem unnecessary. You could have done the thinking, not on paper or aloud, but 'in your head'. Admittedly, this can be difficult: the mathematician sometimes won't get very far without his scribblings. Still, this would seem to be a contingent failing, not an essential feature. The discursive thinking which you do overtly could surely, at least in principle, be done covertly, in the privacy of your own mind. In summary: you can engage in reflective, discursive thinking either with or without jottings on paper or uttered speech – there may or may not be an overt performance involved.

We will concentrate first on the cases of discursive thought which *do* involve some public activity of speaking or writing. This might initially seem a perverse strategy – why not go straight to the central cases of purely private thought? Our roundabout route will, however, prove fruitful: in particular, it will help us to separate issues which can otherwise easily get muddled. So to repeat, our initial question will concern the nature of *overt* processes of thought.

Now, despite the common-sense observation that it is often difficult to think through a problem without (say) jotting down some notes, it remains immensely tempting to suppose that the public aspects of the performance are in some way an optional extra and the thinking itself is *always* an internal process. The difference between thinking aloud and thinking in one's head is (we are tempted to say) the difference between switching on and switching off an outward accompaniment to an underlying inner process – and it is this inner process which always constitutes the thinking itself. Wittgenstein noted the attractions of this picture:

> Is thinking a kind of speaking? One would like to say it is what distinguishes speech with thought from talking without thinking. – And so it seems to be an accompaniment of speech. A process, which may accompany something else, or can go on by itself.   (1953: §330)

Consider again the case where you think through your philosophy aloud: what makes this a case of thought? Surely, the argument goes, it can't simply be that you utter certain words – a parrot might do that, and what we are interested in is precisely the difference between you and a parrot. So the inevitable inference seems to be that the difference between you and the parrot is something else that goes on behind the scenes, something that accompanies your words, but doesn't accompany the parrot's utterances. And this essential inner accompaniment, which could have occurred all by itself, is the real thinking.

Let's dub this theory about the difference between your talk and the parrot's the *inner accompaniment theory*: and let's next ask what kind of thing, according to this theory, is the essential inner process which must accompany thoughtful overt speech.

4   How are we to proceed? Well, another temptation can beguile us here, which is again noted (though certainly not endorsed) by Wittgenstein: we are inclined to suppose that

> in order to get clear about the meaning of the word 'think' we watch ourselves while we think; what we observe will be what the word means. (§316)

And if we try to catch ourselves in the process of thinking, what do we notice? Nothing physical, we want to say: when engaged in thought, we surely do not observe the operations of neurones or any other relevant physical processes. A Cartesian argument becomes dangerously inviting: since the notion of thought is quite different from the idea of any physical process, we must necessarily understand the one as quite different from the other. And thus we quickly arrive at the dualist idea that thinking is an incorporeal process.

We should immediately point out, of course, that the Cartesian argument just sketched is invalid. It does not follow from the premise that our *ideas* of thinking and of any physical process are distinct that thinking itself isn't a physical process (cf. III.7, XIV.3). The dualist conclusion is thus without adequate support; and it also faces a battery of queries and problems. For example, where do the supposed incorporeal processes of thinking take place? How can they enter into causal relations with the physical world – as deliberations surely do when they lead to action? Do these incorporeal processes march in step with the physical speech activity they may accompany or can they go much faster than speech? Can they occur unnoticed? And so on.

It is not simply that these questions have yet to be answered: there seems to be no way they *could* be answered. It is not as though we know what incorporeal processes are, and are just having some difficulties in giving a detailed account of those processes which are cases of thinking. The difficulty centres on the very notion of an incorporeal process itself: it is a notion that fails to do any real work, and is more a cloak for ignorance than anything else. Wittgenstein puts it succinctly:

> Thinking is not an incorporeal process which lends life and sense to speaking, and which it would be possible to detach from speaking, rather as the Devil took the shadow of Schlemiehl from the ground. – But how 'not an incorporeal process'? Am I acquainted with incorporeal processes, then, only thinking is not one of them? No; I called the expression 'an incorporeal process' to my aid in my embarrassment when I was trying to explain the meaning of the word 'thinking' in a primitive way. (§339)

In summary: as we would expect by this stage in our discussion of the mind, the idea that thought is an incorporeal process should be firmly resisted.

5   We are considering the theory that the difference between your contentful thinking aloud and the parrot's echoing your utterances is that there is in your case a parallel process of inward thought accompanying the outward speech. Trying to avoid the temptation to go in a dualist direction, what can we say about this putative inner process?

Very little, it seems. Indeed, such supposed parallel processes seem peculiarly elusive. Wittgenstein challenges us to try the following experiment:

> Say a sentence and think it; say it with understanding – And now do not say it, and just do what you accompanied it with when you said it with understanding! (§332)

If the inner accompaniment theory is correct then you should easily be able to strip off the overt utterance from a case of thinking aloud and repeat the essential thinking by itself: but this seems difficult, to say the least. Of course, you can echo the overt performance of thinking aloud with the covert performance of running through the same words in your mind. But it would surely be quite wrong to say that *this* sort of inner process is what accompanies all cases of thoughtful speech. First, it is experientially false to say that every time you think aloud you are simultaneously running through the same words in your mind (is this trick even possible?) Second, it would be a theoretically useless manoeuvre to try to differentiate your original thoughtful performance from the parrot's by saying that you are concurrently rehearsing the same words in your mind – for inner speech can be as contentless as outer speech! Suppose, for instance, that Jill learns a Japanese poem by heart, without acquiring the slightest idea what the words mean. When she rehearses the poem, could she still claim that she is engaged in significant discursive thought on the grounds that she is accompanying her recital with a simultaneous recital of the same words under her breath? Of course not. She is merely parroting the Japanese words, and no amount of inward parroting of the same words can possibly change the situation.

Wittgenstein's challenge, then, seems unanswerable: and we can make a connected, more general point. Just as it is non-explanatory to try to account for perception in terms of an inner process of 'seeing in the mind's eye', or for action in terms of an inner act of will, it is again entirely non-explanatory to try to account for thoughtful speech in terms of an accompanying inner process of thought. For we will still be left with the question of what it is about this supposed covert process which makes it a case of *thought* as opposed to something else. And this is a question of the very same kind as the one we started off with, when we asked what makes a given overt performance count as an instance of thought.

If all this is correct, the inner accompaniment theory is in dire trouble.

6   We need therefore to reconsider the difference between your thoughtful speech performance and the parrot's thoughtless gabbling. And the differences are manifold. For a start, as you think through your talk on philosophy, you understand the meaning of the words you use – unlike the parrot, and unlike Jill when she

recites her poem. Again, your performance is intelligently directed to certain ends, in particular towards the acquisition of new beliefs: you want to discover exactly what are the right things to say on your chosen topic. The parrot, however, just squawks to get a peanut; and while Jill's purposes may be more complex – perhaps she wants to impress Jack – she is not engaged in a reflective project of discovery. In short, then, your performance is distinguished from the parrot's and from Jill's by your background capacities and purposes. This suggests the following view: what makes your linguistic performance a case of thinking aloud is not that it is accompanied by a parallel process which is the real thinking. Rather, it is the setting, the context and – in a very broad sense – the manner of the performance that counts.

This is, of course, all highly reminiscent of Ryle's remarks about what might at first sight have seemed to be a quite different kind of case. Driving thoughtfully, he said, is not distinguished from driving without thought by being accompanied by some other process which is the thinking itself. Likewise, discoursing thoughtfully (we have just suggested) is not distinguished from mere parroting by being accompanied by a parallel process of thought. In each case, the thought is not a separate process from driving or discoursing: rather it is the context and manner of the driving and the discourse which makes them both exemplify thought.

This account of (some instances of) thought can initially seem counter-intuitive, so let us pause to make it absolutely clear. We are *not* denying that there can be internal processes of thought: the mathematician can choose to do his calculation in his head, for example. But consider the case where someone calculates aloud (to stay with that example). Then what we are denying is that this overt performance counts as a case of thinking aloud because it is accompanied by a parallel inner calculation, or by some other inner process which is the *real* thinking. On the contrary, the overt juggling with figures counts as exemplifying thought because it is done with understanding and with intelligent purposes. And understanding what one says is not a matter of accompanying one's words with an inner running commentary (or we will again be faced with the question of how we understand *that*) but is a matter of one's ability to use and respond to uses of the words. Calculating thoughtfully is thus rather like driving thoughtfully: what matters are the setting and manner of the performance together with the abilities which are in play.

7   Our arguments over the last four sections have mainly concentrated on just one kind of case of discursive thought which involved thinking aloud. We must now widen the scope of the discussion, and we really need to do this in two directions. First, there are cases of thought which involve public performances other than overt speech. Second, there are of course all the cases of purely private discursive thought.

But before turning to these cases, let's pause to note a general point arising from our discussion. In the examples we have discussed, the overt talking or vocal juggling of numbers count as processes of thought because of (a) the agent's purposes in engaging in these performances, together with (b) his understanding of the sounds used. This is very schematic, but one thing is immediately clear: there is nothing here which is inimical to our general functionalist approach to the mind. We have already argued at length that such an approach can cope with the fact that agents have intentions and purposes in their actions, so (a) requires no new discussion. As for (b), the agent's understanding what he does or says, this indeed deserves extensive investigation. The question of what it is for signs to mean something, and for agents to understand them, is the central question for the philosophy of language, and is the topic of some of the best and most subtle work in the whole of contemporary philosophy. We cannot even begin to explore the issues here, except to say that again there need be no special difficulties in this area for the physicalist. Whatever the fine details, words in some way have meaning in virtue of being used for such purposes as the expression of beliefs or desires; and understanding their meaning involves knowing how to use the words and symbols for such purposes, and respond to uses by others. So the ideas of meaning and understanding swim in the same conceptual orbit as notions such as purpose, belief and desire. But these latter notions can be accommodated in a functionalist framework; hence – even in advance of any close investigation – it is entirely reasonable to expect that the ideas of meaning and understanding can also be fitted into the same framework.

So far, then, our treatment of thought seems entirely in keeping with our general functionalist perspective. But, as we said, the discussion now needs to be opened up in two directions. Fortunately, the extension of our approach to cover non-vocal cases of overt thought introduces no radically new issues, and hence no new problems for the physicalist: we need not delay over it. Consider, for instance, the mathematician who jots down symbols on paper instead of reciting his calculation aloud. His writing displays thought, but not necessarily in virtue of any concurrent processes. The difference between him and a child who doodles the same shapes is not that the mathematician is engaged in some duplicate activity behind the scenes. It is once more the context of understanding and the intelligent purposiveness of his activity which makes the difference. The same general approach should allow us to cope with other cases of public discursive thought.

The cases of purely private discursive thought, however, do present us with some new problems. We imagined your composing aloud a discourse on philosophy: but you could have done this in your head. Likewise our mathematician could perhaps have done his symbolic manipulations mentally, if they were not too complicated. And more mundane thought, like arranging a menu, is quite standardly done in one's head. So what is involved in such cases of purely internal thought? And what is the relation between thinking something aloud or on paper and thinking just the same thing privately?

On the discredited inner accompaniment theory, the second question at least was easily answered: for on that theory thinking something publicly and doing it privately involve exactly the *same* inner process of thought occurring, either with or without an associated outward performance. But on the Ryle/Wittgenstein account, the speaking or the writing (or whatever occurs in the public case) *is* the thinking. So the processes which constitute the thinking in the public cases must, by hypothesis, be absent in the cases of inner thought. But then, in such cases, what does constitute the thinking?

There is undoubtedly a troublesome question to be answered here: but it is extremely important to see that it doesn't uniquely concern the nature of internal discursive thought. The issue at stake is much more general, and concerns the relation between doing something overtly and doing it in one's head, whether it be rational reflective thought or anything else. Consider, for example, humming a tune out loud and running it through in one's mind. In most cases, humming a tune would not be said to involve reflective thought: but it is still something that can be done either overtly or covertly. So the question about the relation between public and private performances cuts right across the question of the nature of discursive thought. There can be inner activities which are not cases of reflective thought, and cases of thought which are not inner activities. Wittgenstein memorably suggests that we should try to separate out the two issues by imagining 'people who could only think aloud (as there are people who can only read aloud)' (1953: §331). With respect to such people, the question of the nature of their inner performances would fall into abeyance: but we would still be left with the independent question of the nature of thought.

In order to clear up the question about the nature of inner discursive thought, therefore, we need to say something about the quite general problem of what it is to do something in one's head as opposed to overtly.

8   Let's very briefly review the position which we have reached. Our target is to get clearer about the nature of the sort of inner reflective thought processes which are arguably distinctive of the human mind. We have now suggested that our enquiry really decomposes into two separable sub-problems, questions that can easily be muddled if one concentrates only on the case of private thought. First, what makes a process count as one of discursive reflective thought whether it is overt or covert, outer or inner? And second, what is the relation between doing something publicly and doing it in one's head? If we can sketch an answer to each of these questions which is compatible with our overall physicalist/functionalist view of the mind, then this will enable us finally to scotch the Cartesian suggestion that private rational thought must be an incorporeal process. We have made some progress towards answering the first of our two questions in a way consistent with functionalism. So what of the second question?

Consider again the example of running through a familiar tune in your head. What goes on in such a case? There are presumably some relevant brain-processes, maybe even some discernible twitches in one's vocal cords. But that only specifies the matter of the process: what of its form in Aristotle's sense – i.e. what makes those physical processes *count* as running through a tune in one's head? In earlier discussions we have found it helpful to elucidate the form of a mental happening in terms of its causal role. So let's try the same tack here: let's try saying that a brain-process counts as running through a tune in one's head by virtue of its causal role. Now, this raises the question 'what *is* its role?' And the obvious way to answer this is indirectly, by comparison with the case of humming or singing aloud. In other words, the suggestion goes, a process counts as running a tune through in one's head because it has many of the same causes and effects as running the tune through out loud. On the cause side, the same musical knowledge and the same memories will be in play whether the tune is hummed aloud or run through silently. And on the effect side, there seem to be roughly the same results either way, as far as the consciousness of the agent himself is concerned. If he sings aloud, then as a causal consequence he hears a tune, which involves – on our general theory of perception – an uptake of information, broadly construed. If he runs through the tune under his breath, then he again acquires much of the same information: he reminds himself vividly and in detail of the way the tune goes, so that he can perhaps (for example) now answer questions about the tune much better than he could before the inner performance.

This treatment of the particular case of running a tune through in one's mind obviously generalises: let's say, as a rough account, that an internal process counts as ϕ-ing in one's head if it has sufficiently many of the same causes and effects as ϕ-ing publicly. On this sort of theory, a process counts as thinking through a philosophical problem in one's head, for instance, if it is of a kind that has for the agent sufficiently many of the same causes and effects as would thinking through the problem out loud. We should take 'causes' here generously, to include the causal setting of the performance (the agent's purposes and capacities for understanding), and the relevant effects will largely be the acquisition of new beliefs. Likewise, a process counts as working out a mathematical problem in one's head if it has a sufficiently similar causal role to working it out on paper.

Note, by the way, that you *perceive* the overt performance of (say) working out on paper how much paint you need. Indeed, there would be no point in doing the written calculation if you couldn't see how the figures worked out: you acquire beliefs about the amount of paint you need by acquiring beliefs about the process of calculation itself. Hence given that doing the problem in your head has similar causal powers, we should expect that you will again acquire beliefs about the needed quantity of paint via acquiring beliefs about the course of the calculation. But this requires you to have beliefs about the mental process of calculation – so in the jargon of XV.4, you will be conscious$_f$ of your mental performance. Thus it naturally falls out of our account that mental arithmetic or other inner discursive processes will involve, in a good sense, conscious thought.

Our little theory of what is involved in φ-ing in one's head has evident attractions; but for current purposes, its most significant feature is that it is entirely congenial to the physicalist. The processes which constitute internal thought will be, for him, like the processes that constitute overt thought, at least in being straightforwardly physical; there is certainly no need to invoke any mysterious incorporeal processes. What makes these internal happenings count as thought is a question of their causal role, and this is something which can be described without recourse to any Cartesian mysteries.

9   We have argued in §7 that the general distinction between processes which exemplify discursive thought and those which don't can be captured in broadly functionalist terms. In §8 we then argued that the distinction between doing something overtly and doing the same thing in one's head can also be accommodated within the same framework. By combining these two accounts, we reach a physicalist theory of the initially worrying case of internal discursive thought.

Now, we certainly haven't covered in this chapter every sort of case which falls under that protean term 'thought'. But we conjecture that the general approaches which we have adopted can be developed to cover other cases too. And we are tempted to conclude with a much bolder speculation. Let's acknowledge that there are many kinds of mental phenomena which we have not discussed and will not be treating in this book (e.g. emotions, moods, memory). All the same, given that our general functionalist approach can cope with things as disparate as sensations and discursive thought, it now seems plausible to claim that the approach will work across the board. In other words, we suggest that there are no mental phenomena that will in the end prove recalcitrant to our style of physicalist theory.

XVII

REASONS AND CAUSES

1   In the previous chapter, we argued that what makes a bit of discourse (overt or covert) count as an instance of thought is a matter of its setting – more specifically it is a question of the purposes which are in play and the capacities for understanding which are engaged. We intentionally left it vague how the relevant purposes and capacities relate to the discourse, but it would be entirely in keeping with the spirit of our earlier discussions to take the connections here to be *causal* ones. A bit of discourse (or symbol-shuffling, or piano-playing, or whatever) counts as exhibiting thought because it has the right kind of causes.

The notion of causality has been crucially woven into our theory of the mind ever since we endorsed a causal account of perception in Chapter VIII. Then in Chapter IX we arrived at the following view: intentional actions are things done for reasons in the light of which the agent's behaviour is comprehensible – in other words, an intentional action is something done because of appropriate beliefs and desires. It is entirely natural to take this, too, as a causal theory which identifies actions as events *caused* by beliefs and desires. This interpretation fits neatly with the position we reached in Chapter XII, where we argued that beliefs and desires are physical states identified precisely by their causal function in producing behaviour. Our argument surely implies that the relation between actions and the mental states which explain them must indeed be a causal one. Again, causality plays a crucial role in the functionalist theory of sensations sketched in Chapter XV.

Some philosophers would argue, however, that our whole approach has been misguided. In particular, they would claim that it is a mistake to give the notion of causality a pivotal role in the philosophy of mind. Their anti-causal arguments have been directed mainly against the thesis that a person's reasons are the causes of his actions. So in the present chapter, we will try to go

237

some way towards repelling attacks from this quarter: this will also give us the opportunity to make some points that will prove useful in our discussion of free action in the final chapter.

2   Consider for a moment the following two claims:
(A)   Jill blushed because she suddenly realised that Jack was trying to seduce her,
(B)   Jill left the party early because she suddenly realised that Jack was trying to seduce her.

We can all agree on two initial points about this pair. First, (A) reports an undoubtedly causal relation between Jill's sudden thought and her consequent blush; her thought led, by some causal mechanism or other, to the blush. Second, while we can loosely say that both (A) and (B) give the reason why something happened, putting it this way obscures an important difference. (B) gives Jill's reasons for leaving; it explains something that she intentionally did. By contrast, (A) does not give Jill's reasons for blushing – for the blushing was something that happened to her, outside her control, and not something she did with a purpose. In short, it is true both that (A) makes a straightforwardly causal claim, and also that (B) is an importantly different sort of claim from (A). Can we infer, then, that (B) is *not* a causal claim? Well, not that easily! – it could be that the difference between (A) and (B) is simply a difference between two species or types of causal statement.

Now consider the following claims:
(B)   Jill left the party early because she suddenly realised that Jack was trying to seduce her,
(C)   Jill's limbs moved thus-and-so because such-and-such neural events occurred,

where we imagine the description of Jill's bodily movements in (C) to be completed so as to fit the action mentioned in (B). This time, therefore, we have two claims which are in some sense about the same happening, but which propose notably different kinds of explanation for what occurred. (B) offers an explanation within the framework of everyday folk psychology, while (C) offers a purely physical explanation. These are undoubtedly different kinds of explanation, in the sense that they appeal to different sets of explanatory principles. So could we argue as follows: (C) involves a simple causal 'because', (B) offers a different kind of explanation

XVII: Reasons and Causes

from (C), and hence (B) does not involve a causal 'because'? Well again, we cannot show so easily that reasons are not causes – it could be that the difference between (B) and (C) is once more a difference between two species of causal statement.

The moral is simple: we cannot baldly infer from the fact that the rational explanation of action is not like some other kinds of causal explanation that it must itself be non-causal.

Here is another argument. Causes must precede their effects: so causal explanations are in a sense backward-looking – they explain happenings by reference to other things that occurred earlier in time. But now consider a claim like

(D)   Jack is going into the pantry because he wants a beer.

This, it seems, is simply equivalent to

(E)   Jack is going into the pantry for the purpose of getting a beer.

And (E), it might be said, doesn't even *appear* to be a causal claim any more. For there is nothing backward-looking about (E): on the contrary, it explains Jack's behaviour by mentioning something in the future, namely his getting a beer. In short, genuine causal explanations are backward-looking, while explanations by reference to someone's desires are forward-looking. Hence desire explanations are not causal explanations, and so desires cannot be the causes of action.

This too is a terrible argument. Suppose we grant that (D) is equivalent to (E) – though the point is debatable. Let's also allow that there is a sense in which (E) is forward-looking. What we must firmly reject is the suggestion that the sense in which (E) is forward-looking is incompatible with its being a causal claim. After all, the agreed equivalence between (D) and (E) makes it absolutely clear what the forward-looking character of (E) actually amounts to. It is just that (E) explains Jack's behaviour by reference to his desire for a beer, and this desire is, like most desires, directed towards the future – which is simply to say that Jack desires that he *will* very shortly have a beer. But although it is directed towards the future, the desire itself of course exists right now, just before Jack acts. Jack's desire, his having a purpose in mind, precedes his action: so – at least as far as the time factor is concerned – it could be a cause.

3   Causal explanations, to repeat, explain happenings by reference to something else that occurred earlier in time. An event and

its cause must therefore be distinct occurrences. Suppose, for example, that we ask why the bridge fell down (i.e. what caused it to fall). Perhaps the bridge collapsed because it was struck by a hurricane, or because some well-placed explosive was detonated, or because a herd of elephants stampeded across it, or ... . Each putative explanation mentions some earlier event distinct from the collapse of the bridge, and claims that this other event was responsible for the collapse. Quite plainly we are not merely being given a fuller description of the collapse itself. On the contrary, the explanation relates the collapse to a different happening and says that the one event caused the other.

This simple point that cause and effect must be distinct occurrences has suggested to some philosophers a third line of argument against the thesis that reasons are causes. This argument, as we shall see, rests on the claim that typical explanations of action do not mention any event distinct from the action itself; and it is inferred that these explanations must therefore be non-causal. The argument turns out to be doubly mistaken.

First, let's expound the argument quite uncritically. Suppose Jack is waving his arm out of the window as he drives along: somewhat mystified, you ask what's going on, and get the answer 'Ah, he's signalling a left turn; he still uses those old-fashioned hand-signals!' Now, this reply may well explain Jack's odd behaviour, and it explains his behaviour by making it clearer exactly what he is up to. We thought that he was aimlessly flapping his arm: it now turns out that he was signalling. Looked at in the first way, Jack's behaviour was puzzling: looked at in the light of the fuller description of his action as 'signalling a left turn' the mystery evaporates. We will call an explanation which merely offers us a fuller description of what the agent is doing an *explanation by redescription*. Explanations of this kind are very common. Jill is writing her name twenty times over: what on earth is she up to? Signing her day's correspondence, testing out a new pen, seeing whether the paper is good enough for writing letters on, or ...? It seems that in order to resolve the mystery we again need an explanation by redescription. But such a redescription of what Jill is doing is in no way a causal explanation, for it doesn't mention any event distinct from the action itself.

In summary then, we have two contrasting styles of explanation – explanation by means of fuller description of the event itself, and genuine causal explanation which necessarily also refers to other states or happenings. The explanation of human action typically involves the former, non-causal style of explanation. And hence the reasons which are mentioned in such explanations cannot be causes.

So much for exposition; now for criticism. The most obvious difficulty with this argument lies in its final assumption: it is taken for granted that an explanation of an action by reference to the agent's beliefs and desires falls squarely into the class of explanations by redescription. But this presumption only has to be explicitly stated to be seen to be false. Suppose we say, for example, that Jack went to the pantry because he wanted a beer and believed that the beer was in the pantry. In this case we are quite evidently *not* merely redescribing Jack's behaviour, and that behaviour alone: rather we are linking this stretch of behaviour with two other things, a desire and a belief, and claiming that these two other things were jointly responsible for the behaviour. To put it another way, this explanation – unlike a pure explanation by redescription but like a causal explanation – does indeed mention distinct occurrences. Hence, even if many other explanations of action are non-causal because they are simply explanations by redescription, this fact is simply irrelevant to the thesis that reasons are causes: the explanation of an action by reference to the agent's reasons plainly involves more than mere redescription of that event itself.

There is another weakness in the argument. Suppose you point to a child's spots and ask, in worried tones, 'what are they?' The doctor reassuringly explains that there is nothing to worry about – 'They are just a heat rash'. Now we might say that, in a sense, all the doctor has done here is give a redescription of the spots. But of course, her remark encapsulates a diagnosis; these spots are *caused* by heat rather than a measles infection. So the explanation by redescription here is itself implicitly causal. This illustrates an important general point: what appears on the surface to be a mere redescription of an event may very well encapsulate a causal claim. It is therefore simply a mistake to suppose that there are really two radically different modes of explanation, explanation by redescription and causal explanation. Consider again our earlier example, where we explained Jack's arm-waving behaviour by saying that he is signalling: if it is to be true that Jack is signalling a left turn, must it not be the case that his wavings spring from (roughly speaking) a desire to signal a left turn together with the belief that *this* sort of wave will do the trick? So why shouldn't we say that even the redescription of someone as signalling makes certain implicit claims about the causes of his behaviour? Like the heat-rash case, the explanation by redescription here – far from being positively non-causal – is itself arguably a disguised causal explanation. An appeal to this sort of case will therefore not be enough to demonstrate the supposedly non-causal character of the explanation of action.

4   For the rest of this chapter, we will be discussing a fourth, and much more interesting, argument against the thesis that reasons are causes. This argument, which is often dubbed the *Logical Connection Argument*, will also be found to be open to serious objections. But this time we should perhaps signal at the outset that the many issues at stake here are still hotly debated: we will have to be content to examine just a few early stages of an important on-going dispute.

The Logical Connection Argument has two premises which we might call *Hume's Principle* and the *Logical Connection Thesis* respectively. Both these premises need explanation to make them comprehensible and plausible. So we will devote this section to explaining Hume's Principle (without critical comment), and §5 to elucidating the other premise. Then in §6 we will put them together to produce the Logical Connection Argument.

What is it for one event to be the cause of another? We have already touched on this question in IV.5, but our discussion there was very inconclusive. We considered, but in the end rejected, the idea that wherever there is causality there is an underlying causal mechanism at work. Let us therefore return again to basics – which means, in this case, to Hume's classic discussion of causality.

Hume starts by pointing out that if we carefully observe a situation where, as we would say, a cause produces an effect we will in fact perceive nothing more than one event *followed* by another.

> When we look about us towards external objects and consider the operation of causes, we are never able, in a single instance, to discover any power or necessary connection, any quality which binds the effect to the cause and renders the one an infallible consequence of the other. We only find that the one does actually in fact follow the other. The impulse of one billiard ball is attended with motion in the second. This is the whole that appears to the *outward* senses.   (*Enquiry* VII.1)

Now, Hume of course realises perfectly well that when one says that an event *C* causes another event *E*, one means something *more* than that *C* happened and then *E* happened afterwards. But what more? Hume's answer emerges in the following passage (which we have slightly abbreviated in order to eliminate an irrelevant distraction).

> Here is a billiard ball lying on the table, and another ball moving towards it with rapidity. They strike; and the ball, which was formerly at rest, now acquires a motion. This is as perfect an instance of the relation of cause and effect as any which we know. Let us therefore examine it. It is evident that the motion, which was the cause, is prior to the motion, which was the effect. *Priority* in time, is therefore a requisite circumstance in every cause. But this is not all. Let us try any other balls of the same kind in a like situation, and we shall always find, that the impulse of the one produces motion in the other. Here therefore is [another] circumstance, *viz.* that of a *constant conjunction* betwixt the cause and the effect. Every object like the cause, produces always some object like the effect. Beyond these circumstances of priority and constant conjunction, I can discover nothing in this cause. The first ball is in motion; touches the second; immediately the second is in motion: and when I try the experiment with the same or like balls, in the same or like circumstances, I find, that upon the motion and touch of the one ball, motion always follows in the other. In whatever shape I turn this matter, and however I examine it, I can find nothing farther. (*Abstract*)

In short, then, if the particular event *C* is to be the cause of *E*, there must be a quite general pattern of *C*-type events being followed by *E*-type events.

This central Humean claim fits in well enough with many of our ordinary ways of thinking about causality. For instance, suppose that someone doubts whether your pressing the switch was the cause of the bell's ringing: the first thing to do in order to persuade her is to press the switch a few more times. If the bell continues to ring every time then this will show that the original sequence of events wasn't a mere coincidence. Other things being equal, we would all be strongly inclined to agree that pressing the switch does indeed cause the bell to ring (even if we can't yet see how the two can be connected). The existence of a *general* correlation between events of the two kinds is taken to be an essential mark of a causal link. Consider another example: suppose you are trying to discover the cause of a particular disease. Then you wouldn't be content to locate factors which seem to be roughly associated with it: you want to isolate something (a virus, a poison, a neural degeneration or whatever) that is *always* associated with the disease.

It is rather tempting to agree with Hume, therefore, that an assumption of constant conjunction is built into our conception of causation. To put the point more formally: it is a necessary condition of an event C being the cause of another event E that these two events fall under some true universal law which says that if an event of the first kind occurs then an event of the second kind will always follow. So, for example, if it is to be true that on a certain occasion applying heat caused this particular metal rod to expand, then there must be a background general law which covers the case, e.g. the law that all metal expands when heated.

Hume adds to this basic point about constant conjunction a very important rider. The universal covering laws which back up particular causal claims are laws whose truth is to be established by experience: they cannot be established by pure reflection (unlike, say, logical or mathematical laws). Consider again the example of the billiard balls:

> Were a man, such as Adam, created in the full vigour of understanding, without experience, he would never be able to infer motion in the second ball from the motion and impulse of the first. It is not anything that reason sees in the cause, which makes us infer the effect. No inference from cause to effect amounts to a [logical] demonstration. Of which there is this evident proof. The mind can always conceive any effect to follow from any cause, and indeed any event to follow upon another: ... but wherever a demonstration takes place, the contrary is impossible and implies a contradiction.   (*Abstract*)

What Hume means here is this. Suppose we *could* conclusively demonstrate (i.e. logically prove by pure reasoning without appeal to experience) that if C happens, then E will happen. Then it would be a logical absurdity to claim 'C happened but E did not follow'. But while that claim may be false as a matter of fact, it is never a logical absurdity: on the contrary, the mind can always conceive without contradiction of C happening and any event at all following next.

> There is no demonstration, therefore, for any conjunction of cause and effect. It would be necessary, therefore for Adam to have *experience* of the effect, which followed upon the impulse of these two balls. He must have seen, in several instances, that when the one ball struck the other, the second always acquired motion. If he had seen a sufficient number of instances of this kind, whenever he saw the one ball moving towards

the other, he would always conclude without hesitation, that the second would acquire motion. (*Abstract*)

Adam's appreciation of the constant conjunction between impulse and movement can only be gained through experience. Generalising, we can say that all our beliefs in constant conjunctions are necessarily justified by appeal to experience rather than by pure reflection. Let's say that an *empirical* truth is one which cannot be established by pure reflection independently of experience: then Hume's second point is that covering laws about constant conjuctions are, in this quite familiar sense, merely empirical. We should note, by the way, that Hume actually held what is arguably a stronger thesis, namely that causal laws are *contingent* – i.e. they are not necessarily true, but only happen to obtain. But as we noted before (XIII.7) it is a matter of some current dispute whether empirical truths – i.e. things that can only be established experientially – have to be contingent. Fortunately we needn't tangle here with the metaphysical notion of contingency, and can concentrate on the less contentious idea that causal laws are empirical in the sense indicated.

In summary, we can state Hume's Principle (as we will be calling it) as follows. If it is true on a particular occasion that event *C* caused event *E*, then there must be some general law relating *C*-type events to *E*-type events – and further, this general law must be, in the sense just explained, an empirical truth.

5   We will leave for the moment the question whether Hume's Principle is in fact true, and turn next to the Logical Connection Thesis.

Suppose we explain Jill's action of opening the window by saying that she did so because she wants some fresh air in the room and believes she can get it simply by opening the window. Without pre-judging the issue whether this 'because' is a causal 'because', we can ask what general principle of explanation is being used here. For obviously enough, in advancing this explanation of Jill's action, we imply that there is more than just a once-off, idiosyncratic relation between Jill's belief and desire and her action on this particular occasion. On the contrary, we are plainly employing some *general* truth about how beliefs, desires and actions interrelate: the question is 'what is the relevant general truth?'

Now, we have touched on this question before, in XII.1, where we suggested that the Fundamental Principle at stake is something like this: if someone desires that *p*, and believes that *p* will come about only if she does *X*, then (in the absence of countervailing desires) she will tend to do *X*. There are two important points to make about this principle. The first point we noted in XII.3 – namely that this common-sense principle is very imprecise, and there doesn't seem to be any way of sharpening it up to make it absolutely clear-cut. Perhaps it is true that if Jill desires that *p* more than anything else, and thinks that *p* will come true only if she does *X*, then she will do *X* *so long as nothing untoward happens*. But there would seem to be no clear way of specifying all the different sorts of untoward happenings which can muck things up. Jill might suddenly faint, or suffer paralysis or a cerebral haemorrhage. Or, without any obvious malfunction of the brain, she may suffer one of those curious lapses in attention or rationality which occasionally affect us all. It seems, therefore, that the best we can hope for is some general truth relating reasons to actions which is qualified by the vague clause *barring unusual physiological or psychological mishaps*.

Another way of putting this same point is as follows: the Fundamental Principle relating beliefs and desires to action does not state (and cannot be sharpened up into something that does state) a *constant* conjunction between reasons and actions.

The second point to make about the Fundamental Principle concerns its status. Does it report an empirical matter of fact which can only be established by experience, or is it open to demonstration by reason alone? Is the principle an empirical one or is it perhaps true by definition? In XII.3 we suggested it is plausible to hold that the second option is the correct one. Suppose that Jill believes that doing *X* is required to achieve *p*, but she has absolutely no tendency at all to do *X*. Then would it make sense to go on to say that, despite this, she desires that *p* more than anything else available? It is very tempting to say that this doesn't make sense at all. By definition (as one might say) if you desire that *p* more than anything else then this is to be in a state which will produce actions of a kind you think will make *p* true. We don't have to do empirical experiments to determine whether people try to fulfil their strongest desires: simple reflection on the very concept of a desire is enough to show that this must be so. There is, in other words, a logical connection (and not merely an empirical one) between beliefs, desires and the appropriate actions.

Of course, it is an empirical question whether Jill has this belief or that desire – that question has to be settled by experience, by looking at what she does and says. To repeat: what isn't empirical, or so it seems, is the pattern of *connection* between her beliefs, her desires and her actions.

All this might suggest the truth of what we can call the Logical Connection Thesis. In so far as there are general principles involved in the explanation of action by reference to an agent's beliefs and desires, these principles are *not* empirical truths about constant conjunctions. They are principles about the logical connections between concepts, and quite unlike Humean covering laws.

6   We can now put the two premises of our argument together. First, we have Hume's Principle. If it is true on a particular occasion that event C caused event E, then there must be some general law relating C-type events to E-type events – and further, the general law must be empirical. Second, we have the Logical Connection Thesis. The general principles relating reasons to action are neither strict universal laws (being only expressions of tendencies) nor are they empirical. Instead, they express logical connections. But if we accept both these premises then it seems to follow that reasons cannot be causes. For consider again the claim that Jill opened the window because she wanted fresh air and believed that she would get fresh air by opening the window. If this is a genuine causal claim then – by Hume's Principle – the cause and effect here must fall under an empirical general law. But – by the Logical Connection Thesis – there are no empirical general laws relating reasons to actions. Hence that claim about Jill is not a causal claim. In other words, Jill's reasons for her action are not the cause of her action.

Unlike the arguments which we examined at the beginning of the chapter, this one (the Logical Connection Argument) is worth taking seriously. We will show in the next section, however, that the argument is invalid: even if we accept both premises, we are not committed to accepting its conclusion. But before showing that, it is worth pausing to point out some difficulties in accepting the premises as they stand.

First, consider Hume's Principle again. This principle, at least in its present form, seems to be very dubious. Which isn't to say that a particular statement of the form '*C* caused *E*' can be true in the absence of *any* backing truth about general causal tendencies. The point is that the required backing truth needn't have the Humean form of a *universal* law relating *C*-type events to *E*-type events. For, given the complexity of the causal factors that can affect the course of events, there is liable to be *no* true universal correlation between *C*-type events and any other type of event; any specified regularity can be upset by further intervening causal factors. Consider Hume's billiard balls again. True, the impact of one ball on another is usually followed by motion of the second ball – so long as the latter isn't glued down, or simultaneously hit from the opposite direction, doesn't explode or evaporate, and so on. In other words, the law about colliding billiard balls apparently needs to include some clause to the effect that motion will ensue *other things being equal*. Generalising, the best we can usually say with respect to some pattern of events is that, *other things being equal*, *C*-type events are followed by *E*-type events. Or as John Stuart Mill puts it:

> All laws of causation, in consequence of their liability to be counteracted, require to be stated in words affirmative of tendencies only.
>
> (*System of Logic*: III.x.4)

On the face of it, this point eliminates one of the alleged distinctions between causal explanation and the explanation of action by reference to the agent's reasons. It now turns out that in neither case do we employ strictly universal laws: in both cases the relevant general principles are 'affirmative of tendencies only'.

Still, it might be argued that there remains the other distinction between the two cases. In the causal case the general principles in question are empirical, whereas in the case of the explanation of action, the principles are (roughly speaking) true by definition. But again, this supposed contrast is open to serious question. For a start, there are very general grounds – though we cannot investigate them here – for being suspicious about that alleged distinction between the 'empirical' and the 'true by definition'. And even if one *is* happy with the general distinction, it is far from clear that the principles involved in the explanation of action are non-empirical. As we have already remarked in Chapter XII, the Fundamental Principle standardly functions in the explanation of action in conjunction with other principles, and these other principles *do* typically seem to be empirical principles which are not true by definition. Consider again the Consequence Principle, as we called it: the range of application of this principle – i.e. the question of what sorts of connection human beings are normally capable of making between their beliefs – surely has to be settled by experience.

However, all this is preliminary skirmishing. There are perhaps reasons to be sceptical about the premises of the Logical Connection Argument in its present form; but it would take us too far afield to launch into an investigation of the relevant issues here. So let us now, for the rest of the chapter, give the benefit of the doubt to defenders of the Argument, and proceed on the assumption that the premises are, despite our doubts, true. What we now need to show is that, even if the premises are true, the desired conclusion still does not follow.

7   Suppose that on page 5 of *The Times* there is a report of a hurricane; and on page 13 of the *Guardian* there is a report of the collapse of a bridge. Then it may well be true that the event reported on page 5 of *The Times* caused the event reported on page 13 of the *Guardian*. But quite obviously, not even the most committed Humean would want to say that this causal truth requires there to be a universal covering law relating page 5 events to page 13 events *described like that*! It would be daft to expect there to be any law running 'All events which are reported on page 5 of *The Times* result in events reported on page 13 of the *Guardian*'. If there is a law relating the two events in question, it must be framed in quite different sorts of terms.

It is scarcely less implausible to hold that there are strict universal laws relating hurricanes to bridge collapses, described in those rough, common-sense terms. If there are relevant laws to be had – as the Humean supposes there must be – then they will be couched not in terms of 'page 5 reports' or 'hurricanes', but in much more precise terms concerning pressure-gradients, structural rigidity and the like. Putting the point more generally, a defender of the Humean Principle must allow that causal laws may often be framed in quite different terms from the particular everyday causal statements they support.

This point, as Donald Davidson has argued, is enough to sabotage the Logical Connection Argument. Consider again the claim that Jill opened the window because she wanted fresh air and believed that she would get fresh air by opening the window. If this is a true causal claim then the cause and effect here must fall under an empirical general law (by Hume's Principle: remember that for the sake of the present argument we are assuming that this is true). And – by the Logical Connection Thesis, which we are also temporarily assuming to be true – there are no empirical general laws couched in psychological terms relating reasons to actions. But so what? The most that this shows is that the laws relating a particular belief and desire to an action are not themselves framed in everyday psychological terms. *It doesn't follow that there are no laws at all relating Jill's particular state to her action.* We have just seen that it is a common occurrence for the law which backs up a particular causal claim to be framed in very different terms from the original claim: why shouldn't that be the case here? In short, then, we cannot conclude that the claim about Jill isn't a causal one.

Still, if that claim is to be construed as causal, then according to Hume's Principle there must be *some* law relating the states which are Jill's belief and desire to her consequent action: and what sort of laws are these? Well, in Chapter XII it was argued that beliefs and desires are *physical* states which count as being beliefs or desires in virtue of having characteristic roles in producing behaviour. So, on this view, it will be true that Jill's belief and desire caused her action if the relevant *physical* states of her brain were responsible for the relevant stretch of behaviour. Now, we can expect that any strictly universal covering law relating the particular physical cause and effect here will certainly *not* be couched in everyday terms but in complex neuro-physiological terms. If there are Humean laws relating reasons to actions they will not be framed at the relatively superficial level of everyday talk but at a more sophisticated scientific level. Davidson puts it like this:

> The laws whose existence is required if reasons are causes of action do not, we may be sure, deal in the concepts in which [the rational explanations of action] must deal. If the causes of a class of events (actions) fall in a certain class (reasons) and there is a law to back each [particular] causal statement, it does not follow that there is any law connecting events classified as reasons with events classified as actions – the classifications may even be neurological, chemical, or physical.
>
> (1963: 17)

In summary: the fact that there are no *psychological* laws relating reasons to action doesn't mean that there cannot be some *other*

type of law relating a particular belief and desire to an action. So –
as far as Hume's Principle is concerned – beliefs and desires could
still be causes of action.

Why does all this matter? What is the point of pursuing the
debate whether beliefs and desires are or are not strictly speaking
the causes of action? Well, as we noted at the outset, there is a
general issue at stake here concerning our view of the role of
causality in the overall theory of the mind. We have therefore tried
in this chapter to fend off one major line of attack against our
approach. But the issue about reasons and causes is also of crucial
importance in the context of debates about the nature of human
freedom. And that brings us to the last topic we will be discussing.

XVIII

CAUSALITY AND FREEDOM

1   We begin with three reminders. First, it is a deeply entrenched presumption of science that all physical changes are to be explained entirely in terms of physical causes. To use the terminology of IV.6, where we discussed and endorsed this idea, the physical world is 'causally closed'. Immaterial causes are not to be contemplated: rather, physical changes – with the exception of any entirely uncaused random happenings – are brought about by antecedent physical events, in accordance with the laws of physics.

Second, we humans belong to the physical world, at least in the sense that there is no more to our make-up than ordinary organic stuff. Hence our bodily movements, being just so many more physical events, must themselves have entirely physical causes. For example, a particular arm movement is caused by muscular contractions which are triggered off by events in the peripheral nervous system whose causes can in turn be traced back to highly complex neural events. For further light on the workings of individual neural cells we naturally look to their biochemistry, which is ultimately underpinned by the fundamental laws of molecular physics.

Third, we have claimed it as a virtue of our broadly functionalist account of the mind that it allows us to speak of mental states while still acknowledging that we are (as far as our matter is concerned) purely physical beings. There is, for instance, no incompatibility between saying that a certain arm movement has purely physical causes and saying that it is caused by a desire, because on our view desires *are* physical states.

However, this kind of reconciliation of physicalism with a part of our everyday folk psychology seems to many philosophers not to take us very far. They argue that there are other crucial elements of our everyday ways of talking about each other's actions which cannot be squared with the idea that our behaviour is entirely brought about by physical causes. Consider, in particular, our

252

practice of holding people responsible for their actions, of blaming them for their wrong-doings and praising them for their good acts. This practice seems an ineliminable part of our moral outlook; it seems inconceivable that we should abandon it. Yet surely, the argument goes, people can only be held accountable for their actions if they are genuinely free agents, capable of choosing between alternative courses of action. So if our mental states and our actions are physical happenings, and like everything else in the physical world are bound into a nexus of causes and effects, then how can there really be room for the crucially important notion of free action?

This worry has been very clearly expressed by Isaiah Berlin, who writes that

> unless we attach some meaning to the notion of free acts, i.e. acts not wholly determined by antecedent events or by the nature and 'dispositional characteristics' of either persons or things, it is difficult to see why we come to distinguish acts to which responsibility is attached from mere segments in a physical, or psychical, or psycho-physical causal chain of events. (1969: 71)

But is there really an insuperable difficulty here for a physicalist view of man? This question touches on a tangle of issues belonging to metaphysics, the philosophy of science and moral philosophy as well as to the philosophy of mind: the issue of free will really deserves another book to itself. All we can do in this present chapter is to reach some very modest interim conclusions; but we hope that these will be enough to show that our overall physicalist position isn't *obviously* incompatible with everyday conceptions of free action.

2   It will, of course, be agreed on all hands that what we do can sometimes be caused in such a way as to block ascriptions of responsibility. Suppose you are swept off your feet in a storm and land in the middle of a flower patch; then you may have ruined the flowers, but it was not an intentional, blameworthy action of yours – indeed, it wasn't an action at all in the strict sense introduced in Chapter IX, for what you did was caused by a natural, impersonal force with no intentional contribution from you. Now, Berlin seems to think that if an action is, in his phrase, 'a segment in a causal chain of events' then it is, in the final analysis, no more a free action

than your landing on the flower patch, care of the storm, would be. To quote again:

> whether the causes that are held completely to determine human action are physical or psychical or of some other kind, and in whatever pattern or proportion they are deemed to occur, if they are truly causes ... this of itself seems to me to make the notion of free choice between alternatives inapplicable.   (1969: 65n)

Berlin's view, then, would seem to classify all causal factors – physical or psychological – as being on a level. The presence of *any* sort of cause, if it brings about a human action in accordance with some law (if it 'determines' the action, to use Berlin's word), is enough to make it an unfree action for which the question of personal responsibility cannot properly arise.

But is this correct? Do we really have to lump all causes together, whether they are storms or rational desires, and treat them all as if they were impersonal forces, so that nothing they produce could be a free action? Aristotle thought not. He distinguishes between types of action (in the broadest sense) precisely according to how they are caused. He writes in the *Nicomachean Ethics*, for instance:

> That is compulsory of which the moving principle is outside, being a principle in which nothing is contributed by the person who acts – or, rather, is acted upon, e.g. if he were to be carried somewhere by a wind, or by men who had him in their power.   (*NE* 1110a1-5)

Something which is in this sense 'compulsory' is a central case of an unfree or involuntary act. For example, your damaging the flower patch as a result of being hurled by the storm would be involuntary by Aristotle's lights, for the force was external and you contributed nothing. Aristotle would regard what was done in such a circumstance as something for which you should not be held responsible – and so far, so uncontroversial. However, when he goes on to contrast the involuntary with the voluntary, i.e. with what is done freely, Aristotle again characterises the latter sort of act in causal terms:

> The voluntary would seem to be that of which the moving principle is in the agent himself, he being aware of the particular circumstances of the action.   (*NE* 1111a23-5)

So voluntary acts are also distinguished by Aristotle precisely by the way in which they are caused. And what is the 'moving principle' of a voluntary action? Well, in *De Anima* we are told that it is desire and practical thought that originates movement (433a9-21). So Aristotle's view comes roughly to this: voluntary acts are those which are caused by desires, in the presence of appropriate beliefs about the particular circumstances of the action. Contrast, for example, the following two cases. (1) You are hurled across the yard by a blast of wind so that you hit a bottle of milk and knock it over. (2) You are thirsty and see a bottle of milk; your desire is aroused and as a result your hands move so that, controlled by perceptual feedback, they tip up the bottle to pour out the milk. In both cases, the bottle empties because of something you do (in a very broad sense), and in both cases what you do is a segment within a causal nexus. Nevertheless, Aristotle would say that in case (2) the causes of the action are such that it counts as a voluntary act, while in case (1) your doings are quite involuntary.

This is, of course, the very briefest sketch of Aristotle's general conception of voluntary action. With its emphasis on appropriate causation by desires and beliefs it is strongly reminiscent of the account we gave in Chapter IX of intentional acts: indeed the Greek word we have been translating 'voluntary' could in many cases, perhaps most, be equally well translated 'intentional'. And already there seems to be a sharp contrast between Aristotle's view and Berlin's. Aristotle grants that an intentional action is a segment in a causal chain of events, but he refuses to draw Berlin's inference that in some way its voluntariness is thereby lost. On the contrary, he holds that such acts are voluntary precisely *because* they are caused in the right way, by desires rather than by storms (or by the tugging of strings attached to one's arms, or by the activation of reflex arcs, etc.). And once we see the plausibility of this rival Aristotelian position, Berlin's inference begins to look far too speedy. Suppose we accept that a normal human action is like being swept off one's feet in a storm in the very general respect of being a segment in a chain of causes and effects: why should we think that that commits us to holding the cases are also alike in point of being unfree? Granted, there are causes at work in both cases; but shouldn't we be impressed by the differences between the kinds of causal factors that are in play in the two cases?

3   Someone who shares Berlin's worry about the compatibility of the idea that our actions are caused with the notion of

responsible free action is likely to protest that our discussion so far has missed the point. For note that Aristotle's notion of a voluntary action is a very broad one: it applies wherever behaviour is suitably brought about by desires and beliefs – and so it applies as much to the child or the animal as to the responsible adult agent. Aristotle himself explicitly acknowledges this:

> both children and the lower animals share in voluntary action.
>
> (*NE* 1111b7-9)

So, the protest will continue, even if voluntary actions in this sense can be 'segments in a causal chain', this is really not pertinent to Berlin's worry. After all, we do not regard animals, nor even small children, as morally responsible for what they do; the ascription of genuine responsibility presupposes not merely voluntary acts in Aristotle's thin sense but fully free actions in some much richer sense. And it has yet to be shown that an action which is caused can be free in this crucial, richer sense.

This objection is perfectly fair: but, as one might perhaps expect, Aristotle has much more to say. In particular, he wants to make a crucial distinction among voluntary actions by characterising some actions but not others as done through *deliberative choice*. We are told in the *Eudemian Ethics* that

> all that has been deliberately chosen is voluntary, but not all the voluntary is deliberately chosen, and all that is according to choice is voluntary, but not all that is voluntary is according to choice.
>
> (*EE* 1226b33-5)

Animals, Aristotle maintains in *De Anima*, are not capable of deliberation:

> Sensitive imagination, as we have said, is found in all animals, deliberative imagination only in those that are calculative: for whether this or that shall be enacted is already a task requiring calculation.
>
> (*DA* 434a5-7)

It is because they have no capacity for discursive thought and reasoning that animals cannot deliberatively choose between options as we can: and the same goes too for very small children. A rational agent, however, can consciously set out to reflect on the ends of his actions, he can evaluate and choose the best means to those ends and act on the basis of such deliberations.

This capacity for deliberative choice is what brings us – as distinct from animals and small children – within the ambit of moral practice and appraisal. The animal or the child is a mere *wanton*, following the tug of its desires in an unreflective way. We, by contrast, can stand back and wonder whether it would really be a good idea to fall for this temptation or to pursue that enticing goal. We can monitor our own performances, weigh up considerations pro and con, deliberately set aside the short-term treat in favour of the long-term benefit, and try to bring our actions into accord with our reflective desires about the sort of person we want to be. Because of this role for deliberation in our actions, it makes sense for others to try to affect our behaviour by trying to affect the course of our deliberations. They can chip in with reasons for or against a certain action; they can praise our past performances in the hope of encouraging us to do well again in the future; and they can object to other actions, try to get us to see them as being wrong in one way or another, in the hope of discouraging repeat performances. Since our actions can be grounded in deliberation, there is point in the practice of mutual appraisal and criticism. It is no good reasoning with a delinquent dog, and there is little to be gained from offering rational considerations to a small toddler; but as we grow up and get better at deliberation, we gradually become correspondingly more open to the force of all kinds of argument, and we become susceptible to moral argument in particular. In short, our developing capacity for deliberative choice sets the scene for morality.

For Aristotle, therefore, the key difference between the actions of beings like ourselves who are fit subjects of moral appraisal and the 'voluntary' actions of animals and small children lies in the role for rational deliberative choice. This isn't to say that *all* our actions are unlike animal actions in stemming from prior reflective intentions: that is, of course, simply false. Indeed, the bulk of our intentional actions are relatively unreflective (see IX.5). Again, it isn't being suggested that only our conscious deliberated performances can be morally assessed; that too is simply false (after all, one thing you can be morally criticised for is, precisely, acting without due deliberation). The claim is only that our capacity for reflective deliberation about our actions provides the general setting for morality.

This insight forms just a part of Aristotle's subtle investigation of free action: he goes on to give important discussions of the variety of conditions that can limit our freedom, such as duress, ignorance, environment and settled character. His treatment of these topics is rich, complex, open to interpretation and, no doubt, imperfect. But let's not concern ourselves with the fine details here. For present purposes, what we should remark is the general *sort* of consideration which Aristotle uses to elucidate the notion of responsible agency. To repeat, he thinks that what crucially matters is that we are agents capable of deliberative choice and – barring cases of duress, acting from ignorance and so on – that this is what makes it appropriate to hold us to account for our actions. And this broad line of approach seems extremely attractive. What more (we might ask) could one possibly wish for by way of an example of the exercise of free will than an action which flows from deliberative choice in Aristotle's sense? Jack is deciding whether to choose the crème brûlée or the cheesecake, or to forego both. He first wonders whether he shouldn't abstain, given his resolution to lose weight; but he thinks his hostess might be a little offended at his spurning the results of her labours, so on reflection he decides that the thing to do on balance is to indulge, while firmly resisting offers of second helpings. That still leaves him with a choice to make, and morality is no guide for the second leg of his deliberations. Jack's particular weakness is for cheesecake; but tonight the crème brûlée looks splendidly enticing, so – just for a change – he takes the latter. Now, this is surely the very paradigm of a freely chosen action: not a very exalted one, to be sure, but none the less free for that. Yet, in characterising it as free, all we seem to be relying on is the folk-psychological description of this familiar sort of situation. Given that there are no hidden complications in the example – given, for instance, that Jack hasn't been hypnotised – then nothing more seems to be required for Jack's taking the crème brûlée to count as a free act than that it proceeds from the described course of deliberation.

4   But where does this Aristotelian account of free action leave us with respect to the worry about the compatibility of causality and freedom?

The suggestion is that free acts are just the normal acts of a reflective deliberating agent in the absence of special circumstances like duress, compulsion or hypnotic control. And while we haven't explicitly investigated what is involved in being a reflective deliberating agent, most of the materials for such an investigation are already at hand in Chapters IX and XVI where we discussed action and thought. The main additional ingredient we need is the idea of a rational agent who not only has desires but also, reflectively, has desires *about* his desires (e.g. he wants not to desire unhealthy foods) and so cares about monitoring his own performances. Without going into details, this additional ingredient wouldn't seem to cause any special new difficulties for our general functionalist theory of the mind. But if (a) we *can* give an account of the notion of deliberative agency within a physicalist framework which is compatible with the idea that what we do is caused, and (b) free agency is just the agency of a reflective deliberating agent, then (c) the idea that we are free agents must be compatible with the idea that what we do is caused.

Aristotle himself thinks of rationally deliberated action as being as much subject to causality as is 'voluntary' animal behaviour:

> The origin of action – its efficient cause – is choice, and that of choice is desire and reasoning with a view to an end.   (*NE* 1139a32-3)

So we still have a head-on clash with the views for which Berlin is our chosen spokesman. According to Aristotle, it is not only the wide class of 'voluntary' actions but also the morally crucial category of deliberated actions which are characterised by their causal antecedents. To put the issue starkly, Berlin thinks that causality rules out free action, whereas the Aristotelian holds that being appropriately caused by deliberation is precisely what makes an action a first-grade example of responsible free agency. We might call this Aristotelian view *the causal theory of freedom*; as we have seen, it has considerable initial attractions. So what kind of attack can the opposition mount in order to defend Berlin's rival view that causality after all excludes freedom?

First, some might want to argue that the causal theory is fundamentally wrong to identify free actions as those caused by deliberation, claiming that free actions are those done for deliberated reasons, and reasons are not causes. But as we argued at length in the last chapter, it is difficult to find any good ground for the alleged contrast between reasons and causes. We can take it therefore that the causal theory of freedom does not fall at this very first hurdle.

Second, and this is a more substantial objection, it might be protested that it is just not true to experience to treat the steps in deliberation as part of a rigid causal chain. Consider Jack's predicament again as he is faced with those tempting puddings. Surely, the objection runs, if this is to be a genuine case of free deliberation, then Jack could in the end have jumped either way: he actually chose the crème brûlée, but he could have gone for the cheesecake instead. This is what real deliberation is like: there is no fixed chain of causes in the proceedings – and were things in fact to be causally determined then (as Berlin insists) freedom would be absent.

This second objection raises a number of issues which are difficult to tease apart. But let's start by granting our imagined protestor the following:

(D)   If the initial psychological facts about Jack (e.g. that he has a wish to lose weight, believes there is crème brûlée and cheesecake to choose from, and so on) are enough completely to determine the course of his deliberations, then his resulting choice would not be a genuinely free one.

Suppose we use the phrase 'psychological determinism' for the thesis that there are absolutely rigid psychological laws governing our mental life, the course of our deliberations, and our consequent behaviour; then (D) in effect says that psychological determinism is incompatible with freedom. This may seem intuitively rather plausible, so for the sake of argument let's grant (D) without further ado. However, this concession is quite consistent with accepting the causal conception of freedom which we have been sketching. The point here is a little tricky to grasp, but it is an important one.

At the end of the last chapter, we argued – to put it very schematically – that prior mental states can cause a resulting action without there being any strict causal laws relating mental states and actions as such. In other words, even if there are no strict psychological laws relating types of mental states to types of action, it doesn't follow that the mental states cannot be the causes of the actions they explain. We argued this on a fairly narrow front, considering just the relation of beliefs and desires to the actions they rationalise: but the point generalises. So, for example, there may be no strict psychological laws which dictate that if you have mental states of a certain type then you will deliberate thus-and-so; but the sequence of mental events in the course of a particular deliberation could still be causally related. For these mental events, given our overall view of the mind, are just physical happenings, functionally described; so they could fall under *physical* causal laws

even if there are no *psychological* laws. Hence, to repeat, deliberative reflection leading to action could be a causal process even if
there are no psychological laws governing the course of a deliberation. In other words, the Aristotelian can claim that deliberated
action has causal antecedents without thereby committing himself
to psychological determinism. So even granted that (D) is true – i.e.
that strict psychological laws would be inimical to freedom – this is
no problem for the causal theory of freedom, which simply isn't
committed to there being that sort of determinism.

Now, this point, which we owe to Donald Davidson, takes much
of the sting out of the objection to Aristotle which we imagined
above. For the essential thought was that our experience reveals
deliberation to be an open-ended, indeterministic affair which
doesn't run along strict causal paths. And the truth behind this
intuitive claim is that deliberative processes *as we conceive them in
everyday folk psychological terms* are indeed not subject to strict
laws which operate at that level. But to use an analogy we used
before, this no more shows that deliberation is not a causal process
than the fact that there are no strict laws describing hurricanes as
such shows that the destructive course of a hurricane isn't a causal
process. In short, then, appeal to ordinary experience – which
means in this context appeal to the deliverances of everyday folk
psychology – cannot be enough to refute the causal account of free
agency.

5   The typical objector, however, will certainly not let matters
rest here. On the contrary, he will impatiently protest that Davidson-
ian points about the non-existence of strict psychological laws are
merely a diversionary tactic. Such points, the objector will argue,
cannot touch the central worry underlying his previous line of
attack. For on our physicalist view, deliberation will be a sequence
of physical events, and so will still fall under laws, albeit physical
ones: and that, according to the objector, is enough to rule out
freedom. In other words, it is not psychological laws *as against*
physical laws which limit freedom: *any* causal laws are enough to
usher freedom from the scene. Consider once more Jack's deliberations about his pudding. If this is a sequence of events governed by
laws, if the steps in his deliberation are part of a (physical) causal
chain, surely it is false that Jack could have plumped for either

pudding. And if, as a matter of causal law, he couldn't have chosen differently doesn't it follow that he did not really act freely?

Let's set out the premises of this enticing line of argument more carefully. First, we have an elucidation of something which the physicalist seems to be committed to, namely that steps in a deliberation – like any other physical events – fall under physical *laws*. And on certain simplifying assumptions (which we will return to in the next section) this is just to say that given the initial state of affairs, e.g. when Jack sets off on his deliberations, the subsequent course of events unfolds as a matter of physical necessity. In short:

(N)   The steps in Jack's deliberation follow one from another by strict physical necessity, which means that things couldn't have gone otherwise with his reflections and his resulting action.

Second, the objector offers what seems to be a simple truism about freedom:

(F)   If Jack couldn't have done otherwise, then his action was not genuinely free.

Putting (N) and (F) together, we derive the dispiriting conclusion that Jack's action in plumping for the crème brûlée was not free after all. Or at least, we can derive that conclusion *if the sense of 'could' deployed in the two premises is the same.*

But is it? Perhaps the sense in which Jack's deliberations *couldn't* have gone otherwise is different from the sense in which freedom requires that Jack *could* have done otherwise. After all, the notion of what one could or could not do is a relative one. As far as the speed of his excellent car is concerned, Jack could have driven from Aberystwyth to Oxford in less than four hours; but as far as his terrible driving is concerned, Jack couldn't have done it that quickly. Again, given her intelligence, Jill could have come top of the class; but in view of her lack of application, she couldn't get anywhere near the top mark. In short, what could be done from one point of view or relative to one set of considerations may be impossible from another.

Take again the case of Jack's deliberating about the puddings: he contemplates what is on offer and plumps for the crème brûlée. Considered from the point of view of everyday psychology there was no necessity about this: there is nothing in our folk theory that *dictates* that, in his psychological circumstances, Jack must have acted the way he did, and couldn't have taken the cheesecake instead of the crème brûlée. In other words, as far as our rather vague folk principles are concerned, the desire for crème brûlée could have – as usual – lost out to the desire for cheesecake. And if it had, the resulting behaviour of taking the cheesecake would still have resulted from a desire and therefore could still properly have been described as one of Jack's *actions*. Hence, from the point of view of folk psychology, things could have gone differently and yet resulted in an action: in this sense, there are other things which Jack could have *done*, and not just other things that could have happened to him. To suppose otherwise is to suppose that there is only one way that Jack could have deliberated and acted consistently with his initially having beliefs and desires of the type he did have: and that presupposes that there are rigid psychological laws in operation. But we have reason to think that there are no strict psychological laws; and hence we are indeed left with a good sense in which Jack could have acted in a different way – to repeat, he could have done so, as far as the rather vague principles of folk psychology are concerned.

Now, the notion of a *freely* performed action is itself part of our everyday common-sense conceptual equipment: it belongs squarely to folk psychology. So it is surely natural to suppose that the sense of 'could have done otherwise' which is relevant to the analysis of our everyday concept of free action is the sense we have just elucidated, the sense which also belongs to the framework of folk psychology. Hence, the obvious way of construing (F) so as to give us a principle that is intuitively plausible is something like this:

(Fψ) If Jack couldn't have done otherwise, as far as folk psychology is concerned, then his action was not genuinely free.

By contrast, (N) obviously involves a different sort of 'could': roughly, the idea is that Jack couldn't have done otherwise, as far as the physics of the situation is concerned. More precisely:

(Nϕ) Things couldn't have gone otherwise with Jack, given his total initial physical state and the laws of physics.

But the sense in which Jack couldn't have done otherwise according to (Nϕ) is plainly not the sense which excludes freedom according to (Fψ), so we can't after all put these two premises together to derive any worrying conclusion. On the contrary, as we argued before, Jack *could* have done otherwise from the point of view of folk psychology, and so his freedom is secure.

6   At this point, we must briefly pause to note for the record an annoying technical complication – though this can really be ignored by those who find the physics confusing.

In the previous section, in order to keep the line of argument uncluttered, we slid from saying that the steps in Jack's deliberation fall under physical laws to saying that (N) the steps follow from one another by strict physical necessity. This was really a mistake: physical laws need not be deterministic – i.e. they need not dictate a unique necessary upshot to every causal process. Indeed the laws of quantum mechanics are indeterministic in just this way. The details here fortunately do not matter, but the essential point can be crudely put like this. It is wrong to think of physical objects as subject to laws which completely determine their history; rather, the causal nexus allows for random occurrences. Hence (N) strictly speaking needs to be modified. We do not propose to investigate the needed modificaton here, however, and will instead adopt the simplifying pretence that we do live in what we might call a *Newton world* governed by absolutely deterministic causal laws, rather than in a *Heisenberg world* with quantum indeterminacies.

The excuse for this decidedly cavalier treatment of modern physics is simply that it doesn't matter very much for our current concerns whether you think we live in a rigidly deterministic Newton world or in a Heisenberg world with random occurrences. On the one hand, the pro-Aristotelian who thinks that folk psychology, including talk of free actions, can be reconciled with physicalism standardly uses arguments which don't depend on the details of physical theory. In particular, he will hold that his causal theory of freedom can be sustained whether we live in a Newton world or a Heisenberg one. On the other hand, the anti-Aristotelian who thinks that causation is incompatible with freedom in a Newton world is going to argue that, if we actually live in a Heisenberg world, then things are even worse. It is bad enough, he will argue, to be subject to a rigid determinism: but how can it be any comfort to discover that something you thought was causally determined is actually the result of something *random*? Being at the mercy of random events, a Berlin might argue, is even less happy a situation than being in a deterministic causal nexus! In short, then, neither party in the debate about the compatibility of freedom with the physical causation of behaviour is going to change sides if it is agreed that we live in an indeterministic universe rather than a deterministic one. Hence, since complicating the physics doesn't radically alter the philosophical position, the simplifying pretence we adopted can be allowed to stand.

7   To return, however, to the main line of argument. The traditional opponent of the causal theory of freedom is not likely to be impressed by our manoeuvres in §5. Indeed by this stage there is likely to be a note of exasperation in his protests: he will loudly maintain that we are still perversely refusing to see his point. From the outset, his difficulty has been in reconciling the idea that our deliberations and actions are physical happenings bound into a causal nexus with the fact that at least sometimes we act freely. And he will insist that his worry need not arise from playing fast and loose with different senses of 'could'. His view is that the existence of strict causal laws governing behaviour are enough to banish freedom, irrespective of their type. In other words, he frankly accepts not only $(F\psi)$ but

$(F\phi)$ If things couldn't have gone otherwise with Jack, given the initial physical situation and the laws of physics, then his deliberation and action were not genuinely free.

And this, combined with $(N\phi)$, *does* lead to the disturbing conclusion that Jack's action was not free after all. So, all our fancy detours discussing psychological determinism and so forth have been strictly beside the point. Everything, says our imagined objector, can turn on $(F\phi)$.

At this point in the debate, however, the proponent of the Aristotelian causal theory of freedom can dig in his heels and ask why we should accept $(F\phi)$. *Once we have distinguished $(F\phi)$ from the more plausible $(F\psi)$, why should we suppose it to be true?*

The idea behind $(F\phi)$ is perhaps as follows. If some course of action must follow, given the antecedent physical situation and the operative physical laws, then there is no *real* sense in which something else could have happened. Hence, since freedom requires a *real* capacity for acting in alternative ways, the fact that our actions fall under physical laws rules out genuine freedom. But this idea has only to be plainly set out for it to look rather suspicious. Why should it be supposed that the only 'real' capacity for alternative actions worth caring about is the ability to escape the normal patternings of physical events? Consider, for example, the virtue of having sufficient strength of moral purpose to withstand the pressures of the mob. This involves having sufficiently firmly held moral attitudes, together with a strongly operative desire to behave in accordance with one's own moral attitudes rather than follow desires one recognises as arising from disreputable social pressures. If Jill has such moral resolution, then she is undoubtedly more free than the stupid and weak-minded Jack who is blown this way and that by the influence of the crowd. There is a good ordinary folk psychological sense in which she has more options for action open to her than Jack – though this added freedom brings added responsibility, for if she too runs with the mob, then her moral failure is all the greater. Now, Jill's greater capacity for standing up for the right is surely something worth having if anything is: it is something which we care about inculcating in our children. And it is a 'real' capacity by any sane standard, something which people really have in varying degrees. But why on earth should it be thought that Jill's relative degree of freedom compared with Jack involves or requires a capacity to leap outside the physical course of nature? Why shouldn't moral strength be a physically based capacity like any other 'mental' capacity, and one which can be possessed or lacked in a determinist Newton world?

And after all, why should we want the capacity to escape the normal patternings of physical events? This might just mean being at the mercy of random events – and what's so great about that? Do we really want our brains to be *less* reliable than computers? In response to such questions, the defender of (Fφ) tends to spin nightmare stories about how terrible it would be to have one's behaviour subject to strict physical laws. We are offered, for example, a vision of the world according to which

> The state of things existing at any time, together with certain immutable laws, completely determine the state of things at every other time ... Thus, given the state of the original nebula, and given the laws of mechanics, a sufficiently powerful mind could deduce from these data the precise form of every curlicue of every letter I am now writing.
> (Peirce 1892: 163-4)

The image is conjured of a being who knows our every move before the event. If we try to outwit his predictions, we find he has predicted these attempts too – every putative exercise of free choice turns out to be completely predictable and so, the suggestion runs, our vaunted freedom is revealed as a sham. It seems irresistible to conclude that if completely deterministic laws apply to man's actions, he is himself an automaton.   (Compton 1935: 26)

Or as Isaiah Berlin puts it in an eloquent passage, the view that everything – including all human behaviour – is physically caused,

for all that its chains are decked out with flowers, and despite its parade of noble stoicism and the splendour and vastness of its cosmic design, nevertheless represents the universe as a prison.   (1969: 106)

But haunting though these images are – the Great Predictor, the Automaton, the Prison – they are merely images, and very misleading ones at that.

Leaving aside the point that, in an indeterministic Heisenberg world, the future course of the universe is not deducible even in principle from knowledge of its current state, why should we suppose that the predictability of an action nullifies its freedom? After all, the fact that it is a racing certainty that a Jack, who is notoriously lazy and self-indulgent, will take the car rather than take a brisk three-mile walk to his appointment doesn't make it in any sense an involuntary act. A lot of our free actions are already highly predictable, and none the less free for that. So why should the entirely abstract possibility of more perfect predictions made by a God-like being with infinite powers be thought to be worrying?

Again, it is simply tendentious to say that if deterministic laws apply to our behaviour, then we are automata. An automaton, properly so-called, is an artefact whose behaviour is not guided by any desires or beliefs, experiences or thoughts. Since, as we have argued at length, we can have such states directing our behaviour compatibly with the truth of physicalism, there is absolutely no reason to say that a deterministic brand of physicalism entails that we are automata.

Berlin's image of the universe as a prison is equally tendentious. Here is Jill sunning herself on the beach of an idyllic Greek island. She has decided, after some deliberation, to blow a small inheritance on the holiday of a lifetime; she carefully chose the island out of twenty tempting locations, and it has fully lived up to every expectation. Happily, she turns over to tan her other side, decides to have another glass of wine, reaches for her book ... *and she is in a prison?*

The image of the physical world as a prison, combined with the reflection that the human body is itself part of that world, suggests a still more evocative notion – the idea of the *body* as the prison of the soul. And perhaps here we get to the heart of the matter. For maybe it is the dualist conception of the person as something fundamentally distinct from his body which in the end underlies much of the appeal of (Fφ). The thought is that, if the doings of the body are physically determined, then the person himself never gets into the story, he can never really affect what happens – the soul is in permanent exile from a physical world that rattles on independently. The threat of determinism is thus seen as the threat of being imprisoned in a body that is, whatever the appearances, really out of our control; and this awesome vision gives life to the suggestion that physical causality must rule out freedom. But of course, if we have established anything in this book, it is that the underlying dualist vision is radically flawed. And in so far as it is this which gives the premise (Fφ) its residual plausibility, then this premise in the anti-Aristotelian argument must be rejected.

8   We have suggested in this chapter that the existence of responsible free action can be reconciled with our overall physicalist view of the mind if we adopt a broadly Aristotelian causal theory of freedom. And we have fended off three sorts of attack on the causal theory, whose roots lie in (a) the false assumption that the causal theorist is committed to psychological determinism, (b) a confusion between different senses of 'could have done otherwise', and (c) a backsliding into dualism. Of course, this hardly *settles* the issue once and for all! The problem of free will is a hardy perennial which keeps re-emerging in new forms. But at the outset of this chapter we declared our aim to be the very modest one of showing that it is at least not *obvious* that our general theory of the mind must be in trouble over freedom. And that, perhaps, we have achieved.

CHRONOLOGICAL TABLE

A list of the philosophers mentioned or quoted in the text, born before this century:

Socrates	*c.*470-399 B.C.
Plato	*c.*428-347 B.C.
Aristotle	384-322 B.C.
Thomas Hobbes	1588-1679
René Descartes	1596-1650
Antoine Arnauld	1612-1694
John Locke	1632-1704
Baruch Spinoza	1632-1677
Gottfried Leibniz	1646-1716
George Berkeley	1685-1753
Thomas Reid	1710-1796
David Hume	1711-1776
Immanuel Kant	1724-1804
John Stuart Mill	1806-1873
C.S. Peirce	1839-1914
H.A. Prichard	1871-1947
Bertrand Russell	1872-1970
G.E. Moore	1873-1958
Ludwig Wittgenstein	1889-1951
Gilbert Ryle	1900-1976

GUIDE TO FURTHER READING

The aims of this Guide are modest. We restrict ourselves to mentioning a handful of references for each chapter, which will provide the reader with a limited amount of supplementary material. Many of the works mentioned will, however, provide further references for the reader who wants to explore topics in greater depth.

Chapter I

For an elementary introduction to mind/body problems, see Campbell 1970: chs. 1-2.

There is a brief discussion of Plato's dualism set against the relevant background of religious beliefs in Crombie 1964: ch. 5.

Chapter II

A clear statement of dualism is given, and a number of arguments for it critically examined, in Churchland 1984: 7-18.

Swinburne argues at length for dualism in Shoemaker and Swinburne 1984. Lewis maintains a dualist position in debate with Williams over the issue of life after death in Lewis 1978: ch. 4.

On interpreting Christian belief in immortality in terms of the spiritual quality of present life, see Phillips 1970: ch. 3. For a more traditional discussion see Geach 1969: ch. 2.

Chapter III

Descartes's Argument (as we call it) is presented in the general context of Descartes's philosophy in Kenny 1968: chs. 2-3. (For dissent over the interpretation of Descartes cf. Wilson 1978, especially ch. VI.3)

Chapter IV

Criticisms of dualism may be found in Churchland 1984: 18-21, Campbell 1970: ch. 3, or Armstrong 1968: ch. 2.iii. A more comprehensive discussion will be found in Cornman and Lehrer 1974: 237-76.

Chapter V

The problem of evaluating theories is well discussed by Chalmers 1978 (see especially ch. 7 on Lakatos).

Chapter VI

Introductory accounts of Aristotle's philosophy of mind may be found in Barnes 1982: ch. 15, or in Ackrill 1981: ch. 5. A more detailed investigation, also relevant to later chapters, is Sorabji 1974.

Chapter VII

Discussion of the three arguments for sense-data will be found in Don Locke 1967: chs. 6 and 11, Armstrong 1961: Parts 2 and 5, or Ayer 1976: ch. 4.

The traditional attribution of a representationalist view to John Locke has been disputed. See Tipton 1977: Introduction.

Note that the term 'sense-datum' is not always understood as we use it (cf. Don Locke's discussion in 1967: 20-3; he uses the word 'percept' for what we have called a 'sense-datum'). Note also that different philosophers have classified the various arguments differently. Thus the argument from hallucinations (as we call it) will sometimes be found under the label 'arguments from illusion', though the latter heading often includes our relativity argument as well. And what we would call an argument from science is sometimes presented as 'the causal argument' or even 'the causal theory' (Ayer 1976). This terminological mess is dangerously confusing, so beware!

Chapter VIII

The belief-acquisition theory of perception appears in Armstrong 1961: ch. 9. Another clear and sympathetic account of the theory will be found in Pitcher 1971: Part 2. Such theories are vigorously criticised by Jackson 1977: 37-49.

Chapter IX

Volitional theories are very effectively criticised in Hornsby 1980: ch. 4. For a seminal discussion of the causal theory of action, see Davidson 1963. The analysis of action is discussed in McGinn 1982: ch. 5.

Chapter X

Hume's view is discussed in Armstrong 1973: ch. 5.4. Ryle's style of behaviourism is critically discussed in Armstrong 1968: ch. 5, and also more briefly in Churchland 1984: 23-5.

Chapters XI and XII

A functionalist theory of belief emerges in Armstrong 1968: ch. 16 and 1973: ch. 2. A more general functionalism has also featured prominently in several important articles by Hilary Putnam – cf. for example his 1975: ch. 21. Another key author is Dennett; see his 1969: §9, and the introduction to his 1978.

Chapter XIII

Ryle's logical behaviourism features in chapters 1 and 5 of his 1949. Central State Materialism is forcefully argued in Smart 1959; the position is further defended in Armstrong 1968: ch. 6 especially. In David Lewis 1966 the dispositional characterisations of the soft version of behaviourism are wedded to an identity theory, thus paving the way for what we have called soft functionalism. The case for eliminative materialism is argued by Churchland in his 1984: ch. 2.5. Davidson's anomalist monism is presented in his 1970.

For a comprehensive discussion of behaviourism and materialism, eliminative and non-eliminative, see Cornman and Lehrer 1974: 279-311. Useful later discussions of the various positions we distinguished will be found in McGinn 1982: ch. 2, and in Churchland 1984: ch. 2.

Chapter XIV

Smart's 1959 is a stout defence of the materialist position on sensations. So too is Armstrong 1968: ch. 14. For a discussion of Wittgenstein's views, see Kenny 1973: ch. 10.

Chapter XV

The idea of 'what it is like' to have conscious states is imaginatively discussed in Nagel 1974. For a critical view of Nagel and more about consciousness, see Wilkes 1984.

Chapter XVI

There is an account of Wittgenstein's views on discursive thought in Kenny 1973. For a clear discussion in the spirit of Wittgenstein's remarks, see Ryle 1968 and 1968a.

Chapter XVII

For Davidson's comprehensive criticisms of objections to the idea that reasons are causes, we refer again to his 1963.

Chapter XVIII

For an elementary introduction to the problem of free will see Williams in Pears 1963. Watson 1982 contains an excellent introduction and collection of articles on free will. For a lively and stimulating discussion, see Dennett 1984.

Our view of Aristotle's treatment of freedom owes something to Charles 1984.

BIBLIOGRAPHY

Both in the main text and in the guide to further reading we have used the author/date system for references to modern authors; but for classic texts we have used a short title, in order to avoid anachronistic citations such as Plato 1975. Detailed references in the text are normally by page number (sometimes, as indicated below, to an accessible reprint). However, for classic texts where there is a standard system of references (e.g. Bekker numbers for Aristotle, or citations by Book/Chapter/Section for Locke's *Essay*), we have used that. When quoting from translated material, we have sometimes departed from the translation cited below.

Ackrill, J. 1981. *Aristotle the Philosopher*, Oxford: Oxford University Press.

Adrian, E. D. 1947. *The Physical Background of Perception*, Oxford: Clarendon Press.

Anscombe, G. E. M. 1963. *Intention* (2nd edn), Oxford: Blackwell.

Aristotle, *The Works of Aristotle Translated into English*, eds. J. A. Smith and W. D. Ross 1910-52, Oxford: Clarendon Press.

Armstrong, D. M. 1961. *Perception and the Physical World*, London: Routledge and Kegan Paul.

— 1965. 'The Nature of the Mind', reprinted in Borst 1970.

— 1968. *A Materialist Theory of the Mind*, London: Routledge and Kegan Paul.

— 1973. *Belief, Truth and Knowledge*, Cambridge: Cambridge University Press.

Ayer, A. J. 1976. *The Central Questions of Philosophy*, Harmondsworth: Penguin.

Barnes, J. 1982. *Aristotle*, Oxford: Oxford University Press.

— *et al.* (eds.) 1979. *Articles on Aristotle* Vol.4: *Psychology & Aesthetics*, London: Duckworth.

Berkeley, G. *Philosophical Works*, ed. M. Ayers 1975, London: Dent.

Berlin, I. 1969. *Four Essays on Liberty*, Oxford: Oxford University Press.

Borst, C. V. (ed.) 1970. *The Mind-Brain Identity Theory*, London: Macmillan.

Campbell, K. 1970. *Body and Mind*, London: Macmillan.

Chalmers, A.F. 1978. *What Is This Thing Called Science?*, Milton Keynes: Open University Press.

Charles, D. 1984. *Aristotle's Theory of Action*, London: Duckworth.

Churchland, P. M. 1984. *Matter and Consciousness*, Cambridge Mass: M.I.T. Press.

Compton, A.H. 1935. *The Freedom of Man*, New Haven: Yale University Press.

Cornman, J.W. and Lehrer, K. 1974. *Philosophical Problems and Arguments: an Introduction* (2nd edn), London: Collier Macmillan.

Craig, E.J. 1976. 'Sensory Experience and the Foundations of Knowledge', *Synthese* 33: 1-24.

Crombie, I.M. 1964. *Plato: The Midwife's Apprentice*, London: Routledge and Kegan Paul.

Davidson, D. 1963. 'Actions, Reasons and Causes', *Journal of Philosophy* 60: 685-700. Page references to the reprint in Davidson 1980.

— 1970. 'Mental Events', in *Experience and Theory*, eds. L. Foster and J. Swanson, London: Duckworth. Reprinted in Davidson 1980.

— 1980. *Essays on Actions and Events*, Oxford: Clarendon Press.

Dennett, D. C. 1969. *Content and Consciousness*, London: Routledge and Kegan Paul.

— 1978. *Brainstorms*, Montgomery, Vermont: Bradford Books.

— 1984. *Elbow Room*, Oxford: Clarendon Press.

Descartes, R. *Philosophical Letters*, tr. A. Kenny 1970, Oxford: Blackwell.

— *The Philosophical Writings of Descartes*, tr. J. Cottingham *et al.*, 1985, Cambridge: Cambridge University Press.

Geach, P. 1969. *God and the Soul*, London: Routledge and Kegan Paul.

Hobbes, T. *Leviathan*, ed. M. Oakeshott 1960, Oxford: Blackwell.

Hopkins, J. 1975. 'Wittgenstein and Physicalism', *Aristotelian Society Proceedings* 75: 121-46.

Hornsby, J. 1980. *Actions*, London: Routledge and Kegan Paul.

Hume, D. *An Abstract of A Treatise of Human Nature*, ed. J. Keynes and P. Sraffa 1938, Cambridge: Cambridge University Press.

— *Enquiry Concerning the Human Understanding*, ed. L. Selby-Bigge 1902, Oxford: Clarendon Press.

— *A Treatise of Human Nature*, ed. E. Mossner 1969, Harmondsworth: Penguin

Jackson, F. 1977. *Perception*, Cambridge: Cambridge University Press.

Kenny, A. 1968. *Descartes*, New York: Random House.

— 1973. *Wittgenstein*, Harmondsworth: Penguin.

Kripke, S. 1980. *Naming and Necessity*, Oxford: Blackwell.

Lakatos, I. 1970. 'Falsification and the Methodology of Research Programmes', in *Criticism and the Growth of Knowledge* ed. I. Lakatos and A. Musgrave, Cambridge: Cambridge University Press.

Leibniz, G. *Philosophical Papers*, tr. L. Loemker (2nd edn) 1969, Dordrecht: Reidel.

Lewis, D. 1966. 'An Argument for the Identity Theory', *Journal of Philosophy* 63: 17-25. Reprinted with additions in Lewis 1983.

— 1983. *Philosophical Papers: 1*, Oxford: Oxford University Press.

Lewis, H. D. 1978. *Persons and Life After Death*. London: Macmillan.

Locke, D. 1967. *Perception and Our Knowledge of the External World*, London: George Allen and Unwin.

Locke, J. *An Essay Concerning Human Understanding*, ed. J. Yolton 1961, London: Dent.

McGinn, C. 1982. *The Character of Mind*, Oxford: Oxford University Press.

Melzack, R. 1973. *The Puzzle of Pain*, Harmondsworth: Penguin.

Mill, J. S. *A System of Logic* (8th edn n.d.), London: Longmans.

Moore, G. E. 1953. *Some Main Problems of Philosophy*, London: Allen and Unwin.

Nagel, T. 1974. 'What Is It Like To Be A Bat?', *Philosophical Review* 83: 435-50. Reprinted in Nagel 1979.

— 1979. *Mortal Questions*, Cambridge: Cambridge University Press.

Pears, D. F. (ed.) 1963. *Freedom and the Will*, London: Macmillan.

Peirce, C. S. 1892. 'The Doctrine of Necessity', reprinted in *Charles S. Peirce: Selected Writings*, ed. P. Wiener, New York: Dover.

Phillips, D. Z. 1970. *Death and Immortality*, London: Macmillan.

Pitcher, G. 1971. *A Theory of Perception*, New Jersey: Princeton University Press.

Plato, *Phaedo*, tr. D. Gallop 1975, Oxford: Clarendon Press.

Prichard, H. 1949. *Moral Obligation*, Oxford: Clarendon Press.

Putnam, H. 1975. *Mind, Language and Reality*, Cambridge: Cambridge University Press.

Reid, T. *The Works of Thomas Reid*, ed. W. Hamilton (7th edn) 1872, London: Longmans.

Russell, B. 1912. *The Problems of Philosophy*, Oxford: Oxford University Press.

Ryle, G. 1949. *The Concept of Mind*, London: Hutchinson.

— 1968. 'Thinking and Reflecting', Royal Institute of Philosophy Lecture, in *The Human Agent*, ed. G. Vesey, London: Macmillan. Reprinted in Ryle 1971.

— 1968a. 'The Thinking of Thoughts– What is "Le Penseur" Doing?', reprinted in Ryle 1971.

— 1971. *Collected Papers 2*, London: Hutchinson.

Shoemaker, S. and Swinburne, R. 1984. *Personal Identity*, Oxford: Oxford University Press.

Smart, J. J. C. 1959. 'Sensations and Brain Processes', *Philosophical Review* 68: 141-56. Page references to the reprint in Borst 1970.

Sorabji, R. 1974. 'Body and Soul in Aristotle', *Philosophy* 49: 63-89. Reprinted in Barnes *et al.* 1979.

Spinoza, B. *Ethics*, tr. A. Boyle 1910, London: Dent.

Strawson, P. F. 1966. 'Self, Mind and Body', reprinted in Strawson 1974.

— 1974. *Freedom and Resentment*, London: Methuen.

Tipton, I. C. (ed.) 1977. *Locke on Human Understanding*, Oxford: Oxford University Press.

Watson, G. 1982. *Free Will*, Oxford: Oxford University Press.

Weiskrantz, L. 1980. 'Varieties of Residual Experience', *Quarterly Journal of Experimental Psychology* 32: 365-86.

Wilkes, K. V. 1984. 'Is Consciousness Important?', *British Journal for the Philosophy of Science* 35: 223-43.

Wilson, M. 1978. *Descartes*, London: Routledge and Kegan Paul.

Wittgenstein, L. 1953. *Philosophical Investigations*, Oxford: Blackwell.

INDEX

Actions
  in animals, 73–4
  distinguished from other doings,
    119–22
  intentional, 120–1, 129–32, 254–9
  volitional theory, 123–7, 133–4
  done for reasons, 129–32, 134
  reasons are causes, 134, 237–51
  folk psychological understanding,
    164–8
  vs. physical behaviour, 171–3
  explanation by redescription, 240–2
  Logical Connection Thesis, 242,
    245–51
  free action, 252–68
Acts of will, 123–7, 230
Actuality (Aristotelian), 77, 79–80
Adrian, E.D., 213
Animals, 16, 49–51, 71–4, 84, 109–10,
  130, 168, 209–10, 213, 224,
  226, 256–7, 259
Anomalous monism, 187–8
Anscombe, G.E.M., 129, 132
Argument from Analogy, 201
Arguments from science (for
  sense-data), 92–5
Aristotle, 71, 75–83, 177–9, 187,
  254–9
Armstrong, D.M., 112–13, 152–5,
  171–4, 186
Arnauld, A., 39
Asymmetry (first/third-person
  knowledge), 147–8, 155–7, 174,
  197
Asymmetry Argument (against Ryle),
  147–8, 155
Automata, 49, 267
Awareness, *see* Consciousness

Beetle in the box, 204–6
Behaviourism, 144–6, 184, 186
  hard vs. soft, 144–6
  logical, 184

Beliefs
  acquired in perception, 103–18,
    170–1
  full-blooded vs. thinned–down sense,
    110, 135, 168–9
  not voluntary, 110, 123
  as reasons, 130–2, 238–51
  as causes, 134, 237–51
  Hume's theory, 136–41, 151
  not episodic, 139–40
  Ryle's dispositional theory, 141–51,
    154–5, 157–8
  Armstrong's functionalist theory,
    152–62
  identity with brain states, 159–62,
    186–7
  folk psychological principles, 163–9
  knowledge of other's beliefs, 173–6
  about one's own mental states,
    211–16
  activated, 212
  thought vs. belief, 223
Berkeley, G., 90–1, 124
Berlin, I., 253–6, 259–60, 267
Blind–sight, 117
Body-hopping, 8, 30
Brains in vats, 32, 35, 209

C-fibres, 182, 221
Capacities (constituting the mind),
  72–84, 177–9
Cartesian Mind, 12–21, 24, 37, 45–61,
  82–3, 100, 143, 158–9
Causal theories
  of perception, 85–6, 103
  of action, 121–2, 134, 237–68
  of freedom, 259–68
Causation
  between Mind and body, 52–9, 82
  involving underlying mechanisms,
    53–5
  dispositions as causes, 153
  involved in inner sense, 156–7

279